THE
COUNTRY
HOUSE
REVEALED

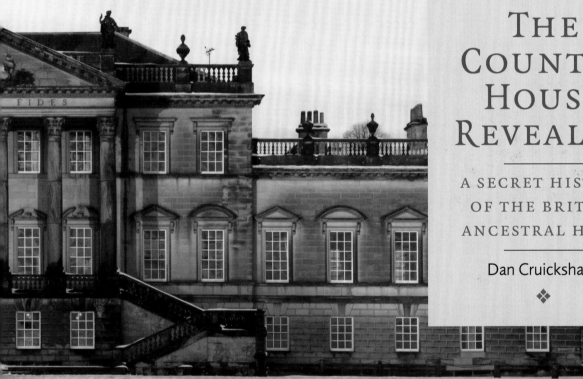

THE COUNTRY HOUSE REVEALED

A SECRET HISTORY OF THE BRITISH ANCESTRAL HOME

Dan Cruickshank

❖

BBC
BOOKS

CONTENTS

ABOVE TOP *Lord Dufferin, who enriched Clandeboye House, County Down, NI when Viceroy of India in the mid-1880s.* ABOVE *The early fifteenth-century Great Hall roof at South Wraxall, Wiltshire, a marvellous Medieval construction with a hidden meaning.*

PREVIOUS PAGE *The author contemplates the vast main front of Wentworth Woodhouse and ponders its true meaning.* OPPOSITE *Entering the hall at Clandeboye is like walking into a Victorian dream of empire and heroic adventure.*

The country house, as it evolved in England, Scotland, Wales and Ireland, is one of the great cultural glories and achievements of the British Isles. Together with their parks, gardens and related buildings, country houses represent an artistic achievement of unquestioned international significance and offer fascinating insights into the society within which they were forged. At its best, the British country house and estate was a subtle organism of architectural distinction that played a key role in the local economy and in national politics. They were microcosms of the larger world and now, where they survive in reasonably complete manner, offer a window into a lost age – indeed offer, in most vivid terms, a particular and often very personal history of the nation.

By tradition the country house was a place in which the family displayed its taste, wealth and pedigree, a powerhouse in which matters of state were debated and decided, and from which its immediate region was governed. But the country house was also home and workplace to a full spectrum of society. The ancestral family presided in the grand rooms or comfortable quarters, but generations of servants also bustled below stairs, in the kitchens, pantries and laundries, in the gardens and in the surrounding estate that – in most cases – provided the economic base to keep the 'big house' and its family going in style.

The country house emerged in England in the sixteenth century as the tradition of fortified dwellings and castles, once the badges of honour,

ancient lineage and prestige, gave way to the ever-increasing desire for accommodation that was fashionable, grand, comfortable and convenient.

In a nation where the wealthy or ruling elite rooted themselves in the country rather than in cities the country house became the emblem of national and artistic identity and destiny, of wealth and pride. But the forces that fuelled the creation of country houses for 400 years – that sustained the creative cycle of country-house construction and rejuvenation – dissipated in the twentieth century. What had become the soul of the nation became, rapidly, dramatically and tragically, seemingly surplus to requirements. The reasons were many and varied, but essentially the times and the world changed. The slaughter of the First World War destroyed spirits, families and fortunes, and the national economy foundered. The political complexion of the nation changed and systems of taxation – Death Duty in particular – undermined the families that had built and continued to attempt to occupy great houses. It's been calculated that in the hundred or so years after 1900, around 1200 country houses were demolished in England alone, while in Scotland, one country house in six disappeared.[1] Demolition escalated dramatically in the years immediately following the Second World War, where, in a world saturated by socialist idealism, the country house was seen increasingly as a thing of the past, perhaps beautiful, but doomed and ultimately a product of elitism and privilege that seemed no longer relevant or admirable.

LEFT *The author inside the staircase hall at Easton Neston, Northamptonshire.*
OPPOSITE *The Marble Hall at Wentworth Woodhouse.*

In Ireland things were no better, and country houses fell victim in vast numbers to taxation and political prejudice. The country house was seen as commemorating years of oppression by English and Anglo-Irish landowners, and, although often designed by outstanding Irish architects, distinctly Irish in character and ornaments in the land, were consigned to oblivion with ruthless abandon.

The massacre of the country house is now seen as one the greatest cultural and artistic tragedies ever to overtake the British Isles. But this makes the survivors more precious, and the depleted numbers that endure are once again recognized as key hallmarks of national identity and high points of architectural endeavour.

This book, and the BBC2 series it accompanies, offers a history of Britain through the stories of six country houses – stories that are intimate, but that also relate to, and throw light on, the larger history of the nation. Each house is of architectural and artistic significance, and collectively they range in date from the early fifteenth century to the early twentieth. They cover a wide geographic spread,

> **The massacre of the country house is now seen as one the greatest cultural and artistic tragedies ever to overtake the British Isles…**

ABOVE *The British country house emerges from under a cloud: Kinross, Perthshire.*

stretching from Perthshire in Scotland to County Down in Northern Ireland and Hampshire in southern England, and each house tells the story of a particular family – its aspirations, achievements and tragedies. They also reveal the different activities that paid for the construction and maintenance of the country house through the centuries, from farming and wool, to coal-mining, imperial administration and stockjobbing. In several cases the houses possess collections of historic objects and archives that are of great national importance and highly relevant to its story and to that of the family who built it. In addition, in several cases the family remains closely connected with the house created for or occupied by generations of its ancestors.

None of the six country houses featured in this book will be greatly familiar to the general reader. This is not because they are relatively insignificant – indeed, they include some of the most important country houses ever built in Britain. There is Easton Neston, the only country house on which Nicholas Hawksmoor, one of the most brilliant architects of eighteenth-century Britain, worked as the lead designer; Wentworth Woodhouse, one of the largest and most perfect Georgian country houses ever built; and Marshcourt, arguably the best country house designed by Edwin Lutyens, now recognized as one of Britain's greatest ever architects.

Of the other three houses, South Wraxall marks, in splendid style, the transition from the fifteenth-century manor, consciously if symbolically fortified, to Tudor country house; Kinross House heralds the arrival of the pure Renaissance-inspired country house in Scotland, while Clandeboye House in Ulster is perhaps the greatest and most eloquent monument in Britain to the nineteenth-century ideal of empire.

By any standards, these buildings are of outstanding national significance. But these six houses are not well known because none of them is currently open to the public, nor, in most cases, have ever been on any general or regular basis. Indeed, the relative obscurity of these buildings, combined with their major interest and artistic

quality, confirms the richness of the repository of history that is still, and despite a hundred years of remorseless demolition, represented by the British country house. So this book and the television series it accompanies offer a privileged view of six of the nation's most fascinating, important and *private* country houses.

What the six country houses featured in this book have in common – besides their historic merit and secret natures – is that they all have, in various ways and to various degrees, faced the threats that destroyed so many of their fellows. The threats have not in most cases come directly from outright demolition, but from those forces that lead to the sale of contents, to dispersal of archives and to the separation of the house from the estate that, by tradition, has generated the money to support the family in the 'big house'. In several instances the houses discussed in this book have, in part, succumbed. In at least three cases, supporting estates have been sold, and in the case of Kinross House, such a detachment is currently proposed, with the house retaining just its immediate garden. This need not be a disaster, but it does limit the house's future options. When the estate, with its potential for offering at least partial financial support, has been detached, the very nature of the country house changes. It can no longer even attempt to be self-supporting or play a significant role in the community by functioning as the hub of a large and local economy. Instead it becomes an isolated if palatial dwelling, whose future is forever destined to be dependent on money made elsewhere or through such business activities – often volatile – that the house itself can accommodate.

Although the future of the British country house now seems relatively secure – its great virtues lauded at home and abroad – major threats remain. Buildings, no matter how artistically, historically or socially important, cannot survive if they do not have a productive use or purpose. It will be interesting, perhaps salutary, to revisit each of these six houses in ten years' time to see which endure, which retain the magic with which all are now bathed in abundance ❖

SOUTH WRAXALL MANOR

South Wraxall, Wiltshire

15ᵀᴴ
CENTURY

Tudor England and the birth
of the country house

❖

THE MANOR HOUSE AT SOUTH WRAXALL, Wiltshire, lies hidden down a narrow lane that once, years ago, was a main road, and the first impression it offers is charming and disarming, for it looks like little more than a terrace of ancient cottages. But there is more – far more – to this extraordinary house that is, in its layers of history, well-worn comfort and gentle beauty, perhaps the perfect English home. The manor is built of a mellow and handsome limestone that is improved rather than withered by age. It's a spellbinding complex of almost-separate structures arranged around a court, and includes an early fifteenth-century Great Hall, a stupendous late Elizabethan barrel-vaulted Great Chamber or drawing room that is flooded with light through vast mullioned and transomed windows, and a delicate gatehouse with the prettiest of late fifteenth-century oriel windows overlooking a large and placid pond. It is, to all who see it for the first time, an astonishing thing – not just an idyllic ancient English home, but a precious architectural jewel and wonderful survivor seemingly untouched since the early seventeenth century. South Wraxall Manor is indeed all these things, but is also something else. It's a parable, an allegory wrought in masonry and mortar. Surprising as it might now seem, the manor was, as its history reveals, once a world of striking, if not bizarre, contrasts, a place of light and shade, of public virtue contrasted with private vices, where ostentatious displays of architectural beauty were created by men whose deeds were ruthless, greedy, even bloodthirsty.

The manor was at one time the centre of an almost lawless land, run and controlled by an ambitious dynasty that in its pride and power felt answerable to none but the king – they were petty princes who, to all intents and purposes, were both judge and jury in their own domain. There are some details of the building that, to the observant and thoughtful, act as a warning of the manor's disquieting past, are reminders that it was once the lair of an almost predatory band of brothers. Outside the entrance to the Great Hall is a group of gargoyles that is most alarming in its imagery once you remember that few architectural objects were created in the fifteenth century just for fun, with no meaning or purpose. Gargoyles can be interpreted in many ways: those that are monstrous and leering can be seen as evocations of spirits that were old long before the Christian age and that evidently lived on in folk memory – that were called upon to protect the house and its inhabitants; then there are grimacing images of Sheela-na-gig that gaily expose their private parts, and smiling images of the Green Man that seem to celebrate the abundant fecundity of creation and commemorate the power of nature and the deep mysteries of the Wild Wood.

But strange as these stone creatures hanging from the eaves and towers of medieval churches and houses may be, few in my experience are so ominous and peculiar as those that congregate on the Great Hall at South Wraxall Manor. Here we see a monstrous and ferocious creation – a lion

PREVIOUS PAGES *The south-facing front of South Wraxall, dating from the early fifteenth century to the early twentieth, possesses a powerful, cohesive and almost disarmingly modest charm.*
LEFT *An early fifteenth-century gargoyle of the Great Hall, showing a frightful beast* *devouring a naked man head first.*
OPPOSITE *A glimpse of the house across the entrance court, showing the double-height porch leading to the Great Hall. South Wraxall is a mellow, idyllic – and somewhat mysterious – ancient English home.*

perhaps, a wolf or a great dog – devouring a man head first, with only his buttocks and well-delineated genitalia yet to be swallowed. And next to this extraordinary apparition is another, equally troubling, but this time showing the head of a man either emerging from the maw of the beast or being eaten legs and buttocks first. What can these mean? Who would choose to decorate their home with such images? What message do they carry? That man eats man? That the weaker go to the wall? That the strong and savage triumph? Are they a warning or are they a proclamation of intent?

After contemplating these images, digesting them, I move inside and inspect the gloomy heights of the Great Hall, where a series of corbels support the superb roof timbers. Most of these corbels are carved as representations of what, at first glance, appear to be weird humanoid lions – lions with no real manes, but almost human faces. Look again,

The visual beauty of South Wraxall Manor's early buildings is a reflection of the quest for, and exercise of, material wealth and power...

ABOVE LEFT *A detail of the early fifteenth-century Great Hall, showing the mighty fireplace and classically detailed timber screen added in 1598–1600.*
ABOVE RIGHT *The early fifteenth-century roof timbers of the Great Hall are ornate and intended to be seen and admired. Particularly striking are the arch-braced collars and cusped wind braces.*
OPPOSITE *The roof timbers rise from a series of corbels carved in a most strange manner. Are they intended to represent humanoid lions or impish monkeys to make a wicked visual pun that monkeys are monks and monks are monkeys?*

though, and they appear to be more like grinning apes or imps, or perhaps monkeys. Are they mocking mankind below, taunting those summoned to the Great Hall to receive summary judgement from the Lord of the Manor, sitting in feudal splendour on his lofty dais? All who raised their supplicating eyes to heaven, in astonishment of terror, would have seen these grinning and almost diabolical creatures, conceived perhaps as parodies of the corps of angels that were often carved within the roofs of fifteenth-century churches. At the very south end of the hall is a pair of quite different corbels. Facing each other are the figures of men – one holding a shield that looks like a page, while the other, clutching an open book, appears to be a tonsured monk. Are they shepherding or exorcizing their impish fellows? And is the monk blessing and condoning the activities taking place in the hall below and thus confirming that the lord of the manor rules – like the king – by divine right and is omnipotent? Or perhaps all these corbels are a wonderful window into the nooks and byways of the medieval mind, which was, we know, mightily amused by all manner of puns and visual jokes and metaphor. The rebus, the visual representation of a name, was a popular jest, so these images may be puns on the word 'monkey' – of unknown origin, but in use from the late fourteenth century – which seems to have been derived from the diminutive for 'monk'. So the roof could be an anti-clerical joke aimed at local monastic orders, showing monkeys as monks and monks as monkeys.

If these are indeed the messages enshrined in this collection of ancient images, then they truly did proclaim – indeed, foretell with uncanny accuracy – the events that were to unfold within this beautiful building.

The visual beauty of South Wraxall Manor's early buildings is a reflection of the quest for, and exercise of, material wealth and power. Nothing or little here seems to do with those lofty spiritual beliefs of the Middle Ages that were expressed through church building. Churches of the fifteenth century possess a Gothic beauty that is

transcendental, while the Gothic beauties of fifteenth-century South Wraxall Manor seem a little sinister – as sinister as the smirking simian monks – rather than angels that turn the roof of its Great Hall from a celestial domain into what one can imagine to be an infernal region. I stand in the Great Hall and stare up at the quizzically grimacing faces and they stare back, as they have done for nearly 600 years or so. As we exchange glances, I ponder this place of veiled meanings and realize that here is a hidden world, created over centuries, and now almost lost in time and through a changing and forgetful world. How much can I rediscover? Many messages, enigmatic or implied, are of course enshrined within the fabric of the building. These I can try to interpret, but, of course, the obvious starting place for my quest is the history of the family that built South Wraxall Manor and occupied it for over 550 years.

THE ORIGIN OF
SOUTH WRAXALL MANOR

The manor of South Wraxall was owned by the Abbess and Convent of Shaftesbury from the reign of King Aethelred in the late tenth and early eleventh centuries as part of the manor of Bradford. In the thirteenth century part of the manor of Bradford was granted to the priory of Mary Magdalene of Monkton Farleigh, near South Wraxall,[1] and in the twenty-fifth year of the reign of Edward III (1352) the Convent of Shaftesbury granted to 'Thomas Scathelok their villain of the Manor of Bradford ... and Editha his wife ... one messuage [and] two virgates, and nine acres of land, and four acres of meadow with ... appurtances in Lyghe and Wrokeshale, within the Manor of Bradford.'[2] What happened to Thomas we do not know, nor do we know if his 'messuage' was erected on the site of the existing manor, but at some point before the reign of Henry VI, who came to the throne in 1422, the Longe or le Long family were in possession of the manor of South Wraxall.[3] 'By what means,' observed antiquarian Thomas Larkins Walker in 1838, 'is not recorded.'[4] The head of the family was then Robert Long, and it would seem that he built the earliest surviving portions of the manor, between 1410 and 1420. Exactly what he constructed, and what survives of his building, is contested. He certainly built the Great Hall, and probably most of the wing to its south that contains the remains of an early kitchen. The kitchen wing, off the low end of the Great Hall, would usually also contain a buttery (for the storage of liquids, bottles or butts) and a pantry (for the storage of bread and other foods). Above these rooms, tainted by smoke and the smell of cooking, would usually be inferior lodgings.

But things seem to have been unconventional at South Wraxall Manor. The buttery is supposed to have been in the low, semi-basement room beyond the north or dais and high-table end of the Great Hall. This may be a memory of Thomas Scathelok's mid-fourteenth-century house incorporated into the early fifteenth-century manor. The large room above the buttery, in the location usually occupied by the family's comfortable, convenient Great Chamber or Solar, may have been the Guest Chamber. Whatever the original use of this room, it was clearly high status because rising above it, and now hidden by later additions, are the timbers of a very fine early fifteenth-century roof, presumably the same date as the surviving roof of the Great Hall. Like the roof of the Great Hall, it has an arch-braced collar construction, and its wind braces are ornamented with cusps and chamfers confirming that – as in the Great Hall – this roof structure was not to be concealed, but to be seen and admired from ground level. The other portion of the existing manor that is generally thought to date from the early fifteenth century is the central portion of the north wing, suggesting that the early fifteenth-century manor was, in general form, L-shaped.

The original pattern of life these fragments suggest is most clear. The house was both a place to display status and power, and a functional machine

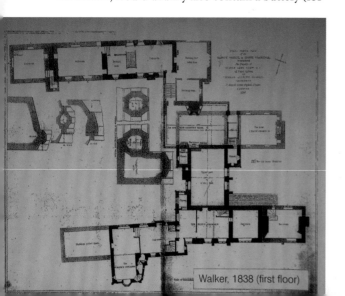

LEFT *Plan of the second-floor level of South Wraxall Manor in 1838. North is to the top. In the centre is the upper portion of the Great Hall, with kitchen range to its south, the Great Chamber (converted into a splendid barrel-vaulted room in about 1600) to its north, and to the northwest a wing, making the fifteenth-century manor L-shaped in plan. The gatehouse was added to the southwest in about 1495 to define the south edge of the entrance court.* OPPOSITE *The view across the entrance court towards the huge mullioned and transomed window, added to the Great Chamber in about 1600.*

Walker, 1838 (first floor)

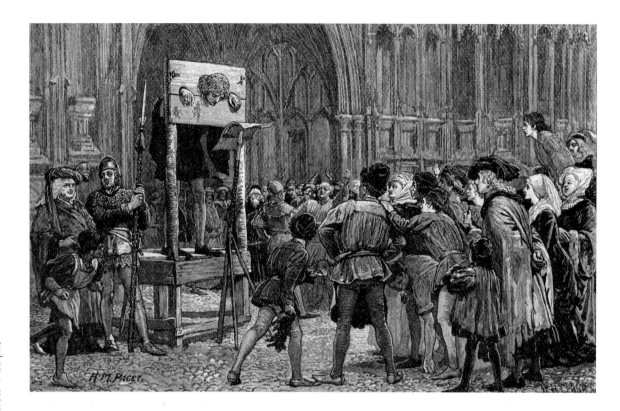

for living. The Great Hall would, in the early fifteenth
century, have been used by the family on a limited
basis – perhaps for feasting on high days and
holidays – and been heated by a central hearth, with
smoke curling up and escaping through a louvre in
the centre of the open roof. To escape smoke and
noisy company, the family would have generally lived
in the comfort, convenience and privacy of their Great
Chamber and bedrooms behind the dais or north end
of the hall. In addition, the Great Hall would also, of
course, have been used by family members for official
business – to receive deputations of tenants and to sit
in judgement as local magistrates.

Off the opposite – south – end of the Great Hall
were the functional service rooms grouped around
the kitchen. At South Wraxall the two-storey range
to the north, perhaps detached from the Great Hall
or connected to it by a timber-built covered way,
was most probably used for family bedrooms or
lodgings. There must also have been stables and
other utilitarian buildings, perhaps built of timber,
whose whereabouts are now unknown or obscured
by later buildings.

ABOVE A nineteenth-century
view of Perkin Warbeck being
pilloried in London following
the collapse of his armed
rebellion for the English throne.
Thomas Long aided in the
suppression of the revolt.
BELOW LEFT & RIGHT
Following the marriage of the
king's son Prince Arthur to
the Spanish Infanta, Thomas
was knighted.

OVERLEAF The south elevation
of the north range, dating from
the fifteenth and sixteenth
centuries, seen through an arch
of the gatehouse.

The creator of this early fifteenth-century manor, Robert Long, remains a misty character, and we have no idea why he chose to embellish his Great Hall with such strange details. The chronicler John Leland recorded in his *Itinerary* of 1535–43 that Robert was the son of 'Long Thomas' a 'stoute felaw'.[5] We also know that Robert was a Member of Parliament, chosen a 'knight of the shire' and a wealthy lawyer whose fortune and power were largely due to the fact that, as Leland put it, Long had been 'sette up by one of the old Lordes Hungrefordes'.[6] The Hungerford family, powerful local magnates in fifteenth-century Wiltshire, used Long as their lawyer and adviser, and evidently elevated him to a key position in the feudal world that they dominated. Through his connection with the Hungerfords, Robert Long became rich, respected and, perhaps, even feared. He certainly seems to have acquired a reputation as a man not to cross and who was happy to manipulate the law in his own favour or in the favour of his clients. A chancery case with which Long became involved suggests that he was unscrupulous and cynical in his use, and abuse, of his power and connections. It seems that he 'maintained' or supported one Edmund Ford in a property case heard in a local court, and then took the rent of the property as the fee for his services. Ford tried to recover the money, but could not get redress in common law 'by cause of grete power, consideration, unlawful maytenance and alliance of the sayde Robert Longe in the sayde shyre'.[7] Robert Long's influence was such that in 1442 he managed to get three of his sons elected with him to parliament, and in the same year was appointed a Justice of the Peace.

Robert Long married twice, one of which marriages forged an alliance with the powerful and local Popham family. He had four sons, John and Henry. The latter was born about 1417, became Sheriff of Wiltshire, a Member of Parliament and married three times, but in 1490 died childless. Robert Long died in 1446 and South Wraxall Manor passed to Henry and then, because he was childless, to his nephew Thomas, the son of John Long and Margaret Wayte. Thomas Long played an important role in the rise of the house of Long – and in the growth of South Wraxall Manor – because he operated and prospered not just locally, but also within the larger framework of early Tudor England. Thomas quickly associated himself with the new Tudor dynasty, established when Henry VII seized the throne in August 1485, and in 1497 was among a body of nobles who went with Edward, Duke of Buckingham to Taunton to meet the king. Thomas made himself useful to the king during the extraordinary events that unfolded in 1497, when a long-standing challenge to Henry VII's right to reign was eventually quashed. The challenge came from a mysterious character named Perkin Warbeck, who claimed to be the Duke of York and son of Edward IV. The Tudors claimed he was a Fleming or French adventurer and opportunist, but – just possibly – he was who he claimed to be. What is more certain is that Thomas Long's display of loyalty to Henry VII during the last days of Warbeck's strange battle for the throne did much to boost the stock of the Long family at the Tudor court. He became one of the inner circle of men who could be trusted and relied upon. Royal recognition of Thomas's worth came in 1501 when, as part of the celebrations of the marriage of the king's son, Prince Arthur, to the Spanish Infanta, Thomas was knighted.

REFLECTIONS OF GRANDEUR
By this time Sir Thomas Long was himself married – to Margery Darrell of Littlecote, Wiltshire – so was connected through this marriage to the powerful Seymour family of Wolf Hall, among whom was soon to be numbered Jane Seymour, a future queen of Henry VIII and mother of a king. In addition to the Manor of South Wraxall, Sir Thomas was also in possession of Draycot Cerne – probably through inheritance from his father, John.

Draycot now became the main seat of the Longs (where Sir Thomas was buried in splendour in 1508), but South Wraxall underwent a key addition that was calculated to impress visitors with the new status of the family. Some time around 1495 to 1500 a gatehouse was added to the west, linked to the

kitchen range south of the Great Hall, to start to define a courtyard in front of the west elevation of the hall. But this was not a serious defensive gatehouse – it was an ornamental affair, raising the status of the modest manor to a mini, if symbolic, castle – the residence of a minor noble. The gatehouse, standing on what was then a public road, also offered an opportunity for a satisfying and very visible display of the Long family's newly acquired badges and emblems of honour and high birth. Above the arch was placed a most handsome and projecting oriel window with traceried and cusped windows that offered splendid views along the road. To each side of the arch are heraldic devices that proclaimed the Longs' grand connections and pedigree. On one side was placed a stag's head (now lost), which was the crest or emblem of the Popham family into which Robert Long had married. Opposite there still survives a

peculiar device – a Marshall's fetterlock – essentially an early type of padlock used to secure the chains or fetters binding prisoners or felons. This was an emblem of the families of Draycot. Between these two emblems, at the top of the arch and below the oriel, is a stone panel carrying the arms of the Long family. These emblems must date from the second half of the fifteenth century, but exactly how and when they were acquired, and their original legitimacy, is now impossible to determine. All that can be said is that in the Middle Ages, certainly into the fifteenth century, rural England formed an isolated and insular world in which powerful lords of the manor ruled over all whom they believed – and that the feudal system confirmed – were subservient. Just as the king ruled by divine right, so these local princes saw themselves as God's anointed rulers fulfilling the destiny that providence had decreed.

When serving in local or national armies, as vassals of the regional ruler or the king, these feudal lords of the manor needed to carry a coat of arms so that they could be identified. If they did not have arms granted, or did not acquire them through marriage, they would simply create their own: by usage it would be recognized, and by habit applied in various ways to the ornamentation not only of their persons, but also of their places of residence.

The College of Arms, which now controls the granting of arms, can throw no specific light on the origins or meaning of the Longs' traditional

LEFT ABOVE *The arms of the Long family, featuring a lion, above the arch of the gatehouse.*
LEFT BELOW *The Marshall's fetterlock, a type of early padlock for securing felons, that became an heraldic emblem of the Long family and enriches the gatehouse.*

OPPOSITE *The gatehouse, added to South Wraxall in about 1495–1500, is one of the most architecturally distinguished and characterful features of the manor. Particularly charming is the oriel window, with its fine, cusped arches.*

heraldic display. In 1530 Henry VIII issued letters patent to the Clarenceux King of Arms to conduct an heraldic 'visitation' to establish who had arms, what they were and whether they had any right to them. Only at this period were formal regulations instituted regulating the use of arms. Informed speculation suggests that by this time the Long arms – a rampant white lion on a black background sprinkled with crosses – had been in use for nearly a hundred years. If so, this ancestral use, combined with the rising status of the family, meant that the arms would not have been questioned or curtailed. The only significant clue to the date of the arms comes from rolls drawn up by heralds, showing the arms of prominent individuals or families assembled for a particular occasion, such as a tournament or military muster, at a particular location. The arms of Long appear in no fewer than six rolls of arms dating from 1465 to 1520, so it's clear that the Long lion and crosses were in use by the family from at least 1465.[8]

From this period – around 1495 – the fetterlock appeared like a rash around South Wraxall, a sign, presumably, that newly arrived Tudor families like the Longs felt compelled to display their recently achieved noble status and heraldic badges. It appears, along with other emblems and arms to which the Longs laid ownership through marriage, on shields that were probably placed by Sir Thomas below the timber corbels in the Great Hall. Post-Reformation Tudor England rapidly became something of a meritocracy, as ancient values and certainties, such as the domination of the Roman Catholic Church, were challenged or overturned. Old families were thwarted or made cautious, while the new men were on the march, demonstrating, by their intelligence and cunning, their right to a favoured niche in the turbulent and vastly energetic early Tudor England. But that England, despite the rewards and opportunities it offered to all men of talent, was little more than a tyrannical state, especially after the Reformation, when a religion-based society was replaced by a culture of rampant materialism, greed and raw and personal ambition.

Sir Thomas Long and his wife Margery had seven children, and it was the eldest boy, Henry, who inherited all the property on Sir Thomas's death in 1508. Henry also, it seems, inherited his father's ambition to prosper and rise. What Henry did not, however, inherit was Sir Thomas's knighthood. Such ranks were not hereditary in Tudor Britain (it was not until 1611, when James I initiated the rank of baronet, that certain ranks of knighthood, like titles in the peerage, became hereditary). But this did not bother Henry. Through his father's connections, he managed to attend the coronation of Henry VIII in June 1509, but Henry evidently realized that, to truly establish himself at court, he had to win recognition in his own right – and his chance came in 1513. England still possessed Calais and its immediate territory, and this offered a splendid theatre for warlike contest and chivalric engagement with ever-vigilant and aggressive bands of French knights and soldiers, whether or not England and France actually happened to be at war. In fact, in 1513 they were, technically at least, in a state of hostility. England, the Swiss and the Holy Roman Emperor Maximilian formed an offensive alliance against France, and in July 1513 Henry VIII and 30,000 English soldiers landed at Calais ready for combat. Included in this number was young Henry Long. Soon skirmishing commenced and the Battle of the Spurs was fought – so named by the triumphant English because that day the French used their spurs more than their swords, so anxious were they to flee the field. Related to this victory was an action at Thérouanne during which, in a cavalry action, Henry distinguished himself before the appreciative eyes of Henry VIII. Perhaps the king had his eye on Henry because the ambitious young man had made a point of getting to know the king, even managing to joust with him at Greenwich in 1510. Henry would, no doubt, be familiar with the Long white rampant lion on a black field, and would have recognized his former jousting opponent on the battlefield. This seems to have been a case when brand recognition paid rich dividends, for after the action and in a most chivalric manner worthy of the court of King

> England, despite the rewards and opportunities it offered to all men of talent, was little more than a tyrannical state, especially after the Reformation, when a religion-based society was replaced by a culture of rampant materialism, greed and raw and personal ambition...

ABOVE *The interior side of the oriel window in the gatehouse. From his lodging above the arch the gatekeeper would have had distant views along the public road that once passed immediately in front of the manor.*

Arthur – in many ways the role model for the aspirant Tudor court – Henry VIII knighted Henry Long for his bravery in battle.

This royal act of recognition was the making of the man and, in many ways, the defining moment of Henry Long's life. From now on Sir Henry became a member of the inner circle of Henry VIII's court, as his father had been of the court of Henry VII. He adopted an additional crest for the Long family following his royal reward for bravery – it shows a roaring lion's head with the blood-red hand of a man gripped in its mouth. This is a fierce image that reflects, with truth, Sir Henry's somewhat ferocious and excessive character. He married Frideswide Hungerford, a member of the ancient and much-respected Hungerford family, and had three children; then, around 1517, he married a widow, Eleanor Leversedge, and had nine children. As well as breeding copiously, Sir Henry secured and held a series of official posts, both local and national, all of which gradually enhanced his power, prestige and wealth. Perhaps most useful, or at least most profitable, of these was his appointment as a commissioner for the valuation of the wealth of monastic property in England. This post was probably the consequence of close connections with Thomas Cromwell, Henry VIII's chief minister, whose patronage Sir Henry used to secure a position for his brother Richard, and to gain a nomination for a seat in parliament in 1532. As far as we can now tell, the links between Sir Henry and Cromwell were firm, perhaps there was even genuine friendship. Certainly, Sir Henry played a role in one of Cromwell's great political and personal achievements. Cromwell organized the divorce of Henry VIII from Catherine of Aragon, and orchestrated the monarch's marriage in January 1533 to his ill-starred mistress Anne Boleyn, an action that resulted in Henry's break from Rome and instigated the Protestant Reformation in England. When Anne's coronation feast was held in June, Sir Henry, as a sign of favour, was appointed to serve as a steward.

With a friend like Cromwell, Sir Henry's motives and character seem clear. He wanted to attach himself to a rising star and he was on the make. And if these were indeed his ambitions, then during the late 1530s he was most successful. The role of a commissioner of monastic wealth put Sir Henry in a powerful and well-informed position to participate in what can be called state gangsterism, when Henry VIII, seemingly inspired and guided by Cromwell, used the break with Rome as a God- (or Devil-) sent opportunity to appropriate the accumulated wealth and property of the Church in England. Sir Henry grasped his chance and – along with many other new, ruthless and rising men – laid claim to monastic land following the Dissolution after 1536. In consequence, Sir Henry gained possession, as owner or lessee, of vast swathes of former monastic land and buildings once belonging to St Mary's Priory near Kington St Michael, and Bradenstoke Priory near Lyneham, both in Wiltshire, plus lands appropriated by the Crown from Malmesbury Abbey. The acquisition of this land seems to have been the final act in a long feud that Sir Henry had conducted with Richard Camme, the Abbot of Malmesbury, before the Dissolution. The true origin of the feud is uncertain, but it came to a head when Sir Henry's men attacked some of the abbot's servants who were hunting on land claimed by Henry as bailiff of Charlton Wood and keeper of Braden Forest. One of Sir Henry's men was killed in the fracas, and this provided an opportunity for the removal of the abbot. The way in which Sir Henry

conducted what now appears to have become a blood feud reveals the dark side of the man, and of the tyrannical age when none were safe if they challenged the authority, or provoked the ire, of Henry VIII's inner circle.

An inquest was held and, according to a contemporary account, 'Sir Henry Long ... a man of great authority in Co. Wilts, and being of malicious mind towards the [abbot] because of quarrels between [their] friends and servants ... gave false evidence at the inquest ... declaring that the [abbot] was privy to the murder.'[9] This evidence, uttered by so powerful a witness, was enough to get the abbot indicted by the coroner's jury as an accessory to murder. At the following quarter sessions at Marlborough, Sir Henry packed the jury with supporters, and any attempt to replace them was met with the new impartial jurors being arrested by Sir Henry and imprisoned. This unscrupulous behaviour on Sir Henry's part does

EXPULSION OF THE MONKS BY ORDER OF HENRY VIII.

ABOVE *The marriage of Henry VIII to Anne Boleyn.*
LEFT *A nineteenth-century view of the Reformation of the 1530s and 1540s – a monk being expelled from his monastery.*
OPPOSITE *A detail of the north range. Peacocks still disport themselves at South Wraxall, as they have done for generations.*

not seem to have been out of character. In another case he abused his power as sheriff in a dispute over land with a man called Walter Fynamore, and was accused of behaving 'more like an oppressor, cruel tyrant and extortioner than an indifferent executor and minister'.[10]

In the abbot's trial things did not, initially, go quite as Sir Henry would have wished. Despite all his efforts, the jury proved reluctant to convict the abbot. Sir Henry's reaction was to make a direct appeal to Henry VIII, whose response set the pattern for petty tyrants and oppressors. Rather than displaying the 'indifferent' and impartial majesty expected from a noble prince, King Henry backed his crony Sir Henry. The jury was instructed by the king to find the abbot and three other monks guilty, and if they did not, the jurors were told their names and addresses would be passed to the king. This was threat enough. Fearing they would be marked men and subject to instant and arbitrary arrest, the jurors duly found the hapless abbot and his monks guilty.[11]

Thus did proud and ruthless men like Sir Henry – the epitome of thrusting ambition and greed for

❝ The wealth and building opportunities created by the Dissolution for the new and rising families of England created a frenzy of house building. Many of these families, 'nouveau riche', vied to display their newly won wealth and status…

ABOVE *Beauty and tranquillity. An oriental vase and cusped arches in a low, ground-floor room.*
OVERLEAF *One of the most magnificent and fascinating late-Elizabethan rooms in England. The early fifteenth-century Great Chamber was transformed in about 1600 into a fashionable and comfortable withdrawing room or high dining room. A plaster, barrel-vaulted ceiling and a pair of vast mullioned and transomed windows were added and, most striking of all, a huge fireplace. Packed with enigmatic meanings, messages and symbols, the fireplace is also a dramatic statement that the Continental Renaissance had arrived in style in rural Wiltshire.*

temporal power and plenty – conduct themselves before the Dissolution, and thus after the Dissolution did they acquire beautiful buildings and huge tracts of land that had for centuries been used for the support of the Church and to help sustain an often needy population. Well before the Dissolution, certain monastic establishments had been accused of being mean and materialistic – a strong anti-clerical streak in late medieval secular society must have been fuelled by a certain amount of monastic misbehaviour – but this monastic meanness and misconduct was as nothing compared to the behaviour of the likes of Sir Henry Long. Monastic buildings were abandoned, torn down, remodelled or robbed of materials to create new buildings. The wealth and building opportunities created by the Dissolution for the new and rising families of England created a frenzy of house building. Many of these families, 'nouveau riche', vied to display their newly won wealth and status. The architectural consequences could have defined new levels of vulgarity. But – and this can be seen as one of the paradoxes of history – the visual consequence of this frenzy was not baneful, but utterly poetic. With great and perhaps perplexing irony, from mean and greedy actions came transcendental and eternal architectural beauty. Men like Sir Henry Long may not have been particularly admirable human beings, but they and their age had vigour, invention and a finger on the pulse of creation. Henry VIII's break with tradition was revolutionary and stimulated among Englishmen a new sense of destiny and confidence, of inquiry and exploration, and that encouraged intellectual freedom and artistic invention. It was, after all, the age that saw the English start to establish themselves on distant continents and that ultimately produced Christopher Marlowe, Ben Jonson and William Shakespeare.

The Birth of the English Country House

It was in this mid-Tudor period that opportunity, desire and means coalesced to create an astonishing body of architecture – an architecture given extra punch and originality because it continued the great craft traditions of the Middle Ages, embraced the new Renaissance style seeping into Britain from the Low Countries and France, and accommodated in a most creative manner pioneering ideas about increased comfort, convenience and privacy. Arguably, it was this moment that saw the birth of the great English country house. As Mark Girouard has explained: 'Not only were country houses built in greater numbers [during the Tudor and Jacobean period] than ever before or since in England, but they dominated their age to a greater extent even than in the eighteenth century.'[12]

Today the buildings produced during the Tudor century can be seen to represent a golden age of English architecture – an age that was the bridge between two cultures: the Gothic of the Middle Ages and the Rome-inspired neoclassical that defined the architecture of the two centuries to follow. Tudor architecture was at once rooted in the best of the past – solid construction, beautiful materials and fine craftsmanship – while also being radical, experimental and ground breaking in its use of new materials, such as terracotta, and the generous use of brick and glass that, by permitting large windows, transformed the nature of domestic interiors.

A commentator of the Tudor age, William Harrison, spoke of the desire of his contemporaries to build the 'house beautiful', to 'cast forth ... beames of stately and curious workmanship into every quarter of the country'.[13] These 'beames of stately and curious workmanship' fall, if only lightly, on the very limited works Sir Henry executed at South Wraxall Manor, but fall they do. Draycot was the main family home for the Longs, so there was little need or desire to transform the fifteenth-century house, but Sir Henry did alter at least one major room to capture and reflect the spirit of his age. Harrison expressed one aspect of this spirit – to create beauty through fine craftsmanship, and Andrew Boorde, in his *Dyetary of Helth* (1542), expresses another – the quest for new comforts and an expectation of new levels of civilized behaviour within the home. Boorde's book is, in a sense, a

manual for building and organizing a comfortable, convenient and polite home for the modern man. In chapter three Boorde advises his readers to 'permyt no common pyssyng places be aboute the howse or mansion; & let the common howse of easement be ouer [over] some water, or elles elongated from the howse. And beware of emptynge of pysse-pottes, and pyssing in chymmes, so that all euyll [evil] and contagious ayres may be expelled, and clene ayres kept vnputryfyed.'[14]

Sir Henry's presence at South Wraxall Manor, and the early sixteenth-century desire for comfort, 'stately and curious workmanship' and privacy is expressed to perfection in a small first-floor room just to the south of the Great Hall. It was created in what perhaps had been a large lodging above the fifteenth-century kitchen. It is possible that Sir Henry divided the lodgings into two rooms by inserting a central chimney-stack and wall – both the existing fireplaces date from the early sixteenth century, and both the small rooms, by the

acquisition of their own fireplaces, would have become very desirable because they offered warmth and privacy. Of the two rooms, it is the one to the west and not above the kitchen (so presumably less subject to the smell of cooking) that is the finer. It is now known as the Raleigh Room because Sir Walter Raleigh, a friend in the late sixteenth century of Sir Henry's grandson Sir Walter Long, is supposed to have sat here with a pipe of Virginia tobacco, exhaling smoke and frightening the servants into thinking he was on fire.

Originally 'stately and curious workmanship' was expressed by the fine oak-made panelling, each panel embellished with a carved representation of folded linen, and by the beautifully designed and detailed fireplace. It is a wonderful thing, very much on the cutting edge of architectural fashion as it was evolving in the first couple of decades of the sixteenth century. The wide fireplace opening is framed by a shallow pointed arch, late perpendicular Gothic and characteristic of early

OPPOSITE *The wide, fifteenth-century kitchen fireplace immediately south of the screens passage in the Great Hall.* ABOVE & BELOW *The fashionable fire surround inserted in the south range in the very early sixteenth century by Sir Henry Long. It combines a*

late Gothic pointed 'Tudor arch' with classically profiled mantle moulding. In the spandrels of the arch are initials: on the left, SHL for Sir Henry Long, and on the right (see detail, left) H and E entwined within a lovers' knot, symbolizing Henry and his wife Eleanor united for eternity.

Tudor architecture. But above the Gothic arch is a mantelpiece that takes the form of a classical Tuscan cornice and marks the arrival in England of Italian Renaissance taste – all in all a wonderful fusion. But it's the ornament within the spandrel of the arch that intrigues me. There are carved vines and grapes suggesting the convivial life, the supping of wine, that this fireplace was evidently intended to encourage, and on its left-hand side are the initials S.H.L, commemorating the fact that this fireplace – or perhaps the room – was created by Sir Henry Long. On the right the initials H and E are surrounded and linked by a complex lovers' knot. This refers to Henry and his wife Eleanor, whom he married in about 1517, and implies their love was true, as this fireplace was evidently intended to commemorate, in stone, for eternity.[15] Eleanor Leversedge (née Wrotesley), Sir Henry's second wife, had, by tradition, her own grand room within the house. It is still debated, but it seems that Sir Henry made other additions or alterations to the

manor. He may have added a second kitchen with
bread oven to the east of the existing early fifteenth-
century kitchen (although some argue that this
addition was made two generations later) and
perhaps a set of smart, comfortable and discreetly
located rooms north of the Great Chamber.
Certainly, the first-floor room in this range is still
referred to as Dame Eleanor's Room, but the
fireplace it contains – a fine and extensive affair
incorporating a life-sized, stone-carved vase of
flowers – appears to date from around 1600.

After Henry VIII died in 1547, Sir Henry seems
to have enjoyed a good relationship with Edward VI,
whose christening he had attended in 1537, and
even survived the reign of Mary I, who, after she
came to the throne in July 1553, tried by most bloody
means to reimpose Roman Catholicism on England
and in the process make the nation subservient to
Spain. In fact, Sir Henry lived unmolested until his
death in October 1556. In his will he requested to be
buried at Draycot rather than South Wraxall, and

ABOVE *Nineteenth-century
stained glass in the Long Chapel
in St James's parish church in
South Wraxall village. It shows
the Long arms and roundels
containing images of fetterlocks.*
BELOW LEFT & RIGHT
Edward VI and Queen Mary.

thus revealed the relative status of the two houses and manors. Draycot was by then the more-prized Long possession.

THE LONG SHRINE

Sir Henry's son Robert, born in about 1515, inherited the Long possessions and appears to have done less to the fabric of South Wraxall Manor than did his father. But he did transform the parish church of St James in South Wraxall village. The fabric of the church dates largely from the early fourteenth century, and on its south corner a large chantry chapel had been added – almost undoubtedly for the Long family – a hundred years or so before the Reformation, so presumably by the first Robert Long. Nobody is now sure. Chantry chapels were places in which the living prayed for the dead in an attempt to ease the passage of the soul from purgatory to heaven. In anticipation of the beneficial function of such sustained acts of prayer, those living in the Middle Ages would build and endow chantry chapels so that priests or beadsmen could pray in perpetuity for their souls. After the Protestant Reformation such mystic Roman Catholic practices were dismissed as mere superstition and discontinued. So what was to be done with redundant chantry chapels?

In 1566 Robert Long took a course of action being followed by many. Rather than allowing the chapel's removal or decay, he decided to embellish it and, for the greater glory of the family, make it a grand Long sepulchre and most impressive family pew. Robert, like his father, felt the need to display grandeur. He had entered the Tudor court as an esquire to the body of Henry VIII – a useful position, for it gave him access to the king at most intimate moments that were well calculated for the asking and granting of favours – and later struck the posture of a warrior by serving with Henry VIII's army in 1544 at the siege of Boulogne. But in the mid-1560s he was still elbowing for position and distinction: he was not knighted or made Sheriff of Wiltshire until 1575, so a showy new family chapel was just the sort of status symbol he needed.

The main external alteration to the chapel was the insertion of a door in the south wall, so that while common parishioners entered the church through the main porch, the family could process into its pew in stately and exclusive manner, much as the king's family entered its royal chapels. Above the door are Robert Long's initials, the date 1566 and – to proclaim the family's pedigree – a stone-carved representation of the Pomfret stag and the Draycot fetterlock.

I entered the church through the small door, as the family did for hundreds of years. The chapel, like the church, has been much altered over the centuries, particularly during the nineteenth, when a large, Gothic-style arch was inserted in the north wall of the chapel, connecting it more fully to the nave of the church. But many early details survive, some pre-Reformation, such as the small angled opening – the squint or hagioscope – that permits a view of the high altar, and niches on the east wall for housing sacred images, frowned upon and removed during the Reformation as idolatrous. But most striking is a tomb that stands below the large south window. The effigy of a woman lies on a tall chest. Her face has been smashed in a frenzied iconoclastic attack, no doubt carried out soon after the Reformation, or perhaps in the early seventeenth century by Puritans, who would have seen this image – like the long-lost statues in the chapel niches – as breaking the Second Commandment, which orders the faithful not 'to make unto thee any graven image, or any likeness of any thing that is in heaven above, or that is in the earth beneath, or that is in the water under the earth'.[16] I ran my hand over the shockingly smashed features. This vandalism, this destruction of beauty, was, of course, provoked by fear of divine retribution, for the commandment continues, 'Thou shalt not bow down thyself to them, nor serve them: for I the LORD thy God am a jealous God, visiting the iniquity of the fathers upon the children unto the third and fourth generation.'[17]

Clearly, someone thought in the sixteenth or early seventeenth century that God would assume that the image of this woman was being venerated as a goddess and that He would not be amused. To save all from His jealous vengeance, she – or at least her face – had to be destroyed. It all remains most extraordinary. But despite the destruction, the tomb retains much that is human, personal and revealing. The woman appears to be wearing a widow's veil, at her feet lies a seemingly wriggling lapdog, and the chest on which she lies is still emblazoned with heraldry. No-one is sure whom the figure represents. It appears to date somewhere from 1490 to 1510, but I know I am contemplating a once-eminent Long lady, for the chest is embellished with fetterlocks, and at its centre is a shield bearing a rampant lion placed on a field of crosses. But there are also the arms of both Seymour and Berkeley, suggesting the woman's own family origins, and that she married into the Longs. Consequently, some think the monument was erected by Thomas Long, who married into the Seymour clan, and that it commemorates one of his wife's well-loved and widowed relations, perhaps one of Thomas's aunts through marriage.

THE APOTHEOSIS OF SOUTH WRAXALL MANOR

Sir Robert Long died in 1581, leaving nine Wiltshire manors to his eldest son, Walter. As things turned out, Walter was the last Long to own both South Wraxall Manor and Draycot. He was also, from the architectural point of view, arguably the most important Long in the history of South Wraxall Manor. In the late 1590s he decided to enlarge, glorify and update the house, and in the process, and because of the quality of the works, made it into one of the most important and impressive late Tudor houses in England.

But who was this man who suddenly increased the size and status of the manor? Some answers and insights into his nature are offered by the works themselves, which are in many respects far from merely mute works of architecture or ornament. It is clear that, on a prosaic level, Walter's alterations and additions were intended to bring even greater comfort and convenience – as well as fashion and dignity – to South Wraxall Manor. But Walter also seems to have wanted the new works to carry messages, some clear and conventional, others enigmatic. But before exploring these, it's necessary to explore the man and to ponder what was one of the defining and most revealing events in the annals of the Long family.

Walter Long was one of the wealthiest landowners in the county and also a magistrate and Member of Parliament who operated on the periphery of the royal court and, after serving in a

LEFT ABOVE *The lintel of the door inserted into the Long Chapel in 1566 by Sir Robert Long, whose initials it bears, along with the date and the family's heraldic badges of honour and pedigree – the fetterlock and stag's head.*
LEFT BELOW *A fine tomb, of* around 1490–1500, *belonging to a somewhat mysterious but evidently important female member of the Long family.*
OPPOSITE *The main entry to the church with, beyond it, the Long family chapel, created in* 1566 *within an earlier chantry chapel.*

military capacity in Ireland, was knighted in 1589. But most interesting are his marriages. First, he married Mary Packington and had one child, a son named John Long. Queen Elizabeth was evidently on good terms with the family, and in 1588 gave Mary, or perhaps Walter's mother, eighteen ounces of gilt plate. When Mary died, Walter married Catherine Thynne of Longleat, a former maid of honour to Queen Elizabeth, and with her had four sons – Walter, Henry, Thomas and Robert.

But, if old accounts are to be believed, with this marriage came a darkening shadow. Catherine brooded over the fact that her stepson John rather than her eldest son Walter would eventually inherit her husband's estates and, as in a nursery rhyme, she became a wicked stepmother, determined to get John disinherited. According to one nineteenth-century chronicler, Catherine 'would get her acquaintance to make [John] drunk and then expose him to his father'.[18] Eventually, Catherine succeeded in persuading her husband to disinherit John, but that was not the end of the story. The disinheritance was legally challenged after Sir Walter died in 1610, with the result that the Long estates were divided: Catherine's son Walter got Draycot, and John inherited South Wraxall, as was his due. John married and had four sons and one daughter. The estate passed from elder son to elder son until 1715, when it went to a Long relative, and so remained in the family until well into the twentieth century.[19]

More compelling than this somewhat sorry tale of attempted disinheritance are the epic events surrounding Walter and his brother Henry's blood-curdling relationship with the Danvers family: it makes sixteenth-century Wiltshire look like the Wild West. The origin of the feud between the Longs and the Danvers is now unknown, but it all came to a head in 1594, as explained in *State Papers*, which contain a 'True declaration of the ground of the conceived mislike of Sire Walter Longe, Knighte, & Henry Longe, gent his brother, againste Sir John Danvers, Knighte, his Sonnes & ffollowers'.[20] The papers give an account of 'the Abuses offered by Sir Walter Longe and his Bretheren against Sir John Danvers, his Sonnes & Servauntes' and the 'manie

❝ The epic events surrounding Walter and his brother Henry's blood-curdling relationship with the Danvers family made sixteenth-century Wiltshire look like the Wild West…

ABOVE *Henry Danvers became a hunted man after the killing of Henry Long.*

Insolent behaviours' which culminate with the killing of a Danvers servant by a Long servant, which another left 'daungerouslie wounded'. This was a crude mistake on the part of the Long faction, for the local magistrate happened to be Sir John Danvers, who promptly had a number of the Longs' servants committed to trial for murder. In retaliation, the Long brothers, backed up by a body of their retainers – essentially hired guns – burst into the house of a Danvers' tenant and in the fracas 'a glass of beer was thrown in the face of the principall officer of ... Sir John Danvers'. Fortunately, no one else was killed or seriously injured following this alarming confrontation.

According to the *State Papers*, Sir Charles Danvers, one of Sir John's sons, tried to make peace. He sent 'gentlemanlike letters' to Sir Walter Long, but Henry Long wanted no peace or accord, and in response 'wrote letters of defyance' calculated to inflame 'the quarrel' and 'sundry times'. He sent Charles 'word that wheresoever he met him, he would untie his pointes [unfasten his breeches] and whip him with a Rod – calling him "Ass, Puppy fool and Boy"'. These terms of abuse were about as bad as it could get. This was fighting talk – a challenge! On 4 October 1594 Sir Charles Danvers and his brother Sir Henry led a large body of their retainers in an attack on the Long faction while it dined at a house in Corsham, just a few miles from South Wraxall Manor. What happened next is described in the Corsham Coroner's Court records: 'Sir Henry Danvers ... and others ... with force of arms ... swords etc did assault the aforesaid Henry Long and the aforesaid Henry Danvers voluntarily, feloniously, and of malice prepense, did discharge in and upon the said Long, a certain engine called a dagge [a type of pocket pistol] worth 6s 8d charged with powder and a bullet of lead'. (A law against the carrying of concealed firearms – aimed at thwarting assassins and robbers – made this type of pistol illegal in 1612.) Henry Danvers, it is meticulously recorded, had the dagge 'in his right hand' and did 'inflict a mortal wound upon the upper part of the body of Long, under the left breast, of which wound he instantly died'.[21]

The men of each party must have been stunned. A killing had taken place in the most public manner, and even when committed in rural Wiltshire, by a well-connected local grandee, this was a crime that could not be ignored or covered up. The long-running dispute had now become a most serious blood feud, so the Danvers brothers, in fear of the law and possibly of summary vengeance from the Long faction, fled. Their only hope of avoiding immediate arrest or retribution was to seek protection from any powerful courtier with whom they were connected and, if possible, seek refuge in his home. The High Sheriff of Wiltshire and the county's Justices of the Peace initiated a search for the two men, and for a footboy who, it was said, had been sent into the Corsham house just before the attack to find out exactly where the Longs were sitting. If proven, this elevated the charge against the Danvers from possible manslaughter to possible premeditated murder.[22] But the brothers escaped their pursuers and within hours of the attack arrived at Titchfield, near Southampton, at the home of the Earl of Southampton. He hid them in Whitely Lodge within his park, and the next day had them ferried to Calshot Castle and from there to France.

The arrival of the Danvers brothers at Titchfield was, perhaps, a fateful moment for British culture. When the hunted pair burst in upon the earl, he was hosting a great feast, and among his guests may well have been William Shakespeare. Certainly the earl was a patron and possible inspiration for Shakespeare (the poems *Venus and Adonis* and the *Rape of Lucrece* had been dedicated to him). But even if Shakespeare was not actually at Titchfield when the fugitives arrived, John Florio, one of his closest collaborators, probably was, and Shakespeare would soon have heard about the feud and the killing.

John Florio, an Anglo-Italian, is one of the more extraordinary characters of the late Elizabethan and early Jacobean courtly world. He set himself the task of reforming the manners of the English, and became Italian tutor to the aristocracy, and even to the royal household when James I came to the throne in 1603. Florio lived for some years in the household of the Earl of Southampton, and it was probably here that he met Shakespeare and either inspired and educated him, or merely provided him with insights and information for the cycle of plays that Shakespeare set in an Italian context.

While the Danvers brothers hid in France, their friends brokered a deal with the Crown that eventually allowed them to return from exile upon payment of a hefty fine. It would perhaps have been better for all if this seemingly clever negotiation had not been achieved. In 1601 Sir Charles Danvers became involved in the ill-conceived coup d'état against Queen Elizabeth, launched by the embittered and truculent former royal favourite the Earl of Essex. The coup, aimed at replacing the aged and childless Elizabeth with a 'stronger' monarch capable of founding a stabilizing dynasty, was a miserably mismanaged affair, little more than a riot in the City of London, and easily put down. Essex, Danvers and a number of associates were executed in February 1601 for treason.

Among those condemned to death but ultimately not executed was the Earl of Southampton. One of the actions held against him was his participation in the organization, on the eve of the coup, of a production at the Globe Theatre of Shakespeare's *Richard II*. The play, written in about 1595 and on one level a discussion of the evils of a weak monarchy, was apparently intended as a rallying cry and justification for the rebels. It must have been on the cards, at least in the immediate

aftermath of the rebellion, that the Globe players and Shakespeare would be arrested. In the event, they were not, nor do they seem to have suffered any ill will from the royal court.

Another play that Shakespeare almost certainly wrote in 1595 was *The Tragedy of Romeo and Juliet*, and this could well have been inspired, at least in part, by the fighting between the Long and the Danvers factions. There are many possible sources for the play – including Luigi da Porto's *Giuletta e Romeo* of 1530, and Arthur Brooke's *Tragical History of Romeus and Juliet* of 1562 – but at the very least the high-profile Long and Danvers dispute gave the subject of feud and lawless factional street fighting a relevance and topicality. The placing of the tale in Verona may have been due to Florio's influence, but in the mid-1590s Shakespeare regularly used Italy as a parallel world in which to set plays dealing with subjects of domestic interest and import but that, if set in England, could have been seen as too topical, political or inflammatory, and thus suppressed by the censorship authorities.[23]

ABOVE *The execution for treason of Lord Essex in 1601. Sir Charles Danvers was executed at the same time.*
LEFT *John Florio, a probable inspiration for Shakespeare and observer of the bloody feud between the Long and Danvers factions that was possibly one of the sources for Romeo and Juliet.*
OPPOSITE *The Earl of Southampton, a patron of Shakespeare and protector of the Danvers family.*

The circumstances of the bitter and bloody feud with the Danvers – and the killing of his brother in particular – must be reflected in Sir Walter's remodelling of South Wraxall Manor, must, to a degree, have inspired it and be alluded to in the many messages enshrined in the architecture and ornament. At the very least the scale and ambition of the works proclaim that the Longs are alive and well, are still very much in business and a power to be reckoned with.

The updating seems to have started in the Great Hall, which is reasonable since it was the first room guests would have seen, and perhaps the only room seen by many casual visitors. Here Sir Walter inserted a large fireplace and constructed a wall flue so that the smoke-belching central hearth could at last be removed. The fireplace carries the date 1598, is embellished with fetterlocks, the Long arms, and Flemish-style strapwork decoration, very much the taste of the time. But it also, almost in pride of place, sports a most curious and larger than life-size face. It could be Hercules, symbolizing strength and virtue, or the Green Man, an ancient nature spirit. Sir Walter also replaced the timber screen in the Great Hall in fine and fashionable manner, with Gothic detail abandoned in favour of classical, and – again – stylized fetterlocks being used as decorative motifs.

The most physically significant of Walter's alterations was to transform the Great Chamber immediately to the north of the Great Hall into a magnificent, comfortable and highly fashionable withdrawing room or high dining room. This room is, in its mixture of meanings, Walter's most complex work. A plaster-made barrel vault, richly embellished with images of human-faced suns and moons, was inserted below the ornamental early fifteenth-century roof timbers and gives the room a stunning monumental quality. This sense of robust scale is reinforced by the insertion of what are virtually walls of glass in both the west and north walls, with the one to the north involving a physical extension of the volume of the old Great Chamber, and the creation of a curious-looking pier that helps support the now-concealed roof timbers. These

windows are vast mullioned and transomed affairs that let light flood into what, with its lowered ceiling height, has something of the feel of a long gallery. The windows in themselves are major statements of wealth because in the late sixteenth century – it's assumed the room was created around 1600 – glass was still a relatively expensive material. But the greatest glory of the transformed room, and the detail that does most to pump up one's perception of its size, is its vast and richly embellished fireplace. It is made of stone, rises thirteen feet to ceiling height, and has a massive presence that makes it feel like the external elevation of a prodigious building. The stone was beautifully carved by Bristol-based masons, but no-one knows who conceived or designed this architectural tour de force. It is one of the greatest, most satisfying and most intriguing fireplaces of Elizabethan England, and demonstrates – in its fine classical details and analogies based on antique culture – that by 1600 the Renaissance world had arrived in even this remote and rural part of Wiltshire. I stood in front of it entranced and puzzled by its meaning, and this of course was just as intended by the person who over 400 years ago conceived this piece of extraordinary architectural theatre. The spectator was to be instructed and informed, but was also meant to be mystified and entertained, taken on a journey of the imagination so that, perhaps, the symbols and forms would develop personal meaning and relevance.

Despite the layers of meaning and the mysteries enshrined in the masonry of the fireplace, one thing is immediately evident. It is the work of an almost post-Christian society. None of the images is biblical, but all relate to the classical world. In a Continental country one would expect, in 1600, to see among the images representations of saints or the Virgin, but one consequence of the Reformation was to clear away such imagery associated with Roman Catholicism, leaving the way open for the triumphal arrival of pagan personages. At each end of the fireplaces are pairs of caryatids or terms, inspired by Greek and Roman architecture, which have tapering bases topped by human torsos and

> ❝ The stone was beautifully carved by Bristol-based masons, but no one knows who conceived or designed this architectural tour de force. It is one of the greatest, most satisfying and most intriguing fireplaces of Elizabethan England…

ABOVE LEFT *Details of the ceiling in the late Elizabethan Great Chamber – images of the sun, and bearded faces within crescents, perhaps representing the moon – suggest that the ceiling was conceived as the vault of heaven, a celestial world. And are the bearded faces within the crescent moons jovial portraits of Sir Walter Long?* ABOVE RIGHT *The slightly worried-looking head that peers from the centre of the fireplace. Perhaps it portrays Hermes, the Greek god of shepherds and boundaries, and guide to the Underworld.*

heads. Each pair comprises a man and a woman, the men neatly coiffured and bearded in late Elizabethan manner, but the women timeless, delightful and each armed with bewitching and enigmatic smiles. Are these figures intended as a marriage of biblical and classical imagery? Are they intended to represent Adam and Eve in antique manner? Perhaps, but we simply don't know; the puzzle is delicious. More obvious, and more strange, is the figure that stands in the centre of the composition, high above the fire opening. It is the great god Pan, with cloven feet and horns. Why? Pan was a god of nature, of shepherds and flocks, and lived in Arcadia. He was also a god of frolic, revels and riot. Well, Wiltshire was sheep country in the late sixteenth century, and the animals a source of much local wealth, and to the Longs the land was no doubt as beautiful as the legendary bucolic paradise of Arcadia. And if used as a room for convivial dining or as a room for merry-making and dancing, Pan was a most appropriate overseer.

On either side is an array of images somewhat easier to identify and interpret. Immediately to the left of Pan, 'Arithmetica' is represented as a female figure leaning casually on a lectern making calculations. To the right is 'Geometria', shown as a figure measuring a globular world with a compass, while a set-square and plumb-line sit at her feet. Beyond 'Arithmetica' is a representation of 'Prvdentia', and beyond 'Geometria' a representation of 'Ivstisia' (Justice) as a young woman holding a sword and scales in conventional manner. But why these attributes, disciplines and values? Walter Long was a magistrate and landowner with authority over many people, so prudence and justice were qualities he most certainly should have possessed and indeed proclaimed. Arithmetic and geometry are perhaps more complex. These disciplines, associated with much-admired ancient philosophers, such as Plato and Pythagorus, can be seen as the abstract building blocks of creation, the essence of the immutable laws of proportion and form from which all that is beautiful – natural or man-made – is wrought. Latin inscriptions under the emblematic figures suggest the importance with which each was viewed. That under arithmetic informs that 'Even or odd, my figures find results. He'll skilfully reckon who me consults.' So all who understand and use arithmetic have the world at their fingertips. Under geometry is written: 'By just measurements I mark off space – How far is Earth from Heaven, and place from place.' Fascinating – geometry is the measure of man, the means by which he can understand divine creation and create divinely on his own accord. Was Walter Long, through the figures and sentiments on this fireplace, announcing himself as a disciple or adept of the rational disciplines of arithmetic and geometry – the basic tools of all designers – and thus revealing himself to be the architect and poet of his own home additions?

Almost equally intriguing is the addition Sir Walter made to a ground-floor room. Just east of the Great Hall was a small room, little more than a closet, but subsequently enlarged, that seems to have been turned into a room of contemplation and reflection, for within it Sir Walter added a remarkable piece of late Elizabethan *memento mori*. This little room was surely intended as a counterpoint to the life, light and vitality of the Great Hall for, on entering, the first thing seen is a large stone fireplace framed by tall and erudite Ionic columns, with – in prime and central place – a

LEFT *One of the pair of caryatids or Terms defining the boundary of the fireplace opening. Perhaps they are Renaissance images of Adam and Eve, or representations of Terminus, the Roman god who, like Hermes, protected boundaries.*
OPPOSITE *The central portion of the fireplace. Above the* Hermes *head stands another protector of shepherds and flocks – the great god Pan, denizen of Arcadia and the lord of frolic, revels and riot. On each side of Pan are personifications of arithmetic and geometry, each with appropriate attributes and implements. And everywhere are faces, masks, strapwork and classical motifs.*

ARITHMETICA

GEOMETRIA

Par impar numeris vestigo rite subactis
Me pcte concinne ſi numerare cupis

Menſuras rerum spatiis dimetioræquis
quid coelo dyſia Terra locusque loco

curious little being. Is it an ape, a monkey –
Caliban? It squats above a motto: *Mors Rapit Omnia*
(Death seizes all things). This was a death room,
something like a chapel, where you could escape
from the Great Hall – where life was lived for the
moment, where worldly pride and achievement
were paramount and proclaimed – to contemplate
inevitable and coming death, to ponder upon
eternity. Perhaps here Sir Walter sat and thought
about his brother Henry, killed so violently
around five years earlier. By the beliefs of the age,
reflections upon the grim reality of death and
decay were necessary for the afterlife of the soul.
You could experience a 'good death' only if you
became mentally prepared, accepted that life
and worldly riches are transient, and remembered
that in life is death, ready to 'seize' you when
least expected. This room, surely intended as a
place of sombre meditation, was to help the living
come to terms with their mortality, to live each day
as if it were their last and, in the process, help ease
the inevitable passing from this world to the next.

To each side of the strange and unsettling
ape-like figure are cartouches ornamented with
peculiar staring faces and emblazoned in Latin
with sentiments. One states that 'Every man is the
architect of his own fortunes' and the other observes
that 'To be praised by the good, and to be abused
by the bad, is praise alike'. These are fairly
unexceptional statements, seemingly like mottos
in Christmas crackers, but perhaps they offer a little
more insight into the character and actions of Sir
Walter Long, and refer specifically to his feud with
the Danvers. It's hard not to think of Sir Walter
sitting in front of this then-new fireplace when in
February 1601 he received confirmation that Sir
Charles Danvers had been publicly executed as a
traitor. Revenge was one of the defining emotions
of the age, so the news may well have been received
with grim satisfaction. But, then again, perhaps Sir
Walter was a bigger man and would have taken a
more philosophical view – 'By just measurements
I mark off space …'.

On the first floor Sir Walter added at least two
more fireplaces to the house, not as spectacular as

those on the ground floor, but still fine pieces of
work. In the chamber above the death room is a
large stone fireplace incorporating full-height
Ionic columns carrying a deep and richly decorated
entablature so that it all looks rather like a porch
or portal. Above the loggia on the north side of the
house is Dame Eleanor's room, and in it is another
of Walter Long's fireplaces – this time furnished
with small Ionic columns set above larger Doric
columns and, high up in its centre, a stone-carved
vase of flowers. It's all very feminine and fitting
for a room that had belonged to a great lady of
the dynasty.

Walter's works are fascinating documents that
imply much about his character, interests and
aspirations. But perhaps now, over 400 years
later, what is most important is that this man,
and his passions and obsessions, created with his
barrel-vaulted Withdrawing Room one of the most
moving and visually exciting late Elizabethan
interiors in England.

Mors rapit omnia

"By the beliefs of the age, reflections upon the grim reality of death and decay were necessary for the afterlife of the soul...

OPPOSITE *The monumental fireplace of about 1600, incorporating large Ionic columns, that dominates the 'death room' adjoining the convivial world of the Great Hall. The fireplace, with its ornamentation and scripts, is conceived as a moral compass and a memento mori –* *a warning that in life lurks death, which comes without warning to level all.*
ABOVE *In the centre of the fireplace is an unsettling image of an ape or monkey squatting above a Latin motto that translates as 'Death seizes all things'.*

THE LAST OF THE LONGS

With hindsight it is now possible to see that the division of lands that took place in 1610 greatly weakened the power, wealth and prestige of the Long dynasty. The Draycot branch managed to continue a steady climb, becoming baronets in the seventeenth century, and in the eighteenth century rebuilt their manor handsomely. But South Wraxall Manor, although it remained in the ownership of the Long family until the mid-1960s, became something of a second home that, although maintained, was not extended or radically altered to reflect changing fashion. By 1665 the house was in dual tenancy, as revealed by leases dating from 1654 and 1660.[24] At about this time the house was inspected by the antiquarian John Aubrey, who, between 1659 and 1670, documented the whole county of Wiltshire. He recognized South Wraxall Manor as one of the great houses of the county, and was particularly taken with the heraldic stained glass in the windows of the Great Hall. Now long gone, this glass would not only have proclaimed the genealogical connections and pride of the family in glowing colours, but also have bathed the hall with beautiful hues. The lost glory of this glass is hinted at by the coloured drawings preserved in Aubrey's publication.[25]

In about 1710 the death room was extended slightly to the north, and its walls panelled, as were those of the room above, and a charming octagonal and stone-domed garden house constructed near the pond. A few years later a handsome early Georgian staircase was installed in the south range, and in the very early twentieth century a tenant named E. Richardson Cox added a square-sided bay to the south front, a corridor and staircase to the east of the Great Hall, a utilitarian kitchen block to the north, and seems to have fiddled a little with the early eighteenth-century panelling and staircase. These are all relatively minor things so that, to a miraculous degree, the house remains predominately as Sir Walter left it. The last Long to live in the manor – Sara Morrison (née Long) – retains fond memories of the house as a warm family home, and also recalls one of the more unlikely moments in the house's history. Sara

inherited after her father, the 2nd Viscount Long, was killed in Holland in 1944. She lived in the house after the war, but, as she puts it, like a 'house guest' of the man to whom she let it. The man was the 2nd Viscount Rothermere, proprietor of the *Daily Mail* and one of the great press barons of the age, so for a few years South Wraxall Manor became a hub of Rothermere's press empire.

South Wraxall Manor is now owned by the musician John Taylor and his wife, the fashion designer and entrepreneur Gela Nash Taylor. The house has been repaired and furnished in the most sensitive and appropriate manner, and has, as most agree, not looked better for decades. It is once again the most comfortable, relaxed and beautiful of English homes, and any ghosts that may have lurked in the shadows – spectres from its life as a ruthless powerhouse in the days of the Plantagenets and Tudors – have been well and truly laid to rest ❖

ABOVE *The handsome fireplace of c.1600 above the death room. Like that in the room below, the fireplace is framed by Ionic columns and entablature and looks like a portal. Any sentiments that might have been written within the strapwork frames have long been lost.*
OPPOSITE *An octagonal, domed garden building of c.1700 that stands near the pond to the south of the manor.*

KINROSS HOUSE

Perthshire, Scotland

LATE

17TH

CENTURY

Restoration architecture
in Scotland

❖

KINROSS HOUSE STANDS GRAVE AND solemn, an object of perfection and precision that seems to defy place and time. It was constructed well over 300 years ago in the often-troubled borderlands south of the Scottish Highlands, yet in its confident and sophisticated classical design seems to be of a later age and less turbulent location. The almost uncanny nature of the house is emphasized by the near-miraculous state of its exterior preservation. The sandstone from which it is built – and that was won from a local quarry – seems hardly weathered by time. The beautifully calculated and cut ashlar blocks of almost marbled sandstone are not streaked with rain or blunted or pitted by frosts, but mostly stand as clean and crisp as the day they were cut and laid.

My first glimpse of the house, in the late summer of 2010, was memorable. As I turned into the long, straight drive from Kinross town centre, the house exploded into view, its precise stone façade directly in front of me acting as a screen to conceal the landscape beyond, its curving wings, flanking pavilions and walls revealing a baroque sense of space and theatrical display. All leads the eye to the house, where the wide window spacing gives it an unexpectedly Italian feel – so arrival was like turning from a Scottish high street into a corner of Tuscany. Despite its age, the house still possesses the power to shock, to surprise.

The story of Kinross House is, in many ways, the story of its age, and its history is entwined with that of Scotland. It was conceived and built at that moment when it seemed that Scotland's political and economic independence from England could be sustained, and when it was timely and appropriate for Scotland to assert its own cultural identity. Its architecture can be read as a proclamation of faith in a better future, a declaration that late seventeenth-century Scotland was – in its architecture at least – among the community of cultured and progressive European nations. In its design, Kinross House looks beyond the influence of English prototypes to the fountainheads of architectural inspiration in the late seventeenth century – Renaissance Italy, France and the Low Countries.

But the most direct and immediate story Kinross House tells is about the Restoration of Charles II in 1660, and this is because it was designed by a man who had served Charles while in exile, was well rewarded after the Restoration, and dreamed of founding an aristocratic dynasty with Kinross House as its power base. That man was William Bruce.

WILLIAM BRUCE

Believed to have been born at Blairhall, Fife, between 1625 and 1630, William Bruce was the second son of Robert Bruce. The family was Episcopalian and, although of modest means, had Royalist and aristocratic allegiances, and a claim to gentility, for they were related to the family of the Earls of Kincardine, with William's first

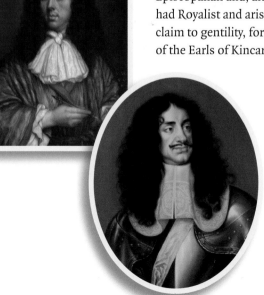

PREVIOUS PAGES *Kinross House in evening light. Constructed during the later 1680s, the house possesses a solemn and pristine classical perfection that still startles.*
RIGHT ABOVE *William Bruce, painted in about 1664 by John Michael Wright. Bruce is attired casually in a dressing-gown and holds a port-crayon, a type of drawing implement, suggesting his architectural intentions.*

LEFT BELOW *Charles II, whose restoration to the throne gave Bruce his change of power and fortune.*
OPPOSITE *Detail of the entrance elevation of Kinross. The pedimented porch, designed by Bruce, was not added until the early twentieth century. Above the porch are carved military trophies and the Bruce coat of arms.*

cousin created earl in 1643. Records are scarce, but William Bruce – too young to fight in the English Civil War, even if inclined to do so – seems to have been educated at St Andrews University and spent most of the 1650s in the Low Countries and France, where he operated as a merchant and ship's captain. There is little reason to doubt that his residence abroad was any more than a business obligation, and certainly he was not regarded in official circles as a Royalist exile. But as an Episcopalian, Bruce would have been excluded from the Presbyterian ascendancy in Scotland and from the puritanical circles of the English Commonwealth, so his life abroad might, to a degree, have been enforced. But, if so, it was ultimately to reap rich rewards.

Papers relating to William Bruce's activities at this time survive in the family archive of Andrew Bruce, the current Earl of Elgin and Kincardine, a descendant of William Bruce's cousin Alexander Bruce. I met Lord Elgin at Broomhall, Dunfermline, a beautiful neoclassical house started in the late 1790s for the 7th Lord Elgin, who brought the Parthenon Marbles from Athens. Although frail and now in his eighties, the current Lord Elgin was impassioned when we explored the life of his somewhat mysterious ancestor. To offer insights into the life of William Bruce, he produced a series of letters, preserved in his family for generations. These were written by Sir Robert Moray and sent to Alexander Bruce, brother to the Earl of Kincardine, but refer frequently, and evidently affectionately, to 'Will' Bruce. Moray and Bruce were well-known Royalist exiles – Moray being within the intimate circles of the Stuart court – and both were to play key roles in English society after the Restoration of 1660. But during the 1650s Moray and Alexander Bruce were impoverished exiles, proscribed in their own land and forced to busy themselves and earn a living in whatever way possible. Alexander was part-owner of a ship with William, and both were based at Rotterdam and La Rochelle, while Moray was at Maastricht, where Charles and the Stuart court were in exile. William and Alexander Bruce seem to have traded in coal, wine and timber between Scotland, the Low Countries, England, France and Norway.

Lord Elgin and I leafed through the ageing papers and found a letter Moray sent to Alexander Bruce from Maastricht, dated 6 October 1657: 'I send you this from Will … in short his voyage and pains have made him no gains, but diminished his stock very much.' So Bruce's effort to trade wine and timber very quickly failed but, Moray observed, 'he takes it most virtuously to my great joy'.

In this same letter Moray revealed a little of William Bruce's wider, cultural interests. He had, Moray writes, 'lighted on a gentleman in the Rochelle that is a musitian and paints, and he hath taken him in boarding in his house'. This suggests the manner in which William acquired and honed the knowledge of architecture that he was to display with such astonishing skill when he returned to Scotland after the Restoration. He received no formal training as an architect; indeed, no gentleman did in seventeenth-century Europe. The only people trained in the art and science of building were masons – artisans of often humble background, who tended to inherit the knowledge and secrets of their trade through family connections or guilds. Gentlemen with a passion for architecture took a different route. Architecture, like poetry, painting, music or philosophy, was among the liberal arts with which all cultured gentlemen were expected to be familiar. To have an understanding of the Orders and canons of classical architecture was one of the expected tokens of education and civilization, often honed by enthusiastic gentlemen through observation on the Grand Tour – when they would hope to inspect ancient ruins in Rome – and by studying Renaissance architectural treatises, such as Sebastiano Serlio's *Tutte l'opera d'architettura*, published from 1537, Andrea Palladio's seminal *Quattro libri dell'architettura* of 1570, and Vincenzo Scamozzi's *L'idea dell'architettura universale* of 1615. When a gentleman amateur actually practised architecture, perhaps working in collaboration with a mason who might contribute technical and practical advice, he would be known not as an architect, but as a surveyor or comptroller of works, as was the case with Sir Christopher Wren and

> To have an understanding of the Orders and canons of classical architecture was one of the expected tokens of education and civilization, often honed by enthusiastic gentlemen through observation on the Grand Tour...

ABOVE *The garden elevation matches the entrance elevation so that the house – with no significant architectural or hierarchical difference between back and front – can be enjoyed in the round, like a perfect sculptural object.*

Sir John Vanbrugh in the late seventeenth and early eighteenth centuries. This established gentleman's route into the practice of architecture must have been the one followed by William Bruce. While in Europe travelling as a merchant, he had the opportunity to see and study exemplary works of contemporary architecture, especially in the Low Countries and France. This may have ignited a passion that was fuelled by reading and that – as with music and painting – could have been refined and guided through professional instruction.

Another letter caught my eye that offers an insight into the nature of Bruce. Dated 13 April 1658 from Maastricht, in it Moray tells Alexander Bruce that 'Will is so very stout a skipper and hath been so often drowned that he thinks no more of a leak and a storm than other people think of a stumble of a horse at land.' Lord Elgin reflected on the contents of the letters and made an important point: they clearly confirm that William Bruce was close to the Stuart court in exile and was in regular contact and on intimate terms with some of its leading members. Suddenly, these ancient and chatty letters took on a very different complexion. Were they, I asked, in some manner documents of state, part of the machinery of cunning and subtle manoeuvre that led, in May 1660, to the return of Moray and the Stuart court to Britain and the Restoration of Charles II? For the Restoration to take place, secure communications were essential between the court in exile and potentially supportive factions in Britain, and William Bruce was in an excellent position to act as messenger. He was a merchant used to travel, and no doubt a familiar sight on quays in Scotland, France and the Low Countries, an intrepid sailor and, it would seem, a brave and daring individual. Perhaps most importantly, he was close to the Stuart court through friendship and blood and could be trusted with the most delicate messages.

Two days after Charles was proclaimed king, Moray wrote to Alexander Bruce. Like so many of his letters, it touches on William Bruce: 'I remember

before Will parted he told me he was advised to think of putting in for some place or employment. Pray let us talk of it.' So Will Bruce, having served the Restoration in some manner, was now 'advised' to look to the new Royalist regime for a reward – some 'place or employment'. But what exactly had William Bruce done to deserve a reward?

The story has arisen, over the generations and presumably based on now long-lost contemporary evidence, that William did indeed make the most of his mercantile travel contacts and experience and act as a conduit of communication between the court of Charles in Maastricht and General Monck, governor of the Commonwealth forces in Scotland. Certainly William seems to have been a familiar figure coming and going at the port of Leith near Edinburgh, and filed away in the Scottish National Archives is a most revealing, if ultimately enigmatic, document. It is a passport issued to William Bruce dated 7 September 1659 and permits 'the Bearer hereof, Mr. William Bruce, with his servant, Horses ... and necessaries to passé about his occasions on this side of the ffryth [firth] and other parts of Scotland and to Repasse without molestation'. It is not now clear if merchants travelling between Leith and the continent in the 1650s required passports for each trip they made. It seems highly unlikely that landing passes were required, and examples, if they existed, do not appear to survive. But this document is, of course, far more than a landing pass. It allowed Bruce to travel at will all over Scotland – to come and go – with horse and servant, 'without

LEFT *Corner detail, showing a Corinthian pilaster capital and entablature – beautifully designed and crisply carved.* OPPOSITE *The south elevation. The side elevations match each other, but are fundamentally different from the main elevations because they contain shallow mezzanine windows between ground and first floors. These small windows serve sets of low-ceilinged rooms created at each end of the house.*

molestation'. In a troubled land, with suspicious officials on the prowl, this was quite some document to possess. And there is more. The passport also permitted Bruce 'to keepe his sword in his lodgings till he Returns into Holland' – a seemingly odd statement, but one that reveals Bruce was allowed to be armed. This suggests he was not only trusted but also, since a sword was a token of status, permitted to carry with him the means to appear in the style of a gentleman.

But the most remarkable thing about this passport is the signature with which it is validated. It is given under 'the hand and Seale' of George Monck himself who, in September 1659, was arguably the most powerful man in Britain and even then determining the fate of the nation. The passport contains one last ringing phrase. Its bearer, guarantees Monck, was 'doing nothing prejudiciall to the Commonwealth of England'. Quite what Bruce was doing is not made clear, but if he was carrying secret messages between Charles in the Low Countries and General Monck, then based at Dalkeith, this is just the kind of travel document he would need. At the very least this document establishes a link between Bruce and Monck and confirms that Bruce was granted a freedom to travel through Scotland by a man who was not only all-powerful, but who must have known that Bruce was in contact with Charles and his court.

RESTORATION REWARDS FOR BRUCE

The significant role William Bruce played in the Restoration is confirmed, in somewhat circumstantial manner, by the profitable places and employments he was quickly granted by the newly established Crown. They were significant and lucrative. In 1660 he was appointed Clerk to the Bills and in 1665 Clerk of Supply to the Lords in Council, both of which posts enabled him to collect fees from parliament and from those petitioning parliament. In 1667 Bruce was appointed Collector of Taxes for payment to the royal forces, and also a collector of the cess, a land tax that was among the principal sources of revenue in Scotland. In addition, in March 1671 he bought himself into a syndicate that paid the Crown £26,000 for the right to collect certain revenue, notably duties payable at the Port of Leith, over a five-year period. All additional money collected above the £26,000 could be retained by the syndicate. Bruce, who had once traded on the quays of Leith as a merchant and flitted over them as a clandestine messenger engaged on high and delicate matters of state, now trod them as a tax collector, pressing hard personal profits.

Through the 1670s Bruce continued to be viewed as a deserving recipient of lucrative sinecures. For example, in 1676 he was appointed one of the Commissioners of Excise for Fife and, as was the custom of the time, retained a significant proportion of the government money that passed through his hands. One reason, no doubt, for Bruce's good fortune was the high position at court enjoyed by his old companions Sir Robert Moray and Alexander Bruce, now the Earl of Kincardine. Moray was based in London and an intimate adviser to the king who, through Moray, continued to use Bruce as a trusted messenger between London and the Duke of Lauderdale, the Secretary for Scotland. Lord Kincardine served on the Treasury Commission for Scotland and used Bruce as a well-rewarded revenue collector.

During the decades after 1660, Bruce became immensely rich and powerful, was created a baronet in 1668, and started his social ascent. By the mid-1670s Sir William Bruce had a dream. He wanted not just to amass a fortune, but also to found an aristocratic dynasty that would be a political power in the land. He had married Mary Halkett, the daughter of Sir James Halkett of Pitfirrane, in 1662[1] and by c.1670 had a son named John, and soon a daughter named Anne. But Bruce needed something more – a great house and an estate that would bring him status, prestige and, ideally, control over local courts, perhaps even access to a parliamentary seat. So a power base was needed, preferably one that was close to Edinburgh, and to help Bruce make the transformation from merchant-on-the-make to Scottish aristocrat it was desirable that the estate should embody a sense of history, of ancient pedigree and Scottish destiny.

"Bruce, who had once traded on the quays of Leith as a merchant and flitted over them as a clandestine messenger engaged on high and delicate matters of state, now trod them as a tax collector, pressing hard personal profits…

ABOVE George Monck, painted in 1668 by John Michael Wright. Monck was the Commonwealth general who turned king-maker and orchestrated the restoration of Charles II in 1660. Bruce almost certainly acted as a vital and discreet messenger between Monck and the royal court in exile.

In 1675 just such a property presented itself to Bruce. The Earl of Moreton, a member of the ancient and noble Douglas family, owned the vast Kinross estate, which included Loch Leven and its island castle, and a loch-side mansion house. But in the mid-1670s Lord Moreton was in debt, as were many noble families after the troubles of the 1650s and 1660s, and Bruce – ever the opportunist – was able to turn the earl's problems to his own advantage. Bruce may have been involved in putting financial pressure on the earl, and certainly seems to have helped him settle some of his more pressing debts. In return for his assistance, Bruce acquired the Kinross estate at a most advantageous price and set about making his dream a reality. The estate carried with it the hereditary sheriffdom of Kinross-shire and a pocket seat in the Scottish parliament.[2] (A pocket seat had a very small electorate over which a patron could easily gain power, usually corruptly, and so have undue unrepresentative influence within parliament.) Acquiring such a seat gave Bruce additional power and allowed him to sit in the Scottish parliament as Shire Commissioner for Kinross from 1681. But, equally important, the acquisition of the Kinross estate bestowed ancient dignity upon the house of Bruce, for the land carried within it one of the historic 'shrines' of Scotland.

That shrine was the castle on the island of Loch Leven, where Mary Queen of Scots had been imprisoned following her unpopular third marriage, to Lord Bothwell, which provoked aristocratic rebellion and a brief civil war in Scotland. Bothwell escaped, but Mary was captured and forced to abdicate in favour of her infant son James, fathered by her second husband, Lord Darnley. After her escape in 1568, she took refuge with her cousin Elizabeth I in England, until her intrigues with Spain, her Roman Catholic faith and her pretensions to the English throne obliged Elizabeth to execute her in 1587.

Mary, a tragic and ill-advised woman, would probably have been forgotten, indeed, condemned by history if not for her doting son. He became James VI of Scotland and in 1603, after becoming James I of England, set about rehabilitating his mother's reputation and elevating her into some kind of martyr and nationalist Scottish heroine. It was a difficult trick to pull off, but he achieved it, partly by moving his mother's body from Peterborough Cathedral to Westminster Abbey and placing it in a chapel opposite and equivalent to that occupied by the tomb of Elizabeth I.

It is now hard to say exactly how Mary was perceived in late seventeenth-century Scotland by men such as Bruce. Had James's campaign to reinvent his mother as a stoic and long-suffering queen of Scotland worked? Had he managed to cast upon her some of the lustre of the Virgin Queen? For a socially ambitious individual like Sir William Bruce, whose rise was so intimately associated with the Stuart Restoration, the fact that Mary had been a queen of Scotland and was the great-grandmother of the reigning monarch was probably enough to make her admirable. Certainly, as Bruce pondered the transformation of his new estate into his

dynastic power base, the castle on the small island in Loch Leven in which Mary had been imprisoned played a galvanizing role in his vision.

WILLIAM BRUCE AS ARCHITECT

One of the many posts that Bruce obtained from the Crown was Surveyor-General and Overseer of the King's Works in Scotland. The appointment, with an annual salary of £300, was made in January 1671 by the Earl (later Duke) of Lauderdale, who as Secretary of State for Scotland ruled the land on the king's behalf as a semi-autonomous viceroy. Bruce must have been Lauderdale's personal choice for he had employed the amateur architect in the previous year to help with the remodelling of his own home, Thirlestane Castle, Berwickshire. The appointment as Surveyor-General made Bruce the official and senior architect in Scotland. What ability or qualification did he have to hold such a post and to operate effectively? In fact, not only had Bruce worked at Thirlestane, but by 1671 he had a small body of architectural work to his credit. Also, having been sent in 1663 by Lauderdale on a mission to northern France, Bruce probably knew some of the most modern and influential French country houses at first hand, notably the just recently completed Chateau de Vaux-le-Vicomte at Maincy and the Chateau de Balleroy in Normandy. Vaux-le-Vicomte, designed by Louis le Vau, possessed a spectacular formal garden designed by André Le Nôtre, while the Chateau de Balleroy, designed in the 1620s by François Mansart, also had a garden by Le Nôtre but

LEFT ABOVE *The Chateau de Vaux-le-Vicomte, Maincy, France. Completed in 1661 to the designs of Louis le Vau, it was one of the most influential houses in mid-seventeenth-century Europe and most probably visited by Bruce in 1663.* LEFT BELOW *The garden elevation of the Chateau de Balleroy, Normandy, France,* designed in the mid-1620s by François Mansart, with house, outbuildings, garden and landscape organized around a long, straight axial route. OPPOSITE *View from the 'garden hall' in Kinross House along the axial route that passes from the entrance gate, through the house and garden, and terminates at Loch Leven Castle.*

– perhaps more memorable for Bruce – the house, outbuildings, garden and landscape were all organized around a long, straight axial route.

Both these chateaux incorporate dramatic and precisely organized plan forms that were reflections of the hierarchies of aristocratic society. Such plans were entirely unprecedented at this time in Scotland and would surely have gripped the imagination of the socially ambitious Bruce. Both possess versions of the double-pile plan, which envisages two parallel sets or 'piles' of rooms on each principal floor, with each set separated by a central corridor. Then a relatively novel idea in Britain (Inigo Jones seems to have introduced it to grandiose British architecture in the Queen's House at Greenwich, built 1616–35, although here it was – bizarrely – a narrow lane rather than a corridor that separated the parallel 'piles' of rooms), this made it possible to enter one room without passing through another, as had been usual in European houses throughout the Middle Ages and into the early seventeenth century, and so introduced new and refined ideas about comfort, convenience and privacy.

❝ These pioneering chateaux combined the double-pile plan with another idea, the enfilade, which involved aligning doors between rooms to create a spectacular vista through the house and a route of parade…

ABOVE *The Fish Gate within the high wall that surrounds the garden at Kinross. The axial route through house and garden continues through the gate across the water to Loch Leven Castle.*
OVERLEAF *The garden front of Kinross House looking from the Fish Gate along the straight axial route, here defined – as Bruce intended – by planting and flower beds.*

These pioneering chateaux also combined the double-pile plan with another idea, the enfilade, which involved aligning doors between rooms to create a spectacular vista through the house and a route of parade. At formal gatherings the parade through the rooms – of different sizes and types – was used to reflect and confirm the social status of guests. All would gather in the larger rooms at the start of the route and then be filtered out at various doors so that only the grandest, or those on most intimate terms with the host, would reach the inner sanctum of state bedchamber and its adjoining closet. Essentially, the deeper a guest penetrated towards the more private rooms on the route, the higher their status.

The experience that Bruce had gained on his European excursions and through his minor building projects was evidently enough for the astute and cultured Lauderdale to appoint him Surveyor-General. Certainly, when now pondering Bruce's early works, it seems clear that he had indeed made the most of his life on the Continent and studied seminal buildings in the Low Countries and France, read widely and may even have employed a tutor when living abroad in the 1650s, or a mason for advice when back in Scotland. As early as 1664, a portrait painted by John Michael Wright shows Bruce holding a drawing instrument suggestive of architectural intent (see page 52), but it was 1667 before he undertook his first architectural commission. This, like much of his early work, was for a friend. For around five years, until about 1672, Bruce worked with the veteran mason John Mylne, enlarging – essentially rebuilding – Leslie House in Fife for the Earl of Rothes. The result was a vast barrack of a classical palace organized around a courtyard, with tall and austere elevations (most was destroyed by fire in 1763, and the surviving range grievously damaged by fire in 2009). Leslie House, with its pediments and Palladio-inspired proportions, first-floor *piano nobile* and classical simplicity, was a considerable – even pioneering avant-garde – achievement in a land where castellated country houses remained the norm.

In Scotland the Renaissance had entered gingerly, influencing the design of occasional elevations and providing a new vocabulary of architectural details to be combined with traditional and sometimes outlandish Gothic forms. This was largely the case because new, full-blown Renaissance classical architecture was simply not wanted by the older families, who saw towered, pinnacled and battlemented residences as the badge of ancient power and lineage. As one Scottish noble told his son in 1632, when explaining why an ancient tower should be preserved during the rebuilding of their house, 'it makes it looke lyk a castle and henc so nobleste'.[3] English visitors could misunderstand the reasons for the preservation of old fortified structures and even be frightened almost witless by what appeared to be the expression of a bellicose spirit. As the antiquary Thomas Kirke wrote in 1679 after a journey through Scotland: 'All the gentlemen's houses are strong castles, they being so treacherous to one another that they are forc'd to defend themselves in strongholds ... the people are proud, arrogant vain-glorious boasters, bloody barbarous and inhuman butchers.'[4]

The current Lord Strathmore is most forthright about Bruce and his acquisition of the Kinross Estate. Exploiting the hard-pressed Lord Moreton's debts to acquire the estate was, says Lord Strathmore, unforgivable, 'not the action of a gentleman'. This, combined with Bruce's decision to build a showy new house on a virgin site, simply proved that he was nothing but a *nouveau-riche* opportunist. Clearly, powerful old families in Scotland have long memories, and there are some actions that can never be forgiven.

Bruce's second foray into architecture appears to have come in 1668, when he altered and extended an existing tower house at Balcaskie to serve as his home, rather than to sweep it away or build on a new site. In 1670 Bruce started with Robert Mylne, the king's master mason, on the limited remodelling of Thirlestane Castle. Despite the drawing instrument – a port-crayon tipped with a sliver of chalk, graphite or crayon – that Bruce holds in his portrait, there is no evidence that he ever made an architectural

drawing. Probably, as the professional relationship with Mylne implies, Bruce had the ideas, provided information about classical design, supplied fashionable models, offered critiques of design, and left the mason to actually produce the drawings that were required to execute the works.

The following year, 1671, Bruce secured the post of Surveyor-General and started work on the most prominent and high-profile architectural project in Scotland – the enlargement and remodelling of the palace of Holyrood House in Edinburgh for the king. Bruce's work at Holyrood is erudite and sober, notably the arch clad with paired giant Doric columns and the courtyard elevation clad, Colosseum-style, with tiers of Doric, Ionic and Corinthian pilasters. All appears derived from study of Andrea Palladio's late sixteenth-century designs, and influenced by fashionable new buildings Bruce would have known in the Low Countries – notably the mid-seventeenth-century Amsterdam City Hall (now the Royal Palace) by Jacob van Campen, and Maastricht City Hall by Pieter Post, and with which Sir Robert Moray was involved. Also, royal buildings designed in London just before the civil war, primarily Inigo Jones' and John Webb's designs for the rebuilding of Whitehall Palace for James I and Charles I, appear to have provided a reference point. Bruce's work at Holyrood is able rather than inspired. It provides a dignified and fashionably classical setting for the royal court and its offices, such as the Privy Council, in Scotland, but it does not set the heart afire. It is charming but irredeemably provincial. But Bruce's architecture, like most aspects of his life, was soon to undergo dramatic change.

THE KINROSS ESTATE

When Bruce acquired the Kinross estate in 1675 he moved into the old house formerly occupied by the Earl of Moreton and started to design his new dream home. He also laid out a formal garden, designed and located to be seen to advantage from the new house when it was actually built. The garden is, in a sense, a clue to the meaning of Bruce's almost visionary designs for his new estate.

He had created a French-style formal garden a few years earlier at Balcaskie House – arguably the first of its type created in Scotland – but the formal garden he designed at Kinross was to be more than just a bigger and better expression of a prevailing fashion in garden design. It was, in a sense, to root Bruce and his burning ambitions into the very landscape of Kinross.

It seems his first move – perhaps inspired by the relation of house, garden and landscape at Chateau de Balleroy – was to define an east–west route through the portion of his estate lying between Kinross town and Loch Leven. At the town end were gate piers and lodges, then the straight route continued virtually due east, following the central path in the formal garden, and terminated at Loch Leven Castle on an island in the loch, in which Mary Queen of Scots had been imprisoned in 1567. This castle was the focus of Bruce's grand layout, with its central axis over a mile long. Either he saw the castle, with its tower and crenellations making it the epitome of Scottish ancestral and noble architecture, as casting lustre upon his dynastic ambitions, or he wanted in some way to associate himself with Mary Queen of Scots. Whichever the case, he was clearly attempting to appropriate history that was not his own. And it was along this straight route that he proposed – when the time was right and he felt his position and income assured – to place his great mansion, his powerhouse. It was an extraordinary vision; placed centrally and astride this controlled and manipulated landscape, with town at one end and castle at the other, was to be the Bruces' ancestral home – one elevation facing towards sunrise, the other to sunset. Here the Bruces would dwell as the lords of all they surveyed, princes in their own domain, their ambitions and aspirations enshrined in the very landscape, in harmony with the turning of the Earth.

While Bruce collected taxes, amassed money and honed his architectural skill by designing for others, he held back from building at Kinross. He probably designed and redesigned his own mighty house, but he did not build. However, he did collect – books for his library, paintings and fabrics for his

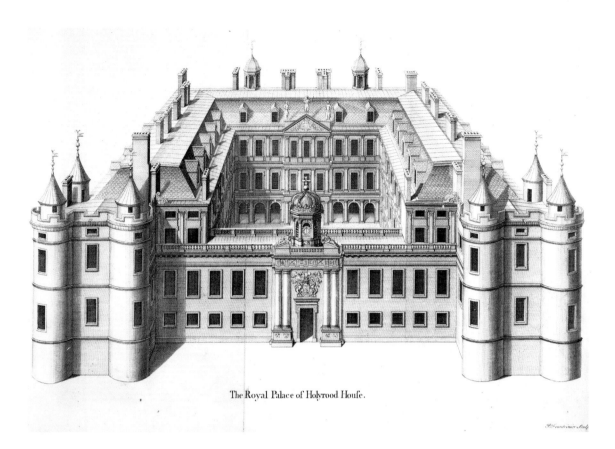

The Royal Palace of Holyrood Houfe.

> ❝ Bruce's work at Holyrood is erudite and sober, notably the arch clad with paired giant Doric columns and the courtyard elevation clad, Colosseum-style, with tiers of Doric, Ionic and Corinthian pilasters …

ABOVE *The royal palace of Holyrood House, Edinburgh, as it appeared in the eighteenth century. As Surveyor-General and Overseer of the King's Works in Scotland, Bruce was, from 1671, responsible for repairing, enlarging and remodelling the castle. His designs include the entrance, framed by paired, giant Doric columns, and the sober, column-tiered courtyard elevations.*

future home. The Bruce papers in the National Archives in Edinburgh offer many intriguing insights into the way he planned and designed his great house at Kinross. Among the 'Accounts' recording objects ordered and purchased by Bruce is an entry for 21 December 1676, showing that he bought a number of books for his library from George Leslie, and these included not only copies of Homer's *Iliad* and the *Naked Truth* with 'Marvel's defending it', but also – for the sum of £4.16s – a copy of 'Palladio's Architectura' [sic].[5] Palladio's *Quattro libri*, or *Four Books of Architecture* (1570), are arguably the most inspirational and influential architectural works ever published. In them he set out theories for sound construction, illustrated and described his erudite analysis and reconstruction of seminal ancient buildings, explained his system of harmonically related proportions that would lead to the creation of universally beautiful buildings, and displayed his own works in which his proportional systems were applied. By the late seventeenth century, Palladio had assumed the character of an architectural god, with his theories and designs applied and copied throughout Europe and its colonies. The belief was that Palladio, through study, insight and trial and error, had discovered the key to the beauty of ancient architecture, a beauty that was based on the immutable and divine laws of nature.

Many architects at this time, no doubt Bruce included, believed that to follow the example and prototypes offered by Palladio was to work with the very building blocks of God's creation. When he started to build Kinross House, Bruce included not only a French-style enfilade, but also rooms that in their proportions and dispositions reflect Palladio's theories. In his *Quattro libri*, Palladio included a description of the seven proportions that, he proclaimed, would produce the 'most beautiful' rooms. These are a circle, a square, a square and a third, the diagonal of a square, a square and a half or 2:3 in proportion, square and two-thirds, and a double square. The key is that all these proportions are extensions of, or closely related to, the same basic unit – the square or its three-dimensional equivalent, the cube. Even the diagonal of a square proportion – otherwise known as root two – if extended to root four, becomes a double square. So this proportional system, organized around the square, was used to create a series of harmonious shapes, all of which relate to one another. For Palladio this integration, the fact that proportions used were 'commensurate', was vitally important; it was the key to getting all elements of a building – its plan, its elevations, its details, such as window and door openings – to relate in a pleasing manner. Bruce certainly seems to have embraced this theory. Kinross House, when built, possessed a plan similar to some of Palladio's villas and rooms that, in plan, were square, of 2:3 proportion and even, with the first-floor saloon, double-square in plan.

LEFT ABOVE *A window embrasure and seats in the early fourteenth-century Loch Leven Castle, serving the floor that, in 1567, accommodated the imprisoned Mary Queen of Scots. She must often have sat upon these seats, looking across the loch and dreaming of escape and freedom.*
LEFT BELOW *Kinross House, seen from Loch Leven Castle,* *presides over the waters of the loch like a Renaissance palazzo on the Venetian lagoon.*
OPPOSITE *Looking towards Loch Leven Castle from Kinross House. The straight route through the garden is an evocation of Bruce's design of the 1680s, but the general planting pattern dates from the early twentieth century.*

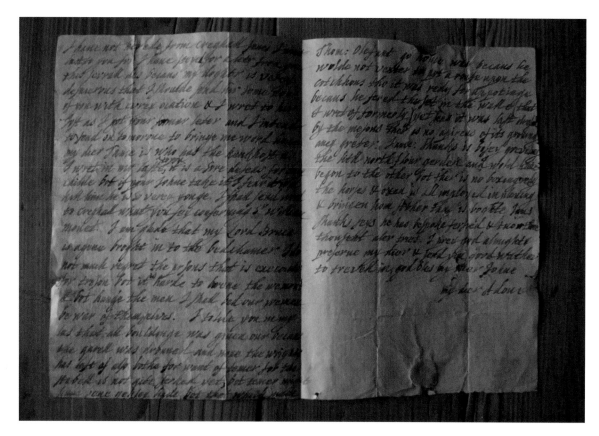

But through the late 1670s and early 1680s Bruce resisted the temptation to build. He had the land, the money, the power and the will to do so, but something restrained him, even frightened him, and he remained in old Kinross House, looking out upon his maturing garden with its central axis orientated towards a house that still did not exist. Then, in 1685, his great patron Charles II died. Had Bruce left it too late? In the light of Charles II's death, would he now lose his posts and his position? Strangely, it seems that this was just the moment that Bruce had been waiting for. He knew, of course, that all he was depended on Charles, and he had known that Charles would soon die. It seems that Bruce waited for this to happen, waited to test his relationship with the new king – Charles II's brother, James II – to see what way the wind would blow before committing himself to the construction of Kinross House. Initially, all went well.

In late 1685 Bruce was in London, dancing attendance upon the new king, attempting,

"Kinross House is one of the most beautiful, serene and dignified classical houses ever built in Britain. For Scotland, it's the nation's first true and complete Renaissance-manner classical house, possessing a quality and architectural power of international significance...

ABOVE *A letter to William Bruce from his wife Mary, dated 3 November 1685, displays great affection and satisfaction that her husband is receiving intimate attention from the new monarch, James II. She is, Mary tells her husband, 'glade' that he has 'agane' been 'brought to the bedchamber' of the king.*

successfully it would seem, to renew the friendly relations he had enjoyed with James in Edinburgh in the late 1670s. Among the letters from Mary Bruce to her husband, currently preserved in the Charter Room at Kinross House, is one that's remarkably revealing, capturing precisely the optimism that must have prevailed in the Bruce household at the time. The new king was on the throne and it seemed, for the Bruces, that all was well in the world. They had survived the transition of monarchs. The letter from Mary is dated 3 November 1685 and – direct and immediate in its emotion, and with spelling that is wayward even for its age – displays great affection for William, who was in London with John and seemingly sorely missed: 'My dierest harte, I will not sofer [suffer] myselfe to repine so long as I get frequent letrs from my dier that alwes tells me that you are in good helthe and your son.' Despite missing her husband and son, Mary understands that their attendance at court is necessary for the family's future: '... if you continoue in your masters faver I will be wel plesed what ever sockses [success] you have hade in your partiqular att this time.'

The 'master' was, of course, King James II, who had been on the throne since February 1685. Later in the same letter Mary confirms the current status of Bruce's relationship with the king: 'I am glade that my Lord Bruce is agene brought in to the bedchamber.' This is a most revealing statement. Bruce, evidently on more than one occasion, had visited the king at court – probably in Whitehall Palace – and made the full circuit of the rooms, while lesser men had been filtered out at various doors in the sequence – hall, ante-room, presence chamber and so on – and had made it all the way to the state bedchamber, where he was received by the king. This was a sign of the greatest intimacy and favour. The Bruces, their fortunes depending on royal patronage, were right to be pleased. Clearly, Bruce's time at the court in London had been well spent, not least because in April 1685 James II had appointed Bruce to the Scottish Privy Council, an advisory body that was, in effect, the government of Scotland.

Bruce had reached a giddy height in the power structure of Scotland, indeed of Britain. The reward of the earldom he craved, which would seal his creation of an aristocratic dynasty, could not be far off. Feeling at last secure of his income and position, he started to build his mansion at Kinross, which was clearly underway by November 1685, for Mary concludes her letter by informing Bruce that 'all bouldinge [building] was given over because the qarell [quarry] was drowned and nowe the wrights has left of also ... for want of temer [timber]'. But the garden, started nearly a decade earlier, and the park were in a happier condition and still being improved: 'Jame Shanks is busey greveling [gravelling] the little north flour garden' and has 'bespoke ... two or three thousant aler [alder] trees.'

KINROSS HOUSE

For me, Kinross House is one of the most beautiful, serene and dignified classical houses ever built in Britain. For Scotland, it's the nation's first true and complete Renaissance-manner classical house, possessing a quality and architectural power of international significance. In a way, the house symbolizes Scotland's aspiration, during the last decades of the seventeenth century, to join the community of European nations as a sophisticated, modern and independent power. Kinross House is truly a most extraordinary achievement. Something quite amazing had happened to Bruce and his architectural ability during his years of brooding. His work at Holyrood House is pleasing but not exceptional, while that at Kinross possesses a sureness of touch, a perfection of design and construction that puts it in quite another league, that makes it one of the most compelling buildings in Britain. Given its power and importance, it's worth spending a moment attempting to dissect Bruce's design, to discover the buildings that influenced him, and to understand the way he distilled, fused and transformed them in such creative a manner in his designs for Kinross House.

It now seems obvious that Bruce wanted, through his design of Kinross House, to declare cultural and architectural allegiances with continental Europe rather than with Britain, to connect with the big, prevailing, international architectural ideas. His deference to Palladio – a hero also of English architects since the early seventeenth century – was part of this, which meant Kinross House shared a common ancestry and visual connection with much seventeenth-century English architecture, notably the works of Inigo Jones, as well as with the bold and simple Dutch Palladian architecture and the sixteenth-century villas in northern Italy by both Palladio and Vincenzo Scamozzi. The influence of seventeenth-century French architecture beyond the enfilade plan is not so clear. Designers of mid-to-late seventeenth-century chateaux in France tended towards verticality, variety and movement of elevation. Bruce at Kinross prefers a grave simplicity and a horizontal stress to his design. Despite what could be perceived as his desire to embrace the 'international classical style' of the moment and look to the fountainhead of Italy, it must be admitted that the most direct prototypes for Kinross House lie in

England and are the work of an amateur architect who has much in common with Bruce.

Roger Pratt was born in England in 1620 into a Royalist family, and emigrated to the Continent in 1642 to avoid the civil war. He travelled in France, Italy and the Low Countries, returned to England in 1649 after the execution of Charles I, and established himself as a lawyer with a penchant for architecture. Like Bruce, Pratt started his architectural career working for friends and relatives. Around 1649–50 he designed a house at Coleshill, Berkshire, for a cousin, Sir George Pratt. This, as it happened, turned out to be one of the most influential houses designed in Britain during the seventeenth century. It was completed in about 1662 and, tragically, destroyed by fire in 1952. Coleshill House possessed a simple, dignified and almost heartbreakingly sombre beauty. The inspirations were the Dutch Palladian architecture Pratt would have seen on his travels, and Palladio via Inigo Jones's pioneeringly Palladian Queen's House at Greenwich, and all was dependent on a system of proportions so subtle that its sophistication was scarcely apparent. For example, the long entrance and garden elevations were each nine windows wide, but with the three at either end of each main elevation more closely spaced than the centre three windows. These centre windows lit the cubical double-height entrance hall on one side and the double-square Great Parlour and Great Dining Chamber on the other. This system of spacing – perhaps inspired by a number of Venetian palazzi

LEFT ABOVE *The Queen's House, Greenwich, in south London, designed by Inigo Jones in 1614 and completed in 1635, was the first fully formed, Palladio-inspired villa built in Britain and a great influence on succeeding generations of British architects.*
LEFT BELOW *Coleshill House, Berkshire, was completed in*

about 1662 to the designs of Roger Pratt. Destroyed in 1952, it possessed a sombre beauty and was one of the most influential houses created in late seventeenth-century Britain.
OPPOSITE *Detail of the finely carved fireplace, dating from 1685 to 1690, in the Oak Drawing Room in Kinross House.*

and some of Palladio's villas – gave emphasis of the most subtle kind to the centre of each of the main elevations. No columned portico was necessary, for the spacing almost implied one, and expressed the dignity, importance and large volumes of the rooms they served.

It was the wide spacing of the central windows at Coleshill that Bruce followed, for all the windows on main elevations at Kinross are set well apart, giving the house a very Italian rather than northern European feel: in the darker north, where light was at a premium, piers between windows tended to be far narrower than in southern Europe. Another great difference between the two houses – and really something of a Bruce innovation – was to light the upper floor at Kinross not by large dormers set in the pitch of the roof (the common seventeenth-century solution in northern Europe), but by very shallow attic windows set within the parapet above the cornice. This visually powerful design helps give Kinross House a neoclassical gravity and sense of Roman authority that anticipates the Palladian revival of the 1720s and 1730s. At Coleshill, ground- and first-floor windows were of identical shape and size (although those on the first floor a trifle more ornamented), reflecting the relatively equal importance of the two floors – a contrast to Palladio's designs in which, almost invariably, first-floor windows are deeper and more ornamented to emphasize the pre-eminence of the first-floor *piano nobile*. This pattern of ground- and first-floor windows of matching shape was followed by Bruce at Kinross with even greater uniformity than at Coleshill, for Bruce's first-floor windows lack any additional ornament.

Another house by Pratt also seems to have been an inspiration for Bruce. It was a mansion, designed in 1664, on Piccadilly, London, for Lord Clarendon, then the most powerful political figure in the land but who was forced into exile when the Second Dutch War of 1665–7 went badly wrong for Britain. Although Clarendon never lived in his mansion, it remained a suitable prototype for all men of ambition. It had a centre block nine windows wide, with a three-window pediment as its focus that was

set on an axis with St James's Street and, rather arrogantly, looked directly down upon the antiquated Tudor gatehouse of St James's Palace. This centre block was flanked by a pair of wings that projected to the depth of three windows, and were each three windows wide. The elevation of the house was a sedate two storeys topped by a central cupola, and possessed a classical gravity that seemed the epitome of taste and power. However, despite the manner in which it gripped the imagination of the nation and its immense influence on other architects, it was torn down by a consortium of speculators in 1675 and replaced with Dover Street, Albemarle Street and Bond Street. So by the time Bruce actually started to build Kinross House, one of his contemporary architectural inspirations was already just a memory.

The main and most obvious debt Kinross owes to Clarendon House is its very shallow but significant three-window-wide end projections that, in most modest manner, echo the wings of their Piccadilly prototype. This type of plan – centre block set between cross wings – had been a traditional permutation for a yeoman or gentleman's house in England since the Middle Ages, and Tyttenhanger Manor, Hertfordshire (c.1665) is a good example almost contemporary with Kinross House. But Bruce's reduction of the cross wing to four shallow projections, each framed by giant Corinthian pilasters and so implying end pavilions, was an inventive permutation of the type. This combination of pilasters and end projections was perhaps inspired by Gian Lorenzo Bernini's abortive but famed design of 1665 for rebuilding the Palais du Louvre in Paris.

Much of the plan of Kinross House is original – indeed idiosyncratic – and no mere shallow copy of Coleshill or other prototypes. For a start, Kinross is two windows wider than Coleshill, so Bruce was able to introduce extra volumes on the ground and first floor so that there were two rooms rather than one between large central staterooms and the flanking closets. The other very obvious difference is the treatment of the main staircase. Rather than placing it in a double-height entrance hall, Bruce

> Clarendon House... despite the manner in which it gripped the imagination of the nation and its immense influence on other architects... was torn down by a consortium of speculators in 1675 and replaced with Dover Street, Albemarle Street and Bond Street...

ABOVE *Clarendon House, Piccadilly, London, designed by Roger Pratt in 1664 for the politically powerful Lord Clarendon, was another possible influence on Bruce when* *designing Kinross House.* OVERLEAF *Details in the basement of Kinross House – ranks of cues in the billiard room and cast-iron kettles in the kitchen.*

created a single-storey hall, square in plan and separated from flanking vestibules by curious screens formed by pairs of Ionic columns (although puzzlingly absent on the earliest surviving plan by Alexander Edwards), with a large, open-well staircase set within the north projection or wing. This asymmetrical placing of the main staircase appears to follow precedent established by English architects. Certainly William Talman resolved, at much the same time, on something similar at Chatsworth, Derbyshire.

The execution of the staircase at Kinross is exceptional, with heavy, square-section oak newels and a moulded handrail framing beautifully carved oak panels lush with acanthus leaves and ripening fruit and flowers. In basic principle and form – although not in detail – the staircase seems inspired by that of the 1630s at Ham House in Richmond, Surrey, which the Duke of Lauderdale occupied as his London base and for which Bruce designed gateways in 1671 and 1675. Certainly the concept of

trompe l'oeil-painted staircase dados echoing the carved handrail that Bruce employed at Kinross was expressed earlier with the Ham staircase. The carver responsible for the beautiful workmanship at Kinross is believed to be the Edinburgh-based Dutchman Jan van Sant Voort.[6]

The main rooms on the ground and first floor at Kinross follow the basic model of Coleshill, except for the addition of the extra four volumes per floor,

with rooms grouped to form apartments and doors aligned to offer vistas through the building and routes for formal parades. But what is substantially different, and most intriguing, is the parallel world Bruce created for service, servants and even surveillance and defence. As at Coleshill, the corridor/vestibules at Kinross, defining the double-pile plan, lead to closets that adjoin those serving the apartments of rooms. In all cases these inner closets could not be entered directly from the apartments, and in some cases only from the central corridor, this suggesting that they had a role in the servicing of the house – indeed, were rooms for servants, allowing them to be on close call – and were not part of the circuit of the polite rooms. But far more significant, the two projecting end portions of Kinross possess one more storey than the central portion of the house. These additional floors take the form of a low mezzanine, of barrel-vaulted masonry construction, inserted between the ground and first floors. The introduction of the mezzanine floors means that the narrow end elevations of the house are quite different from the main elevations because they incorporate an extra tier of windows and, in consequence, the height of the ground-floor windows is lower than on adjoining elevations. This is certainly a peculiar arrangement, especially when observed from within corner rooms, where windows on adjoining walls are of different heights.

The mezzanine levels, and the upper storeys and basement of the house, are reached by a pair of

LEFT ABOVE *A flower and acanthus swirl on one of the staircase balustrade panels.* LEFT BELOW *Spheres grasped by acanthus leaves ornament the top of each newel post.*

OPPOSITE *The massive, open-well oak-built staircase of 1685 to 1690 is the most magnificent interior detail of Kinross House. Montgomery family portraits line the staircase walls.*

secondary staircases placed symmetrically on either side of the entrance hall. But there are also additional discreet, almost secret, routes between the ground floor and mezzanines. Within the thickness of the internal walls, set near either end of the corridor vestibules off the entrance hall, are (or were) very small spiral, stone-built staircases, most of them originally hidden behind cupboard doors (only one of these staircases now survives intact). The precise purpose of these four small and hidden staircases remains somewhat mysterious. At the most mundane level they could have been used by servants to transport human waste in a discreet manner from rooms on the mezzanine to the basement. This is certainly the use implied in contemporary documents. Or perhaps, more romantically, they could have been created to permit secret comings and goings by certain visitors without being observed.

There is one more great oddity about Bruce's plan. The projecting ends of the main elevations give movement and interest to the composition, but also bring a problem and a seeming bonus. Bruce proved

❝ One of the commonplace observations about Kinross is that it's one of the first great houses in Scotland to be designed and constructed with no reference, either symbolic or practical, to fortifications…

ABOVE LEFT *One of the narrow windows at Kinross, located in small rooms created within the thickness of the wall, that command views of the main doors of the house.*
ABOVE RIGHT *One of the very narrow and winding 'page' or service staircases linking ground and mezzanine floors.*
OPPOSITE *Corner showing the relationship of ground-floor windows on the main frontage (far right) with slightly shallower ground-floor window and mezzanine windows on the side elevation.*

himself unable to reconcile the alignment of the doors of the closets within the projecting end portions of the house with the doors of adjoining rooms, so – rather unsatisfactorily – the vista along the length of the house is interrupted. But the bonus of the projections raises issues about the very nature of Kinross House. One of the commonplace observations about Kinross is that it's one of the first great houses in Scotland to be designed and constructed with no reference, either symbolic or practical, to fortifications. But this may not be the case. Within the thickness of the wall, where it projects slightly to form the end 'wings' or pavilions, are tiny rooms, some but not all lit by slit-like windows that offer views across the adjoining elevation. The purpose of these rooms, most fitted with ornamental plaster domes and various ornamental details, has long been a puzzle. Were they miniature closets? Locations for close-stools? Cells in which people could be confined? (Some possess doors with locks that can only be operated externally, which must have led to anxious moments over the years for those who accidentally locked themselves into these claustrophobic spaces.) But there is another possibility. The projecting end portions of Kinross House can be seen as subtle bastions, with these small rooms offering commanding positions from which the main doors of the house can be watched, even controlled and defended, because the narrow windows make very efficient loopholes from which a pistol or musket could be used to beat back intruders.

THE PLANS

The organization of life within Kinross House, and specific room uses, are revealed – or at least strongly implied – by surviving and partly annotated plans of the house. The earliest would appear to have been produced around 1685–90 by Alexander Edwards, an associate or assistant of Bruce. The originals are in the possession of the University of Edinburgh, with copies in the National Monument Record for Scotland.[7] There is also a plan of the house in its setting, showing that a formal garden was intended for the west, entrance side, of the house as well as to the east.[8] The plans are accompanied by an elevation of the entrance front, showing it much as it survives. But intriguingly, the windows are shown as voids. If they were fitted in the 1680s with sliding sashes on counterweights, it would be a very early example of this type of window technology, which seems to have evolved in England and the Netherlands independently during the 1660s and 1670s. There is very strong evidence that sashes were indeed installed because in April 1688 Alexander Eizalt & Co wrote to Bruce about supplying frames for 'Chassie [presumably sash] Windows'.[9] If sashes were not used, the windows would have been fitted with timber mullions and transoms, and fixed and hinged leaded lights. Perhaps significantly, sash windows had been fitted during the 1670s at Ham House, where Bruce would no doubt have seen them.

As expected, the 'Under Ground Storie' or basement is shown on the plans as the service hub of the house. It is beautifully constructed, with stone-vaulted ceilings supporting the ground floor, uniform and boldly detailed voussoir arches to doors and fire surrounds, a double-pile plan arranged around a central corridor, and a very functional disposition of rooms. Externally, the façade of the basement has banded rustication, inspired by Roman architecture, to provide a visually and physically strong base for the smooth-faced stone façades that rise above. The uses listed in the basement include 'Inner Kitchen with Storages

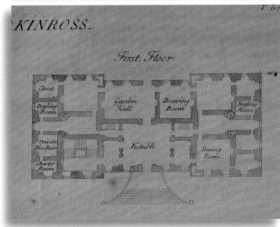

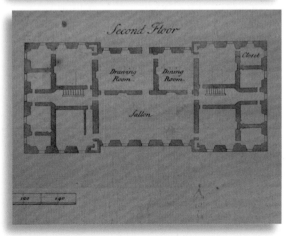

pastrie Owen ... Scullerie for holding of the Wessels ... Scalerie with a boyling Chimney & a division within which is 2 beds for kooks ... Inner woman house' (presumably a dormitory for female servants) adjoining a 'Nurserie'.

On the ground floor the entrance hall from the west is called the 'Westibull', and the small rooms flanking the existing entrance hall and separated from it by pairs of Ionic columns on plinths are shown as separated by solid walls (so are the unusual Ionic screens in fact a later alteration?). The small room to the north, between the hall and the 'Great stair to Parler', is called a 'Waiting roome'. The room to the south of the entrance hall is described as a 'Bedchamber', as is that in the northeast corner of the ground floor. All closets off rooms are described as 'Closets' or, in the case of most of those off the central corridor 'Dressing roomes'. The exception is the closet in the northwest corner, beyond the great staircase, which is described as the 'Charter roome wolted & grated Iron door'. This was the repository of documents and valuables, and was evidently intended to be thief- and fire-proof. Its window on the north elevation is unique, being small in depth and perhaps originally barred.

The square-plan room to the east, which overlooks the garden, and still retains its now much-altered unpainted oak panelling, was a 'Withdrawing Roome', while the small spiral staircases and the mezzanine rooms they lead to are described as 'Backstairs to Intersole [or

LEFT Elevations of Kinross House (top), and plans, as in about 1710, published in Vitruvius Scoticus. The functional and convenient 'double-pile' nature of the plan is clear, with 'piles' of rooms set on each side of, and served by, central service corridors or lobbies. Aligned doors on each level allow a vista and architectural promenade through the rooms of the house. OPPOSITE The curving passages linking the basement of the main house to a flanking building.

mezzanine] garderobe for Servant'. The large, double-height and virtual double-cube room on the first floor is described – Coleshill fashion – as the 'Great Dyning Roome'. The sequence of three main rooms on the first floor overlooking the garden is also described. These, from north to south, are named as 'Withdrawing roome ... Antechamber' and 'bedchamber', thus identifying the main state apartment. The two additional square-plan rooms at the north and south ends of the house are also described as bedchambers. The small rooms off the bedchambers are described as closets, while those off the central corridor and that above the Charter Room are described as 'Little bedchambers off Backstairs'.

The second floor contained a series of bedchambers and closets, but also a 'stand for Musitians', which appears to have been a small gallery, reached through an arch, from which musicians could have entertained guests in the Great Dyning Roome below. This plan and description must be treated with some caution because elements of it, particularly those relating to the upper floors, could have been compiled before the house was actually completed and thus show what was intended rather than record what was created. Two other plans, almost contemporary, tell a slightly different story. One, thought to date from around 1700, is reproduced in Pevsner's *Buildings of Scotland*.[10] It suggests that the Ionic columns in the entrance hall are indeed original, calls the main central room on the garden front the 'Garden Hall', and describes the closet at the north end of the house at ground level and adjoining the Charter Room as 'Sir William Bruce's Closet'. On the first floor the double-height room is called the 'Saloon', and the sequence of rooms to its east, overlooking the garden are – from north to south – the 'State Drawing Room,' the 'Ante-Chamber', the 'State Bedchamber' and beyond it a closet.

Thus, the state promenade through the house is made clear. All is organized as in a royal court, with Bruce apparently conceiving himself as a petty prince in his own palace. Guests would have arrived in the entrance hall, virtually all would have progressed via the great staircase to the huge Saloon, and then the filtering process would have started. Some would have passed into the State Drawing Room and seen into the adjoining Ante-Room, but been excluded from entering it. Here the chosen few would have waited to enter the adjoining State Bedchamber to be received by Bruce. Only those of most intimate acquaintance or of highest status would have retired with Bruce into the Holy of Holies – the closet beyond. This formal plan, revealing and establishing the social status and importance of guests – essentially a mirror of the social structure of the larger world – would not only have permitted Bruce to behave with pomp and display when circumstances demanded, but also, of course, proclaimed that his home was a palace in miniature, the house of a courtier in which the genuine royal court could be expected to arrive at any moment. Kinross was, in the most visible way possible, to be a house fit for a king.

A third set of plans is included in *Vitruvius Scoticus*, a publication that illustrates the works of William Adam and other progressive Scottish classicists. The book appeared in 1812 without a significant text or introduction, so the status and provenance of some of the illustrations remain uncertain, not least that of Kinross House. Its illustration appears to date from around 1710, the year in which William Bruce died, because the engraving describes Kinross as the home of his son John. The entrance elevation is shown much as built (although the pedimented porch was not finally added as designed until the early twentieth century) and the windows are fitted with sashes. On the ground floor, the room behind the west front and to the south of the entrance hall or 'Vestuble' [sic] is described as a 'Dining room' rather than a bedchamber, as on the earlier plans, and what was described as Bruce's closet is a 'Private Dining Room' connecting directly to the adjoining Charter Room. On the first floor the room uses are much as on the 1700 plan, but the 'Ante-Chamber' is termed a 'dining room'. The second floor is not annotated.

> Thus, the state promenade through the house is made clear. All is organized as in a royal court, with Bruce apparently conceiving himself as a petty prince when in his own place…

ABOVE LEFT *The staircase from ground floor to basement, and the view along the centrally placed basement corridor.*
ABOVE RIGHT *The view at ground-floor level, showing the barrel vault supporting the mezzanine floor at the southern end of the house.*

THE DECLINE

Soon after Bruce started the construction of Kinross House in mid-1685 something rather unpleasant happened – indeed, an event that, with hindsight, we can see marked the turning point of his life and aspirations. In May 1686 James II, the man Bruce believed he had wooed and won, turned nasty in a most public and humiliating manner. Bruce was peremptorily sacked from the Privy Council for Scotland after just over a year's service. The reason for this is now lost in history, but Bruce was left very exposed. His previous twenty-five years of success and power had depended on royal patronage, and now he was out. One explanation for Bruce's estrangement from James is that he, like most people, failed to understand just how ruthless and ultimately stupid James would be in his hapless attempt to turn back the clock and make Britain once again a Roman Catholic nation ruled by an absolute monarch.

Perhaps, because Bruce was a man of burning

ambition, James thought that he could count on his unprincipled support. But it's possible that Bruce, as an Episcopalian, felt as threatened and shocked as most of his countrymen by James's conduct and resisted. We do not know. Nor do we know much about his feelings after his dismissal. Perhaps, as a man of the world who had clearly weathered many storms, he felt confident that he would weather this one. Certainly, building works at Kinross proceeded at a steady pace, and accounts confirm that in 1686 the ornate carvings of military trophies above the

entrance door and foliage above the garden door were completed by the Dutch and Flemish masons Peter Paul Boyse and Cornelius van Nerven.[11] These strikingly deep and sculptural carvings appear to have been an afterthought on Bruce's part because, most unusually, they are carved into the main wall of the house in bas-relief form, rather than being carved on stone blocks projecting from the façade of the house, as are the Bruce coats of arms placed above the second-floor centre windows.

At the same time the garden and landscape continued to be planted and improved. Indeed, Bruce's transformations at Kinross seem to have become legendary. On 18 October 1687 Sir Charles Lyttelton wrote to Bruce from London to inform him that the gardens of Kinross were the talk of the town: 'I hear Lady Lauderdale's gardens at Ham are but a wilderness to be compared to yours at Kinross, of which I wish you all the content and true satisfaction your own heart can desire.'[12] By this time, with seeds and trees coming from London, Holland and Paris, the creation of the gardens was costing Bruce about £400 Scots a year.[13]

The reference to Lady Lauderdale is interesting. The Duke of Lauderdale, a ruthless and ambitious politician, had become all-powerful in Scotland after being made Secretary of State in 1660 and, thanks to his close connections with Charles II, became a significant power in England too. Bruce was one of his creatures, but in 1674 had become embroiled in factional rivalry between Lauderdale and his political rivals the Duke of Hamilton and

LEFT Military trophies carved into the beautiful ashlar facing stones of the façade above the main entrance door.
OPPOSITE The garden entrance. The porch, formed with Ionic columns, is original, and here the carvings flanking the first-floor windows depict, in most appropriate manner, flowers, garlands and foliage.
OVERLEAF The north end of the entrance hall or vestibule. The screen, formed by a pair of Ionic columns on pedestals, is probably original, although not shown in the earliest plan of c.1685–90 by Alexander Edwards. The door (left) leads to the staircase hall, while the distant door, with coat of arms above, leads to what was originally the highly secure Charter Room.

IRREVOCABILE

the Earl of Tweeddale. Bruce was, it seems, exposed for passing confidential information to Hamilton, and for this disloyal act Lauderdale stripped him of his post as Surveyor-General and described him as 'the bitterest factionalist partie man of his quality in all Scotland'.[14] This was indeed the pot calling the kettle black. Lauderdale himself was subsequently stripped of all his powers in 1682 and died a few months later a broken man. Bruce survived, but money started to become short and his dream of becoming an earl and founding an aristocratic dynasty must have appeared to be evaporating.

Eventually, James II's foolish behaviour led to his dramatic and speedy fall. In June 1688 seven powerful English nobles invited William of Orange, who was James's nephew and married to his daughter Mary, to enter England with a Dutch army to depose James and save the Protestant religion of the land. William and his army duly arrived, were

ABOVE *The beautifully carved Bruce arms above the door to the Charter Room, off the staircase hall.*

well received, and started on their triumphal progress to London and power. James was captured in December but allowed to 'escape' to France, where Louis XIV gave him, his second wife Mary of Modena and their baby son James a palace and a pension. This established the second Stuart court in exile and the Jacobite intrigue for a return to power in Britain that would not end until 1746, with the defeat of James's grandson, 'Bonnie Prince Charlie', at the brutal battle of Culloden.

William and Mary's elevation to the throne of England, Scotland and Ireland heralded a new age and created opportunities for new men and new families. Bruce, although he did not quite realize it in 1688, was now one of yesterday's men who, because of his long and profitable association with the ousted Stuart dynasty, would be viewed with suspicion. Indeed, as the Stuarts attempted to regain the throne by force, and as the Jacobite cause became militant, times were getting very dangerous and difficult for men like Bruce.

But despite the changes, Bruce pressed on with the completion of Kinross House. Documents from the late 1680s and early 1690s offer insights into life at that time. Bruce was losing his lucrative government posts and had to extract revenue from the Kinross estate – from fishing, farms and rents from tenants. This is illustrated by a document – a Feudal Charter – that Bruce granted to one of his tenants in 1688. This produced a lump sum of money, but reduced Bruce's annual rent income.

Although suffering a shortage of ready cash, Bruce was spending large sums on the house. An account dated 12 January 1692 lists payments made by Bruce to 'Alex. Brand, merchant' for numerous items for the house including 'a pic. of architectorie and frame ... 2 pics. of flower pots in frames' – perhaps the very paintings that survive fixed above doors in the ground-floor Garden Hall and Oak Drawing Room – and 'for your low dyning room 91¼ skins of geld. leather'.[15] These gilded and no doubt embossed leather panels – probably Spanish – were for one of the smaller dining rooms mentioned on the early floor plans. The account records that Bruce paid £219 sterling for the leather,

a colossal sum, suggesting that he was still in funds.

At this time – 1692 – Kinross House was complete structurally and the ground-floor rooms fitted with panelling and internal details such as window shutters and fireplaces. Much of this still survives, notably the panelling in the entrance hall and flanking vestibules, in the Oak Drawing Room and in the southwest closet, which – strikingly Dutch in atmosphere – retains its wall panelling and a superbly carved corner chimney-breast, a semi-domed affair furnished with delicately carved brackets embellished with acanthus leaves, which matches another one that survives in the Oak Drawing Room. The richness of this small room confirms the high status and potential importance of the closets in Kinross House. But although the ground-floor fittings and furnishings were more or less complete, the upper floors seem to have been in a very different state. The floors and room partitions may have been in place, but that was it. The Great Staircase would have led up to a desolate world, its echoing rooms a testament to the hard times that befell Bruce after 1686. Indeed, although Bruce may have used the ground floor of the house for entertaining as his garden could be seen to advantage from there, he did not move into the house when roofed by 1692, but continued to occupy the old house nearby.

In 1693 what Bruce must have long dreaded finally happened: he became a marked man. As an Episcopalian, he had been close to the Stuart court, and it was assumed, rightly or wrongly, that he would favour a Jacobite counter-revolution and perhaps be actively plotting a return of the Stuarts. In this atmosphere of fear and distrust Bruce found himself imprisoned in Stirling Castle in 1693. His wife Mary joined him in prison at Stirling and a letter written on her behalf about the incompetent or corrupt behaviour of the head servant at Kinross reveals only too clearly how the Bruces' circumstances had changed. Mary was worried about household spending at Kinross while she and Bruce were absent and their house nearly empty. Only a year after Bruce had spent a small fortune on leather wall-covering for his would-be palace, his wife was watching every penny. The letter to the Bruces' factor states: 'My lady finds that there is bought beef, also white bread in the accounts, whereas My Lady had ordered there should be no spending [on that?] and that he [the head servant] still takes the same quantities of fish when there is but six servants and their families as when there were twelve …'[16]

Bruce was soon released, but imprisoned again in 1694, then released to Kinross under house arrest. At around this time Bruce, fearing that his land and

money might be confiscated by the state, handed everything over to his son John, who henceforth ran, in name at least, the Bruce interests. Then, on 29 February 1696, the Privy Council issued another warrant for his arrest,[17] and Bruce was imprisoned yet again, this time in Edinburgh Castle.

Despite these repeated and regular imprisonments, Bruce managed to carry on his architectural practice. In about 1695 he designed Craigiehall House in West Lothian for the Earl of Annandale, and a year or so later designed alterations and additions for Craighall in Cupar, Fife, for Sir William Hope, his grandson and then a minor in Bruce's guardianship. Also at this period Bruce got involved in an adventure that was to be not only the last in his life, but, in a sense, the last great adventure in Scotland's history as an independent nation.

THE FALL

Although the Stuart Restoration of 1660 had brought stability and wealth to Scotland, and William III's administration had soon sorted out the chaos caused by James II's brief and wild reign, the country lacked an abundance of wealth-creating natural resources. The relatively small nations of England and the Netherlands had grown rich and powerful through the acquisition and cultivation of productive colonies, so why should not the kingdom of Scotland do the same? Thus was sown the seed of the Darien adventure – a scheme to found a Scottish colony in Central America.

LEFT ABOVE AND BELOW *Edwardian garden details that were installed by Sir Basil Montgomery during his early twentieth-century restoration of Kinross House and its grounds.* OPPOSITE *The garden front glimpsed through the late seventeenth-century Fisher Gate. Cornucopia flank a stone-carved bowl stocked with specimens of the fish that could be caught in the adjoining Loch Leven at the time Kinross House was built.*

The Isthmus of Panama was identified as a likely location for it. True, the area was within the Spanish sphere of interest, but this seemed at the time a minor inconvenience. The plan was promoted by a number of leading Scottish economists and merchants, including William Paterson, who in 1694 was one of the founders of the Bank of England. He envisaged the colony as a haven of free trade for merchants from all nations and argued that its location on a narrow strip of land set between the Pacific and Atlantic oceans was the 'door of the seas and key to the universe'. Who controlled this strip of land, argued Paterson would be the 'arbiter of the commerce of the world'.[18]

Despite their relative poverty, William and John Bruce invested £500 in the Darien scheme.[19] It was not a good investment. From the very start things went wrong for New Caledonia, as the colony was called. The land, next to the river Darien, was hot and humid rainforest, and European-style farming proved impossible; yellow fever, dysentery and malaria quickly became endemic; the local people were not inclined to trade with the Scots; no efficient system of resupply had been established, nor a method for establishing the colony on existing trade routes. Soon these difficulties led to bitter internal strife. A bad situation was made far worse when William III bowed to pressure from English merchants alarmed by the Scottish initiative, and to his own fears of offending the Spaniards who claimed ownership of the area, and decided to distance himself from the enterprise and, effectively, abandon his Scottish subjects. By January 1699 a third of the Scottish settlers were dead from disease or starvation, and by June the settlement was abandoned. Subsequent attempts to refound it failed too. The dream was over. Scotland was humiliated and almost bankrupted.[20]

One can only imagine Bruce's dismay at the collapse of this heroic enterprise. Scotland's dream of economic self-sufficiency was virtually over, as was Bruce's last chance of personal wealth. A letter from Mary, dated 11 January 1699, reveals the family's circumstances: '... as for my cominge to you, there is maney inconveniecs [in] that, Also, in

my aprehension more than I can put in this leter, as the putinge you to a great and niddles [needless] expense now when your purse is growne so leghte [light] for I have hardly aney clos that I coulde be seen into.' But if Mary's financial circumstances were so dire – not even money to travel to Edinburgh or for a decent dress – her spirit and pride were unbroken: '... I am not so humbled for al that is come as to be contente to apier in a contemptable maner ...' This could be Mary's last letter. Within months of writing it, she was dead. Her husband, now probably in his early seventies, was left with a daughter and a son, a vast and still incomplete new house, spiralling debts, and myriad troubles associated with government suspicions about him.

THE 'DYNASTY' FALTERS

Bruce's two children – John and the slightly younger Anne – seem not to have been the source of delight and support that William no doubt would have wished. John had been educated as an architect and potential statesman. He had enjoyed a 'Petit Tour' from 1681 with a well-educated relative of his mother, went to the Netherlands and France, studied in Paris, and was encouraged to observe foreign culture and customs, keep a journal and read widely. But John proved himself slothful, careless of little beyond riding and mixing with elevated society, and disappointed his father by writing sparse letters 'lacking in thoughtful observations'.[21] However, soon after his return to Scotland, John made a useful marriage – to the widow of the Marquess of Montrose and daughter of the Duke of Rothes. But no child resulted from this marriage, so Sir William's hopes of founding an aristocratic dynasty appeared to be finally dashed. But, always a resourceful man, William had a fall-back plan. He had entailed the Kinross estate to his daughter Anne and her husband and heirs in the event that John had no offspring. This would mean the owner of the estate would no longer bear the name of Bruce, but at least Bruce blood would flow in their veins. In the production of progeny, Anne did much better than her brother. In 1679 she married Sir Thomas Hope and had three sons, and

Despite their relative poverty, William and John Bruce invested £500 in the Darien scheme. It was not a good investment. From the very start things went wrong for New Caledonia…

ABOVE *The first-floor saloon. Conceived by Bruce as a vast and dramatic double-cube volume, it was not completed until the late eighteenth and early twentieth centuries.*

after Sir Thomas died in 1686 she married John Carstairs and had four more children.

Bruce may also have had a further plan. Only months after the death of his affectionate and long-suffering wife of forty years, he married again. Could he, despite his advanced age, have been planning to beget a more resourceful son to whom he could leave Kinross? His second wife was Magdalen Scott, the young widow of an Edinburgh merchant. Presumably she brought some money into the family. The circumstances surrounding this unlikely marriage are hinted at in a letter that Bruce received in late 1699 from his son's wife. She had a great affection for his dead wife and reveals a concern that Bruce's conduct and his proposed marriage might damage both the family's reputation and the prospects of his grandchildren. It is evident that by this time the marchioness and John were in possession of Kinross House, while Sir William remained in the old house. In the letter she scolded her father-in-law: 'Alas, Sir, by your reserve [and] letting it publicly appear as if you were a stranger here ... gives your son and me undoubted grounds to see your uneasiness by our being in your house ... we came to please you, ease and divert you ... we are all ready to move upon your desire.' As for the proposed marriage, the marchioness confessed 'that I did wish you never to marry any [and fear] to see the posterity of my dear and excellent Lady Bruce cut off from enjoying what is Sir William's'.[22] The marchioness clearly feared that 'Little Willie', the son of Anne Bruce and much loved by Mary Bruce, might be disinherited if Sir William had a son by his new young wife. But the marriage produced no children, and Magdalen Scott remains a very hazy figure in the history of Kinross House. All that's certain is that her political allegiances were firmly Jacobite, presumably reflecting Bruce's own beliefs, which helps explain the state persecution that characterizes his last years.

Bruce lived in increasing poverty and isolation, presumably still in the old house at Kinross since he no longer had the means to complete the interior of his new house. One of the great ironies about Kinross is that the architectural genius behind this splendid creation probably never lived in it, but always beside it, from whence he could contemplate the great house and garden and ponder upon the transitory nature of worldly power and riches.

UNION AND PERSECUTION

In 1707, owing largely to national bankruptcy and personal impoverishment from the Darien scheme, the ruling elite of Scotland voted to wind up the parliament and, in a sense, sell the nation to England. Although the announcement was greeted by riots in Edinburgh, in May 1707 the Act of Union between the nations was agreed. In simple terms England had full power and control over Scotland. The advantages for Scotland were more nebulous.

In that same year persecution of Bruce reached a new height. King William III had died in March 1702, and was succeeded by a Stuart, but this did Bruce no good. Queen Anne, another daughter of James II, was most unlike her father. She was a Protestant and no pretender to absolute rule, but she was fearful of the Jacobite cause, still very much alive and seen as a serious threat, particularly in Scotland. One expression of her nervousness was Bruce's enforced resignation of his parliamentary seat, in favour of his son. Another was the round-up of potential or suspected Jacobites. A most chilling

LEFT *The ground-floor garden hall or drawing room, with panelling and over-door paintings of flowers that were installed by Bruce.*
OPPOSITE *One of the two fireplaces in the first-floor saloon. The stone bolection moulded fire surround may date from the late seventeenth century; other details are probably of late eighteenth- and early twentieth-century date.*

TO COMMEMORATE
BASIL TEMPLER GRAHAM MONTGOMERY 5TH BARONET OF STANHOPE
THIS MEMORIAL IS SET HERE BY THERESA HIS DEVOTED WIFE
TO RECORD FOR POSTERITY HIS ACHIEVEMENT
IN THE REBIRTH OF KINROSS HOUSE AND GARDENS
THE WORK OF SIR WILLIAM BRUCE IN THE 17TH CENTURY
THEY WERE LONG LEFT DERELICT
UNTIL SIR BASIL
WITH TIRELESS DEVOTION UNERRING JUDGMENT & WITH JOY
BUILT UP THE OLD WASTE
AND RENEWED THEIR FORMER BEAUTY
1902 - 1928
CYNTHIA WIFE OF HENRY KEITH MONTGOMERY LOVED & CARED FOR THIS GARDEN FROM 1937 - 1971

warrant from Kensington Palace, dated 8 March 1707 and signed by Anne, ordered him to be seized on 'suspicion of High treason and treasonable Practices and to bring him in Safe Custody before us to be examined Concerning such matters as shall be objected against him relating to the premises and to be further dealt with according to law'[23] The names appended to the warrant include Lords Pembroke, Godolphin, Somerset, Sunderland, Montrose, Marlborough, Strickland and Devonshire. These were the most powerful men in Britain, with the 4th Marquess of Montrose in particular being a product of the volatile and complex times, for he was not only a rare Scottish supporter of the Act of Union and Lord President of the Scottish Privy Council, but also the son of Bruce's daughter-in-law, the dowager Marchioness of Montrose. To have acquired such powerful enemies as these, Bruce must have been perceived as a very serious threat indeed, and this time there was no quick release.

Bruce was imprisoned in Edinburgh Castle and, although not charged or tried for treason nor stripped of his baronetcy, was detained for many months. It must have been a hellish experience. Old, alone and incarcerated in a dank cell with nothing to

" On my last day at Kinross House I went to the burial ground to pay my respects. On the chapel walls are the names of members of the Bruce family, and in the vault are sarcophagi, but none bears the name of Sir William. His body – his grave – is lost. It seems extraordinary and most sad that the man who created the beauty of the Kinross estate has no memorial…

ABOVE *Panel in a garden pavilion recording the early twentieth-century rescue and regeneration of Kinross House and garden.*

do but dream of what had been, what could have been, of freedom and of his beautiful house and garden at Kinross. Bruce died in 1710, in all likelihood a sad and disillusioned man. He seems to have remained estranged from his son, who died childless later the same year. Virtually all he had gained had been lost, and his vision of an independent Scotland and of a Bruce dynastic power base at Kinross was in ruins.

But despite the calamities that engulfed Bruce and his world, one thing remained – his stupendous creation at Kinross. The house and estate became the property of Bruce's daughter Anne and her second husband John Carstairs. They perhaps moved into the old house near the loch, but the final demolition of this ancient building in 1723 suggests that either Kinross House was at last habitable, or that the Carstairs family had given up all hope of living on the Kinross estate. Whatever the case, Kinross House itself had become famous because of Sir William Bruce's architectural ability. The author Daniel Defoe described it in his 1726 work *Tour thro' the Whole Island of Great Britain* as 'the most beautiful and regular piece of Architecture in Scotland'.[24] By this time the Kinross House and estate was owned by Anne's son James Carstairs, whose son James Bruce Carstairs sold it in 1777, thus putting a full and final end to William's dream of the Bruces of Kinross.

The Kinross estate was sold to George Graham, a wealthy East India merchant, who spent much money on the house – most of the fire surrounds and joinery on the first floor were installed by him – but Graham's primary interest was the income that could be extracted from the land and the waters of the loch. The estate passed through marriage from the Grahams to the Montgomery family, with Kinross House maintained but largely unoccupied from around 1819 until the very early twentieth century. This unusual state of affairs meant that the interior of the house escaped the usual Victorian alterations and 'improvements'. But it didn't escape Edwardian restoration and subtle rearrangement and modernization. In 1902 Sir Basil Montgomery decided to wake the sleeping giant of Kinross, beautify it, complete it and bring it back to life. He rearranged the ground floor, blocking and opening doors, moving fireplaces and knocking small closets into spacious bathrooms. On the second floor he ornamented the ceiling of the Saloon so that it echoes the splendid late seventeenth-century plaster ceiling above the Great Staircase. Outside the house, Sir Basil recreated the formal east garden much as Bruce had designed it, and built various pavilions and seats. It must be said that, by the standards of the age, Sir Basil's works are sensitive and self-effacing, but, more to the point, if not for his enthusiasm, Kinross House would almost certainly fallen into terminal ruin.

At the time of writing (Christmas 2010), Kinross House is set to enter a new chapter. After nearly 240 years of ownership by the Graham and Montgomery families, the house and garden (but not the estate) are about to be sold and the contents auctioned. The future is uncertain. There is no doubt the house will be maintained – it has statutory protection as a building of architectural and historic interest – but the exact nature of its new life is unknown. Will it become even more hidden and exclusive? Will its gardens, as well as its doors, be closed to the public?

Just outside the stone wall that defines and, in a sense, defends William Bruce's garden is a burial ground, and within it stands a chapel – a not particularly handsome neo-Norman affair constructed in the 1860s. It is, as it happens, far more interesting than it looks. It stands on the site of the medieval parish church of Kinross and covers what remains of an ancient vault. It was in this vault, beneath an aisle of the old church, that the body of Sir William was interred in November 1710.[25] On my last day at Kinross House I went to the burial ground to pay my respects. On the chapel walls are the names of members of the Bruce family, and in the vault are sarcophagi, but none bears the name of Sir William. His body – his grave – is lost. It seems extraordinary and most sad that the man who created the beauty of the Kinross estate has no memorial. But of course, in the larger sense, he has. As long as Kinross House endures and continues to inspire and delight generations to come, so will the name and the strange story of Sir William Bruce. ❖

EASTON
NESTON
Near Towcester,
Northamptonshire

18TH

CENTURY

Baroque masterpiece

Arriving at Easton Neston is a mysterious business. A modest drive leads off a public road and winds through an unostentatious park. Buildings appear, perhaps a stables or some other essentially utilitarian structures, then the side elevation of a long, low, red-brick building and suddenly, between gate piers, a diagonal view of a most arresting stone-clad elevation, looking like a complex jewel-box of a building, with its two-storey-high giant pilasters and columns in the rich Composite order, and a façade full of movement, yet

exuding sombre gravity. The long, low storey is a wing, and the tall pavilion is Easton Neston, which, on closer inspection, is seen to be sitting astride a long and dramatic avenue that, although informal, is defined by trees and stretches into the surrounding park as far as the eye can see. All is very startling. Easton Neston is one of the most visually thrilling, enigmatic and secret buildings in Britain. Its exterior was completed around 1702, the only country house built solely to the designs of Sir Christopher Wren's pupil Nicholas Hawksmoor – now acknowledged as one of the greatest and most original architects of eighteenth-century England – and owned for over three hundred years by the family that built it.

Hawksmoor was a master of what is now known as the English baroque style, and perhaps best known for his half-dozen London churches, constructed following the Act of Parliament of 1711 for Building Fifty Churches in London (in fact only a dozen or so were built). These churches – notably St Anne, Limehouse; Christ Church, Spitalfields; St George-in-the-East; and St George, Bloomsbury – are powerful and original works of art. They develop some of the themes pioneered by Wren during his City church-building campaign following the Great Fire of 1666, and achieve a powerful abstraction of form and detail that reinvigorated the classical language of architecture. Hawksmoor explored the special and compositional possibilities offered by cubical volumes, by layered elevations, and by the play of light and shade, to achieve startling and

PREVIOUS SPREAD *The garden front of Easton Neston in early morning winter sun. A relatively compact country house is given tremendous architectural gravity and presence in the relatively minimal manner, notably by the use of the Giant order of pilasters that rise majestically through two storeys.* ABOVE *Christ Church,*

Spitalfields, London, designed by Hawksmoor in 1714 – over ten years after the exterior of Easton Neston was completed – makes clear that Hawksmoor was gradually moving towards ever greater noble simplicity, abstraction and architectural reduction. Indeed he was on a very personal journey to the sublime, with emotional impact achieved through the use of

primary forms and volumes. The portico was added, it seems, only as an afterthought, in 1725–7. OPPOSITE *The entrance elevation of Easton Neston. The pair of Giant order central columns framing the main door may also have been added as an afterthought, to yet further enhance the ever-increasing grandeur of the composition.*

often stupendous results. Easton Neston, although significantly earlier, points the way towards these later, mature masterworks.

Many country houses in the English baroque are among the most visited and loved in the country: Castle Howard in North Yorkshire (1699–1712), where the 1981 television serialization of *Brideshead Revisited* was filmed; Chatsworth in the Peak District (1687–1707); Seaton Deleval in Northumberland (1718–28), which was recently acquired for the nation by the National Trust; and the most impressive of them all, Blenheim Palace (1705–24) in Oxfordshire, built for the victorious general the Duke of Marlborough, and later made famous as the birthplace of Winston Churchill. All are central to our collective idea of British art and history. Easton Neston is one of the most important and pioneering essays of the English baroque style of architecture, yet it is relatively unknown for it has never been open to the public, and remains a most secret and secluded domain. It is a house remarkable for combining the antique gravity of its façade with a fluid and ingenious interior plan. The giant order of the elevation brilliantly leaves behind the Anglo-Dutch classicism that the most recent domestic architecture in England had used, replacing it with something muscular and monumental. The spatial complexity of the interior, with its celebrated staircase, gives the visitor an experience closer to the great German baroque staircase at the bishop's palace in Würzburg by Johann Balthasar Neumann than to anything else in Britain. It is this ability to combine seemingly contradictory elements, in the case of Easton Neston the classical grandeur and nobility of the façade with the baroque freedom and playfulness of the interior spaces, that best characterizes the genius of Hawksmoor.

The story of the house can best be told by placing it within the context of Hawksmoor's biography. Easton Neston was an incredibly important commission for the architect, coming close to the beginning of his independent career. Before looking at the house, it is important to understand who Hawksmoor was and how he came to build at Easton Neston.

The portrayal of Hawksmoor in popular imagination as a diabolical occultist – originally set out in a poem by Iain Sinclair, and developed in Peter Ackroyd's novel *Hawksmoor* and the comic book *From Hell* – has no basis in recorded fact. Nevertheless, Hawksmoor has remained to some degree a mysterious figure. He has elicited a vast array of interpretations from many different fields, many of them seemingly contradictory. The architectural historian Giles Worsley has argued that Hawksmoor was a neoclassicist, keeping the classical spirit alight throughout the baroque period. On the other hand, Pierre de la Ruffinière du Prey has written a book on Hawksmoor's churches that portrays them as attempted recreations of early basilicas and obscurely envisioned ancient wonders. Another architectural historian, Vaughan Hart, sees Hawksmoor as an eclectic storyteller in stone, his buildings thick with symbols and references to antique monuments and freemasonry. In another field Denys Lasdun, the architect of the National Theatre, felt that Hawksmoor's effortless ability to create pure forms and be influenced by history without being a slave to it could show a way to reinvigorate modernist architecture.

These twentieth-century interpretations are all the more extraordinary for flying in the face of an earlier view of 'Mr. Hawksmore' as a jobsworth dullard and perpetual second fiddle to his great contemporaries Sir Christopher Wren and Sir John Vanbrugh. Like Shakespeare, Hawksmoor is in many ways the grammar school boy who was to show up the gentlemen practitioners. He was born in Nottinghamshire some time around 1661 or 1662, but was lucky enough to be employed as Sir Christopher Wren's personal assistant in London at about the age of 18. He did not merely work for Wren, but became part of his household, living with the family at Wren's official residence at Scotland Yard near Whitehall, and eventually becoming his personal clerk. There could not have been a more fertile environment for a young man than Wren's office. Wren was Hawksmoor's senior by some thirty years, and was one of the most commanding intellectual figures of his day. He had started life as a

Easton Neston is one of the most important and pioneering essays of the English baroque style of architecture, yet it is relatively unknown for it has never been open to the public, and remains a most secret and secluded domain…

ABOVE The north wing, originally one of two, was constructed in the mid-1680s (roof timbers have recently been dated to 1683–6), perhaps inspired by a slightly earlier design by Christopher Wren. The exact designer and builder of the wings remain unknown. Hawksmoor was later to call the wings 'good for nothing', presumably because they constrained the width of the frontage of the house he was to design between them.

mathematician and astronomer, but had later moved into architecture. Wren was the architect who had been given the job of redesigning London after the Great Fire of 1666, and although he was not able to implement his plan of turning London into a city of grand approaches and monumental boulevards on a Continental scale, he was nevertheless the architect for many of the buildings that still define London's skyline today – from St Paul's Cathedral to the hospital complexes at Greenwich and Chelsea, as well as the many parish churches still remaining from the fifty built by Wren after the Great Fire. This was an extraordinary opportunity for a young man from the provinces, and Hawksmoor grasped it with both hands. There was no official training for an architect at the time (Wren himself was self-taught), so this was a remarkably thorough architectural education for a practitioner of the era. Hawksmoor might well have been the best-trained English architect of the seventeenth century. Indeed, his professionalism marks him out in an age of gentlemanly amateur practitioners. It was a hands-on apprenticeship: as Wren's personal assistant, he gained an insight into every stage of building, from the office drawing board to supervising work on site, for all the most important works of the day.

Hawksmoor's earliest-known drawings, including one of Bath Abbey from the early 1680s, are mawkish, but it was under Wren's supervision that he learnt the fluid and wonderful style that we know from his later drawings (although, unfortunately, none survive for Easton Neston). Through his skill as a draughtsman, Hawksmoor was increasingly essential to his master, becoming his amanuensis and eventually even his architectural partner.

Wren instilled in Hawksmoor an interest in the pan-European architectural culture of books, treatises and prints, which would become for Hawksmoor a driving passion. The sale catalogue of his library after his death in 1736 shows how prodigious a collection he had amassed by the end of his life. Hawksmoor was an architect who never went abroad. Wren, of course, had got only as far as Paris, but other architects of the English baroque, such as Thomas Archer and James

Gibbs, had their architecture inspired and invigorated by travels to Rome. So much of Hawksmoor's architectural language stems from Rome that it is strange to think he never saw it.

Despite his lack of travel, Hawksmoor was by no means a provincial architect in his scope. It is through his avid bibliophilia that he came to know so much about the history of architecture. Through his library, he kept an eye on contemporary European developments, becoming an expert in contemporary debates in the theory of design and construction. Wren also transmitted to Hawksmoor an interest in the history of architecture, which extended beyond the strictures of classicism. Wren had an interest in the exotic styles of Asia Minor, then still obscurely known in England. An attempt to reconstruct these monuments, known through ancient written sources, can be seen in such works by Hawksmoor as the church of St George in Bloomsbury, London, with its spire an imaginative reconstruction of the stepped pyramid of the Mausoleum of Halicarnassus. As Hawksmoor's obituary stated, 'He was perfectly skill'd in the History of Architecture, and could give exact account of all the famous buildings, both Antient and Modern, in every part of the world; to which his excellent memory, that never

LEFT ABOVE Sir Christopher Wren, the architect who seems to have produced in the 1680s the initial, but ultimately unexecuted, designs for a new house at Easton Neston. LEFT BELOW Sir William Fermor, created Baron Leominster (or Lempster) in 1692, built Easton Neston,

seemingly wanting its design ever grander. OPPOSITE The view of the garden, largely remodelled in the 1920s, from the house. In the distance is the rectangular canal that continues the straight axial route that passes through house, garden and landscaped park.

fail'd him to the very last, greatly contributed.'[1] It is debatable how far we should take this, but it is at least clear from Hawksmoor's letters concerning the mausoleum he designed in the years 1729–36 for the Earl of Carlisle at Castle Howard that he was intensely proud of his prodigious learning in architectural matters.

The age in which Hawksmoor was practising witnessed the birth of antiquarianism in England, a movement he was part of. He is especially unusual for his interest in native Gothic architecture. We get a sense of his fascination with an eclectic range of architectural styles in a letter he wrote to the Earl of Carlisle, describing his journey back from Castle Howard in Yorkshire. Hawksmoor visited and appreciated the Gothic Beverley Minster, which he says 'surpasses anything of ye sort in England', and the wonderful Jacobean house at Wollaton, of which he says, 'The House appears well, and is an admirable piece of Masonry; some true stroakes of architecture ...'. He also paid a visit to a number of contemporary houses (including returning to Easton Neston).[2]

ABOVE The mausoleum at Castle Howard, North Yorkshire. Designed in 1729, and Hawksmoor's last completed work, it is one of the most staggeringly moving buildings in Britain that, in a sense, marks the termination of Hawksmoor's solo career as an architect, which started with Easton Neston.
OPPOSITE Ground-floor plan of Easton Neston, as published in 1715 in Colen Campbell's Vitruvius Britannicus. Based on drawings supplied by Hawksmoor, it shows extravagant wings and forecourt structures that were never executed. Notable aspects of the plan of the house are its dramatic asymmetry – in striking contrast to the symmetry of the main elevations – and spacial invention, notably the way in which the entrance vestibule opens directly into the square-plan and double-height Great Hall to its south.

This appraisal of different types of architecture distinguishes Hawksmoor from the Palladian architects who reached ascendancy later in his life. Unlike Hawksmoor, who used a very diverse range of architectural sources, the neo-Palladians looked to the work of the sixteenth-century Renaissance architect Andrea Palladio and proclaimed the 'rule of taste' governed by the architectural 'laws' perceived to be implicit in Palladio's architecture (see pages 150–1). Hawksmoor believed in more than just the strict observance of rules, as can be seen by quoting from his defence against attacks from the neo-Palladian Lord Burlington: 'Men have generally different ways of thinking and the Opinion of the Proffessours of Arts are exceedingly various, so that if you will not agree to this Maxim, that all Rules should proceed from Reason, Experience and necessity, (as well as laws) then we must submit to the many Caprices of the World.'[3] It is notable that in this sentence 'laws' seems to come as an afterthought and is in parenthesis.

The only known portrait of Hawksmoor is the bust from the last years of his life, kept in the Buttery at All Souls College, Oxford (which Hawksmoor extended from 1716 to 1735 in a most inventive synthesis of Gothic and classical elements). The bust, made of plaster painted black to give it the appearance of bronze, is attributed to Sir Henry Cheere, although it could be by the young Louis-François Roubilliac, who worked in Cheere's studio at the time. We get a better idea of Hawksmoor's personality outside his professional life through the comments in his obituary: 'In his private life he was a tender husband, a loving father, a sincere friend, and a most agreeable companion.' Even the Duchess of Marlborough, who supervised the work at Blenheim and was normally fiercely disdainful towards architects – especially Sir John Vanbrugh, who had designed her palace at Woodstock – had to admit Hawksmoor's talents: 'everybody that knows him will allow him to bee one of the most able in his profession'.[4] In his letters Hawksmoor comes across as somewhat solemn, whilst also capable of moments of tenderness. He is intensely modest, but also proud of his abilities.

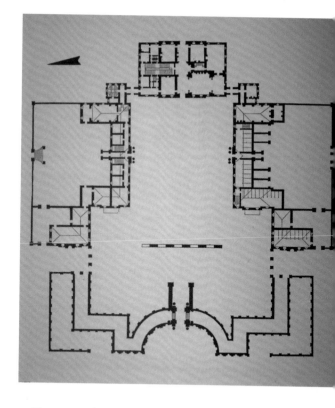

To get a real sense of Hawksmoor, though, we need to look at his buildings rather than what was written by or about him. Unlike the neo-Palladian architects who emerged around 1715, Hawksmoor invested his whole energy in the production of buildings rather than theoretical texts. Through his work with Wren on St Paul's Cathedral, the city churches and many projects for the Royal Office of Works, and with Vanbrugh on the great country houses of Blenheim and Castle Howard, Hawksmoor was involved in a huge proportion of the great buildings of his day. Easton Neston is especially fascinating because it shows that Hawksmoor had a powerful architectural vision of his own. Along with his ominous masterpiece, the mausoleum at Castle Howard, the Gothic spires of Westminster Abbey's west front, All Souls and Queen's College in Oxford, and his solemn and brilliant churches in London, Easton Neston proves that Hawksmoor was not just the equal of his talented contemporaries, but also an architect rarely surpassed in the forcefulness of his imagination.

HAWKSMOOR'S EARLY INVOLVEMENT
AT EASTON NESTON

Easton Neston was Hawksmoor's first major independent commission. It is the building of an architect of enormous promise trying to prove his merit. This involved trying to put everything he had learnt through his association with Wren into the building, whilst also attempting to establish that he was an important architect in his own right. There is indeed no built work by Wren that can be compared to Easton Neston stylistically, so the house also represents Hawksmoor's finding of his unique architectural voice.

Hawksmoor had already been responsible (under Wren) for Christ's Hospital Writing School, London (1692–5, now demolished) and the King's Gallery (begun in 1695) at Kensington Palace, where Hawksmoor was clerk of works. Both projects can be seen as dry runs for creating the stripped-back

ABOVE AND OPPOSITE
ABOVE The two drawings relating to Easton Neston at All Souls College, Oxford, catalogued as Sir Christopher Wren's. The drawing opposite is supposed to be his initial design of the early-to mid-1680s. The style is generally in Wren's domestic manner and relatively humble. Almost certainly, nothing of this design was built, although the nine-window width of the centre block, the distance between the wings and possibly the vaulted form of the basement seem to have been inherited by the scheme as built. The drawing above is more enigmatic. It shows the plan of a large baroque house, with an elevation that breaks forward and is clad in Giant

Doric pilasters. Over these designs is superimposed another, incorporating square, pier-like pilasters without capitals and running straight into a cornice, above which rises a drum and dome, seemingly with a baron's coronet placed upon it. The style of the architecture suggests that these drawings are the work of Hawksmoor, and indeed the domed feature is much like the cupola included in the drawing published in Vitruvius Britannicus in 1715 for an enlarged scheme for Easton Neston.
OPPOSITE BELOW The only known contemporary likeness of Hawksmoor – the bust in the buttery at All Souls College, Oxford.

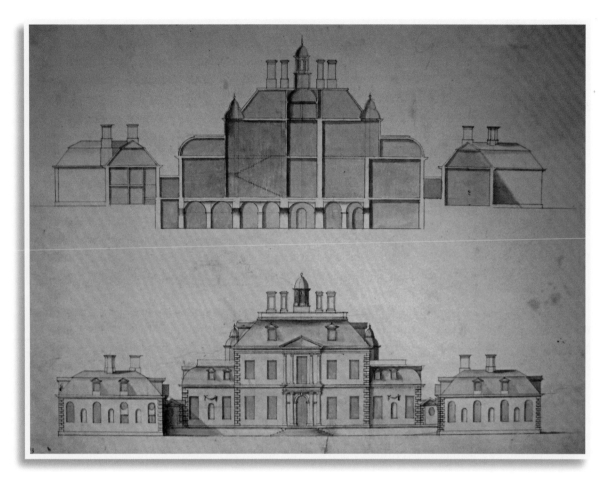

monumentality achieved at Easton Neston and developed in spectacular manner in Hawksmoor's London churches. The King's Gallery especially is an extremely plain building, with simple giant pilasters expressed in orange brick on a brown brick background. Unlike Easton Neston, though, the effect risks being overly severe.

The story of how Hawksmoor came to be involved in Easton Neston is somewhat shrouded in mystery, as it is under-documented. The patron was Sir William Fermor, later to become Lord Leominster. There had been a house at Easton Neston already, although very little is known about it, apart from the fact that it had thrice accommodated Elizabeth I. Work had started on the site, near Towcester (pronounced 'toaster') in Northamptonshire in the early 1680s, about twenty years before the house itself, which is dated to 1702 on the frieze of the garden front. It is uncertain how

far Hawksmoor was involved in this initial project. Some accounts of the house from the 1730s suggest that these early works were carried out by Wren, and two letters about the house from Wren to Fermor survive from this period. Some observers even speculate that the basement of the existing house was constructed in the 1680s under Wren's control

and subsequently altered by Hawksmoor when he built the house above it. A recent dendrochronology analysis of roof timbers in the main house (commissioned by the BBC) shows that the timbers were felled between spring 1700 and 1701, thus proving that the exterior of the house was indeed completed by 1702 under Hawksmoor and not a decade earlier under Wren as has been argued. Rather than actually supervising the construction of the house, it seems likely that Wren was only proffering friendly advice to Fermor, who was first cousin to his second wife Jane, perhaps to the extent of producing designs now in All Souls College, Oxford, rather than actually being employed as his architect.

The brick-built wing that remains from this period (originally one of two) is unlikely to have been by Wren, despite the fact that it is occasionally attributed to him. Hawksmoor was later disparaging of these buildings, saying 'the Wings are good for nothing'.[5] He was extremely unlikely to have used such language in describing the work of his former master, for whom he retained an enormous esteem.

It is uncertain how far this project from the early 1680s progressed. However, in 1692 Fermor married Lady Sophia Osborne. This was his third marriage, and an extraordinary coup, lifting Fermor into the higher echelons of his day. Sophia was the daughter of one of the most powerful and hated men in the land – the Marquess of Carmarthen, made Duke of Leeds in 1694. Carmarthen was loathed for his greed, corruption and unprincipled quest for, and abuse of, power and position. He had been the most important Tory signatory of the invitation in 1688 to William of Orange to become monarch of England, Scotland and Ireland, and was therefore in a position of immense power at court. The dowry from Carmarthen to Fermor was reported to be £10,000 (about £875,000 today), which would certainly have helped towards the cost of a new house at Easton Neston. Within six weeks of the marriage, Fermor was made a baron and became Lord Leominster. He was finally in a position to achieve his grand designs!

The newly ennobled Fermor must have been thrilled that his long-held ambition of having a prestigious country residence (a dream harboured since the early 1680s) would now come to fruition. We can imagine him hoping to confirm his ennoblement by building a house in the new baroque style that had been pioneered at Chatsworth during the 1680s and 1690s for the Duke of Devonshire by the architect William Talman. Fermor might well have looked to his friend Wren again for advice on who to employ. We can surmise that Wren suggested his erstwhile pupil Nicholas Hawksmoor – and the result is a house that equals, or even surpasses, the noble grandeur of Chatsworth, albeit on a smaller scale.

THE EASTON NESTON MODEL

The building history for Easton Neston is not that well known. There is a letter by Hawksmoor from as early as 1686, referring to the levels, but no drawings survive, although a rough sketch by a Colonel Thomas Colpeper might well be of an earlier design (or perhaps even of an earlier house on the site). Nevertheless, there is a fantastic source for the design process because, most unusually, a large and detailed model survives. The Easton Neston model is the most important surviving model for a country house of this period. In 2005 it was bought by the RIBA Drawings Collection for a sum of just short of £180,000, and can today be seen in the Victoria & Albert Museum in London. The model is a beautiful piece of carving in its own right. It is made of oak and can be magically dismantled like a Russian doll to reveal the complexity of the interior, with its plasterwork details carved into the wood.

The model is fascinating both for the way it prefigures Easton Neston as it was built, and also for the way in which it differs from this final product. The complex succession of rooms packed into a relatively tight space is already apparent in the model, although the whole ensemble is slightly lower. The intricacy of this interior is well described by the architectural historian and Hawksmoor expert Kerry Downes: 'Against the sprawl of Castle

ABOVE LEFT *Sant'Andrea, Mantua, Italy, by Leon Battista Alberti. Started in 1462, it's an early example of the Renaissance use of the Giant order in the form of Corinthian pilasters and pedestals rising through three storeys.*

ABOVE TOP RIGHT *The west front of Chatsworth House, Derbyshire, designed after 1696, probably under the control of William Talman, perhaps with Thomas Archer. Along with the slightly earlier south front, an inspirational English example of the use of the Giant order.*

ABOVE BOTTOM RIGHT *The model of an early phase of the*

design of Easton Neston, probably dating from 1693 or soon after. The model, which incorporates a complex interior with volumes much as built, was probably intended as a design tool. Significantly, the Giant order is absent from the exterior, suggesting that the design of the house got more monumental as it evolved, to match the increasing grandeur of the client.

OVERLEAF *The house's entrance front, a composition of great gravity that was surely intended by Hawksmoor to evoke the cultural glory of Renaissance Italy and the splendours of ancient Rome.*

Howard the packing together of state and private rooms at Easton Neston within the width prescribed by the wings, as expertly as items in a Christmas hamper, still invites our wonder.'[6]

However, the exterior of the model is significantly different from the house as built. Although the windows are in the same places, the architectural style of the house is much closer to the Anglo-Dutch classicism of Hawksmoor's predecessors, such as Hugh May or Sir Roger Pratt, than to the baroque grandeur that is commonly associated with him. It does not have the Giant order columns, rising through both floors, that now dominate the façade, but rather it employs an almost astylar two-storey elevation. This transformation from an early design, found in the difference between the model and the final version, corresponds to what we know of Hawksmoor's methodology of going through a series of designs before alighting on the final solution.

The leap forward expressed by the different façade treatment in the model and the final project is suggestive both of Hawksmoor's achievement

specifically, and more generally of the change of style occurring in English architecture at the time. It might be presumed that the change came about in part to proclaim Fermor's recent ennoblement and subsequent rise in status. But the addition also speaks of the new style of which Hawksmoor was a pioneer. Along with Wren's Whitehall designs (1698) and Vanbrugh and Hawksmoor's Castle Howard (1699–1712), Easton Neston is one of the buildings from the turn of the eighteenth century that was to shrug off the prissiness of Anglo-French classicism for the powerful, inventive and emotive freedoms of the English baroque.

Wren had seen the drawings for Bernini's great planned Giant order façade at the Louvre in the 1660s, saying that he would have 'given my skin' to have them. This façade was one of the first buildings to bring the increased monumentality of this type of baroque architecture north of the Alps. Earlier and inspirational examples south of the Alps in Renaissance Italy that expressed the visual punch of the Giant order were Leon Battista Alberti's

church of Sant'Andrea in Mantua, started in 1462, and Michelangelo's buildings on the Campidoglio, Rome, from 1536. Architecture on the grand scale of the European baroque would not, however, be practised in England until long after this moment. Hawksmoor's Easton Neston is one of the pioneering buildings to bring this feeling of immense baroque grandeur to a façade in Britain . Kinross House, Scotland, of the 1670s and 1680s incorporates a Giant order (see Chapter 2), but its pilasters are not closely or regularly spaced, and little more than a gesture of ornament.

It seems reasonable to speculate that the meaning behind the introduction of the Giant order at Easton Neston relates to Fermor's desire to display a sense of dignity that was almost Roman in its solemn grandeur. This speculation is perhaps supported by the details. The order is Composite and Roman (with a peculiar innovative detail, of which more in a moment), and expressed by pilasters rather than columns, with the exception of the centre bay of the entrance front. The main façades are articulated, breaking slightly forward at their ends, then back, and forward once again in their centres. Pilasters rise between all the windows and emphasize the movement of the façade. But the pair of pilasters (placed in front of slivers of 'shadow' pilasters) that emphasize the centre bay of the entrance elevation have two free-standing columns set in front of them, permitting the crowning cornice to break even further forward. Emphasizing the centre bay of an elevation was a

LEFT ABOVE *The east range of the Palais du Louvre, Paris, built between 1667–70 to the designs of Claude Perrault, it is a highly inspirational example of the application of the Giant order.*
LEFT BELOW *Print from the 1560s showing the Piazza del Campidoglio in Rome, where, from 1536, Michelangelo perfected the Renaissance use of the Giant order.*
OPPOSITE *Detail of the entrance front of Easton Neston showing*

the Composite capitals of its Giant order. Hawksmoor introduced a lion's head at the top of the capital between the volutes – a witty reference to the fact that Fermor was created Baron Lempster (or Leominster) in 1692. The visual clash between the capitals on the pilasters and those on the columns suggests that the columns might be an afterthought, added to increase the grandeur of the house's entrance elevation.

conventional and favoured device of the English baroque school. But here the device – if dramatic – is also somewhat strange because the capitals of the pilasters and columns crash into each other in a manner that is positively alarming. Hawksmoor was not a chaste, gentle or polite classicist; he evidently relished the vigour of violent juxtapositions between forms and details, brought about when each reflected the logic and disciplines of their respective proportion or form. For example, the columns and entablature of the west portico of Christ Church, Spitalfields, added over a decade after the church was started in 1714, relate hardly at all to the details of the main body of the building from which they spring. The result is artistically thrilling, almost a collage, and gives the church an authentically antique quality, as if it had been altered or added to over the ages like genuine ancient buildings in Rome. But, it seems to me, the clash of the capitals at Easton Neston is simply awkward. The combination lacks visual or intellectual clarity. Can it be that Hawksmoor was ordered by Fermor to add these columns in an attempt to further increase the visual punch and Roman solemnity of the entrance front? The decisive but generally hazy role played by clients in the creation of definitive architecture is so often underestimated.

THE ARUNDEL MARBLES AND SPACES FOR DISPLAY

An insight into Hawksmoor's work at Easton Neston is offered by the Arundel Marbles. The story of this group of antique statues (one of the most important in the country) is so interesting that it is worth a small diversion. They can now be seen in the Ashmolean Museum in Oxford, in a building designed by C.R. Cockerell (a great admirer of Hawksmoor) and finished in 1845. The story of the marbles reveals the evolution of museum culture in Britain – its genesis being within country houses, and its culmination in the displays within great public institutions, such as the British Museum.

The marbles, or sculptures, were brought to England during the second decade of the seventeenth century by Thomas Howard, the

ABOVE *The Great Hall, looking south, as it appeared until the 1890s – a double-height space of superb architectural quality, with wall niches, stone-built Doric piers set over stone-built Corinthian piers and columns, and with a sense of soaring space. In the 1690s model the hall was separated from its flanking vestibules by screens of columns, but, as built, these were omitted to gain a greater sense of monumentality and space.*

OPPOSITE *The Great Hall, looking south, as it exists today, with a floor inserted above it in the late nineteenth century, walls dividing it from its flanking vestibules, and wall niches flushed over.*

1st Earl of Arundel, who was England's first great art collector. He had travelled around Italy on a grand tour, accompanied by the architect Inigo Jones. On this tour he developed a mania for collecting. To acquire more antique statuary he sent the remarkably picaresque figure of William Petty on a quest around the Mediterranean. Petty appears like a figure out of a *Boy's Own* adventure series: he was a highly intrepid adventurer, willing to go to any lengths to acquire classical sculpture. During the course of his travels he was shipwrecked and subsequently arrested as a spy. On one occasion he even attempted to bribe the imam of a Muslim town to condemn a group of statues as idolatrous, in the hope that they could subsequently be picked up at a cheap price. The ambassador of Constantinople wrote back to Arundel to stress the extent of Petty's daring deeds: 'There was never a man so gifted to an imployment, that encounters all accidents with so unwearied patience; eats with Greeks on their worst days; lies with fishermen on plancks, at the best; is all things to all men, that he may obtain his end which are your lordships service.'[6]

Arundel House, located immediately south of the Strand in London, was one of the most important houses in British history, although it has long since been demolished. It has even been described as an anticipatory British Museum, incorporating a purpose-built sculpture gallery. Arundel was an extraordinary patron, and the house became the locus of English interest in the visual arts. Arundel was the benefactor of England's first great classical architect Inigo Jones, as well as Flemish old-master painters, including Peter Paul Rubens and Sir Anthony Van Dyck. His house was a treasure trove of European late Renaissance culture, and a sign that England was becoming more cosmopolitan and less insular in its outlook.

After Arundel's death, however, the house slowly fell into disrepair, and the colonnade collapsed, damaging many of the sculptures. A number of fragments were taken by barge across the river to be dumped on a patch of waste ground in Kennington, one column drum eventually being used by the merchant and antiquary James Theobald as a garden roller! Fermor was able to take advantage of this disaster by purchasing the greater part of the collection at the nominal price of £300 (about £22,000 today).

Hawksmoor was not just designing a house for Fermor, but a stage set for the famed statues. The whole project was conceived in an atmosphere of classical idealism. We can imagine Hawksmoor, with his 'almost morbid passion for classical archaeology' and 'slightly childish delight in anything Latin',[8] as Sir John Summerson described it, being thrilled and inspired by the marbles. Fermor would have wanted his house to exude an aristocratic atmosphere of scholarship and tradition in a heroic, classical setting. This he would achieve with Hawksmoor's help. Hawksmoor would design theatrical spaces for the display of statuary and architectural promenades, through which the antique marbles were elevated and given a context. The classical language he was using would be the perfect partner to offset the antique sculpture. Like so many country houses in England,

Easton Neston was an attempt to recreate the ancient ideal of villa-living as implied by Roman writers like Pliny the Younger. But it can also be understood in more worldly terms: as an arena for display and a space for contemplation which would show off Fermor's taste, scholarship and sense of history, whilst exuding a sense of permanence. Fermor wrote to Dr John Covel, the master of Christ's College, Cambridge, explaining that 'I am now setting up all my marbles in the manner I intend to leave them in'. He was interested in them not just as *objets d'art*, but as objects for scholarship. As he wrote of an ancient inscription on one of his marbles: 'Wee had much ado to pick it out of its ancient worn characters, but if you find it in any way doubtful wee have here frequent learned men whom I will consult to decypher it better.' In this we can see Fermor pioneering certain aspects of the ethos of public museums that would come into being in the early nineteenth century in the private setting of a country house.

Hawksmoor's flair in creating highly theatrical and exciting spaces within the medium of classical sobriety was the perfect foil to Fermor's collection. The statues are no longer in Easton Neston, and the once double-height hall has been divided horizontally and otherwise much altered, although its original appearance is preserved in nineteenth-century photographs. Blenheim and Castle Howard, the houses Hawksmoor went on to design in association with Sir John Vanbrugh, would also pivot upon remarkable double-height halls. The fact that this motif predates Hawksmoor's association

LEFT ABOVE *The treads on the main staircase have rebates on their underside so that all lock firmly together to help ensure that the great weight of the staircase is carried safely to ground level.*
LEFT BELOW *One of the ancient statues among the collection of Arundel Marbles – supposedly the torso of an Amazon. The Marbles were originally in Easton Neston and an*

inspiration for the design of its interior.
OPPOSITE *The main staircase in Easton Neston is a spectacular affair – beautiful and something of an engineering marvel – that ascends gradually and allowed those using it to study the Arundel Marbles that once inhabited the niches located above its landings.*

with Vanbrugh again proves Hawksmoor's originality. The lessons learnt in these halls would also be put to use in the interiors of his churches, such as the wonderful cube-within-a-cube spaces of Christ Church, Spitalfields, and St Mary Woolnoth, City of London, of 1714 to 1730. It should be said, however, that Hawksmoor's double-height hall at Easton Neston is significantly different from those at Blenheim and Castle Howard. These last two, inspired by Palladio's villas, are set on the central axis of the house and entered directly from the main door. Hawksmoor took a different tack and disposed his double-height hall as a distinct space just off the main access corridor into the house and immediately adjacent to the front door. Indeed, it's possible that Hawksmoor was playing one of his games with history and took as the model for his hall and entrance the Great Hall and screens passage of English high-status medieval houses. If so, this evocation of tradition could be another ploy to root both Fermor and Easton Neston in English history and thus bestow upon them both an air of precedent and admirable ancient lineage.

We can get a sense of the effect of the theatrical spaces in Easton Neston when they had the classical statuary in them from Sir Justinian Isham's diary entry: 'The hall is large and lofty being 40 ft high with several antique statues, busts, &c. about it, the staircase is paved as well as the hall with good stone, hath handsome iron rails with several antiques in niches and the wall is to be painted.'[9] The walls were eventually painted in grisaille in about 1710 by Sir James Thornhill, as can still be seen today. Thornhill was the leading history painter of his day, famous now for his enormous ceiling frescoes at St Paul's and at the Greenwich Hospital. His frescoes on the staircase at Easton Neston (the subject of which remain debated, with the Triumph of Diocletian or scenes from the life of King Cyrus being currently the favoured options) contain figures that seem inspired by Fermor's collection of statues. If so, the statues displayed within the house were also shown as creatures of the artistic imagination, mythologized and set within the context of a famed and noble ancient culture.

Easton Neston's staircase is of a baroque grandeur unparalleled in any surviving English example of the period. The staircase is of two flights in a tall, long and narrow room. The first flight slowly rises by very shallow treads towards a single large window, which on bright days blinds the stair-climber. On turning around at the intermediate level after this gradual ascent, the whole space, with one flight stretching up and another down, suddenly and magically opens up as a magnificent vista, all bathed in light from the large window. The wonderfully tendril-like ironwork banisters that follow this staircase are in the style of Jean Tijou, with a pattern of lyres.

As well as being a work of great visual beauty, the staircase is also something of an engineering marvel. It incorporates huge slabs of stone as landings, with those set between flights being almost entirely supported in wonderfully minimal manner by the stone treads that are themselves linked ingeniously. Each tread has a rebate in its soffit that notches into the tread below. This ensures that the treads are locked together and do not twist or turn. All is like a vast sculpture, and the treads, rather than being cantilevered, as most imagine, are merely stabilized by the walls, on to which pass part of the load they carry. This structural system – something of an English speciality – was not invented by Hawksmoor, but seems to have been pioneered by Inigo Jones in the early seventeenth century at the Queen's House, Greenwich, and later developed by Wren and architects such as William Talman.

Despite the fact that the house is contained within a traditional rectangular box only nine bays wide, the interior is packed with moments of awe-inducing theatricality that can be appreciated in a dramatic sequence. At every turn one is confronted by transformations of scale, between double- and single-height volumes, and also by variations in light and shade. Notable is the event that takes place at the top of the processional staircase. On the top landing is a door that, when opened, offers the surprising view of a giant and monumental niche. But this is only a prelude to the main event. The door

> At every turn one is confronted by transformations of scale, between double- and single-height volumes, and also by variations in light and shade…

ABOVE *The moody shadows of the staircase give way to the light-filled gallery that runs the full depth of the house and has large windows set at both ends. The gallery sits astride the axial route that runs through house and surrounding landscape.*

leads to a long gallery, set at right angles to the axis of the staircase, that runs the full depth of the house. At each end of the gallery are huge, round-arched windows – forming part of the centre features of each main elevation – that allow light to flood into the interior and also offer fantastic views along the axial avenues (and canal-like sheet of water) that stretch in both directions from the house. At each end of the house is a series of mezzanine floors, thus creating three and four storeys over the basement instead of two, and the space to fit in the required number of bedrooms in this relatively small house, whilst also retaining space for grand gestures.

The external expression of these mezzanines is startling. Both side elevations have small crowning pediments to emphasize their centre bays, but thereafter are very different. One side elevation is three windows high, with ground-floor windows matching in size those on the main fronts, but with two tiers of windows above, the top belonging to the attic. The other side elevation is a far more idiosyncratic affair. Its central portion is four storeys high, with the huge, semi-circular-topped staircase window set immediately below the central crowning pediment. On each side of the arched central window and the lofty window below it are placed four storeys of far smaller windows, incorporating squat mezzanine windows squeezed between ground- and first-floor windows. Finally, these smaller windows are flanked by tall windows that echo the lofty height, if not the exact form, of the

windows on the main elevations. This side elevation has, in a sense, a most modern and functional feel because the size and placing of the smaller windows do nothing to deny or confuse their purpose, but – in most honest manner – reflect the location and relatively low status of the rooms and spaces they serve. The windows on the main elevations also carry messages about the meaning of their interiors. The ground- and first-floor windows are of the same shape and size – there is no expression of a conventional *piano nobile* composition in which one storey of windows in an elevation is deeper than the others. But at Easton Neston the ground floor is proclaimed to be the major floor, for its windows are topped with cornices, while the windows of the first floor are not.

The basement is a powerful architectural space, with a central stone-paved corridor and a kitchen with a wide vaulted ceiling of unusual construction. Seemingly, the design of the kitchen vault was altered to make it stronger when it was resolved to construct the vast double-height hall above. The vault below the staircase also seems to gave been strengthened after construction started. Perhaps the basement was constructed in the 1680s as part of the first building campaign and then altered by Hawksmoor in the 1690s.

Easton Neston's role as a centre for classical erudition was not to last for long. When the young Horace Walpole visited Easton Neston in 1736, over twenty years after Fermor's death in 1711, he found the place disappointing. He was especially surprised

LEFT ABOVE *Light floods into the gallery through huge sash windows that are effectively walls of glass. Views along the axial routes that run straight and true into the landscape from both the east and west sides of the house make the point that the house stands at the heart – is the focus – of its own universe.*
LEFT BELOW *A small bedroom on the mezzanine level, lit by square windows set between ground and first floors.*

OPPOSITE *The tall niche in the gallery that visually terminates the journey up the main staircase. It seems inspired by the massive niches in the Pantheon in Rome. The door is one of the curiosities of Easton Neston. Despite the ruthless way it is cut into the panelling, it must be an original Hawksmoor detail, for it leads directly to the main service staircase and is essential for the efficient functioning of the house.*

to see 'a wonderful fine statue of Tully haranguing a numerous assembly of decayed emperors, vestal virgins with new noses, Collosus's, headless carcasses and carcassless heads, pieces of tombs and hieroglyphics'.[10] Walpole's dismay was at least partly caused by the hapless Italian sculptor Giovanni Battista Guelfi, who had been brought to England by Lord Burlington, and who, as one contemporary put it, 'misconceived the character and attitude of almost every statue he attempted to make perfect; and ruined the greater number of those he was admitted [permitted] to touch'.[11]

Fermor's son, the 1st Earl of Pomfret, attempted to complete the interior, notably employing the eminent stuccoist Charles Stanley in around 1735–40 to decorate the dining room with trophies showing hunting scenes and a fine allegorical ceiling. The 1st Earl died in 1753 and his son became deeply financially embarrassed and had to sell all his moveable property. He was a spendthrift who once (according to Horace Walpole, at least!) lost £12,000 (£1 million today) in a single game of

PREVIOUS PAGES LEFT *Detail of the wrought-iron balustrade on the main staircase, showing a baron's coronet and interlocked Ls for Lord Leominster.*
RIGHT *One of the murals on the main staircase, painted in about 1710 by Sir James Thornhill. The murals show scenes from antiquity and the classical world, and in their figures, draperies and composition seem inspired by, and intended to complement and enhance, the Arundel Marbles originally displayed beside them. For example, the female figure on the extreme left, carrying a vase on her head, appears to have been inspired by the headless and limbless torso of the Amazon shown on page 120.*
ABOVE LEFT & RIGHT *The south elevation of Easton Neston (left) is four storeys high, including basement, while the north elevation (right) is five storeys high, including the square mezzanine windows above the ground floor. Each elevation is a powerful composition that reflects the asymmetry of the interiors, with sets of small rooms packed into the ends of the house to reconcile the need for accommodation with the large and dramatic volumes occupied by the double-height hall, the great staircase and the gallery.*
OPPOSITE *A pilaster capital at Easton Neston of conventional Roman Composite design – large volutes set above acanthus leaves, but the top rosette replaced by a lion's head to represent the client's rank as Lord Leominster (Lempster).*

cards. The sculpture collection was bought by the earl's mother, the Dowager Countess Henrietta Louisa, using money from the estate of her daughters, and she presented it to the University of Oxford in 1755.

THE EXTERIOR

It was not just the interior of Easton Neston that was meant to be suggestive of a classical spirit. The façade also has a monumentality and sombreness redolent of classical gravity. But the façade was meant to be eloquent about more than just the ancient world. It was also to express Fermor's new position in society, primarily through the addition of the Giant order to the façade, which rises in Roman manner from a rusticated basement or podium. The building is faced with ashlar from the Helmdon quarries, described by a contemporary as 'the finest building stone I have seen in England'. This stone is remarkably resilient, and the carving can be appreciated today as if it were new. Movement is introduced by the subtle breaking forward and back of the façade, a device that, on sunny days, enlivens the building with moving shadows that seem to mark the passing of time, while the house itself can be seen to stand for eternity. This became a common device of English baroque architecture.

Wren is unusual as an architect for being almost solely concerned with public projects rather than private country houses. Hawksmoor could not look to his former master for inspiration on how to express patrician values suitable for a house such as Easton Neston. Hawksmoor had designed an unbuilt project for a 'Villa Chetwina' at Ingestre Hall in 1688, from which we can see that he was already grappling with ideas about a spatially complex interior. For the exterior, however, it seems likely that Hawksmoor looked for inspiration to the work of his contemporary William Talman, the most prolific country house builder of his age. Hawksmoor looked especially to Talman's south front at Chatsworth, which was the most celebrated house of its day. Like Easton Neston, it is a rectangular box with a Giant order of pilasters on a rusticated basement, surmounted by a balustrade

topped by urns – although, at twelve bays, Chatsworth is much longer, and its order is Ionic rather than Composite. Nevertheless, it ought to be seen as an important influence on Hawksmoor's Easton Neston.

HERALDIC ARCHITECTURE

But Easton Neston is not expressive of Fermor's patrician status through architectural means alone. There is also the addition of heraldic symbols. The balustrade on the top is broken up by a coat of arms, but the most notable feature is the lion's head that replaces the rosette between the volutes in the Composite capitals. The lion functions as a heraldic symbol for Fermor, who had recently been ennobled as Lord Leominster. This addition of an unusual heraldic symbol to the normal language of classical architecture creates what is known as a nonce order. Other important examples of nonce orders in capitals from the English baroque period include the swags created from festoons of sea fruit in the capitals of the King William building in Greenwich, a structure intended for use by veteran sailors. Among the most majestic are the falcons in the capitals of c.1710 at Drayton House, Lowick, Northamptonshire which refer to the heraldic crest of the house's owner, Sir John Germain, and are alluded to in many architectural details throughout the house. Mawley Hall in Cleobury Mortimer, Shropshire, from 1730, offers possibly the most bizarre examples of strange things cropping up in capitals, with round babies' heads, deer, dogs and an eagle nestling amongst the acanthus leaves. However, the most visible example of heraldry in an English baroque building is not on a capital, though it is by Hawksmoor – the church of St George, Bloomsbury, has one of the most peculiar spires ever designed, and has recently been restored to its original glory, as it is seen in William Hogarth's celebrated print *Gin Lane*. The spire, inspired by of the Mausoleum of Halicarnassus, has cavorting around its base the royal heraldic symbols of the lion and the unicorn. Perhaps the most famous example in British architectural history of a nonce

order is the Adam brothers' creation of the British order later in the eighteenth century, influenced by Giovanni Battista Piranesi, who had been studying ancient Roman examples of elaborate and fantastical capitals.

How much the use of nonce orders in English baroque architecture comes from the Italian architect Francesco Borromini, or from a local tradition stretching back to the Elizabethan era of making buildings speak of their occupants' status, is hard to tell, but these examples strongly suggest that both patrons and architects of the period did expect their buildings to be, at least to a degree, eloquent, with messages on a symbolic level. Vanbrugh's work, especially at Blenheim Palace – bristling with images of cannonballs and French cocks being trounced – takes this approach to another level.

If we are to understand the individuality of Hawksmoor's architectural language, it is important to realize that the symbolic elements at Easton Neston do not constitute what is unique about him. He certainly conformed to a slight degree to his contemporaries' need for buildings to be symbolically eloquent, as shown by the Leominster lion. Nevertheless, seeing Hawksmoor's buildings as palimpsests of hidden messages is a limited way of approaching his architecture. Easton Neston's relatively austere character is profoundly different from the profuse and extravagantly symbolic nature of Blenheim Palace. Whether this move towards increased simplification shows a

LEFT *The recently restored tower of Hawksmoor's St George, Bloomsbury, showing the step-pyramid spire around which frolic the heraldic lion and unicorn.*
OPPOSITE *The basement kitchen. The arches supporting the vaulted ceiling are of unusually wide span, shallow rise and finely engineered form.*

The central portion of each arch is narrowed in width so that its weight is reduced without a reduction in the strength. The way these heroic arches are locked together with bold keystones is particularly satisfying, and reveals Hawksmoor's love of the poetic expression of structure and the material of construction.

growing classical spirit, or even a proto-abstraction, Easton Neston's vocabulary is remarkable for its brevity. An idea of brevity seems central to the architectural disposition of all of Hawksmoor's buildings, and is instructive of the divergence in personality between Hawksmoor and Vanbrugh. The power of Easton Neston is achieved with only a highly stripped-back yet impressive order of unfluted Composite columns, the gradual stepping forward of the façade, and a somewhat taut intercolumniation. The architectural historian Howard Colvin describes the effect of this simplicity splendidly: 'With two columns, ten pilasters and a coat of arms, Hawksmoor has designed an elevation besides which Chatsworth is pretentious, Castle Howard rhetorical and Belton almost banal.'[12]

Whilst realizing that it is anachronistic to talk about Hawksmoor's buildings using the vocabulary of abstraction, we might nevertheless see his methodology as the distillation of sources through simplification. It is the genius of the building that this process of stripping back does not result in frugality, but grandeur over grandiloquence. Hawksmoor was rediscovered in the twentieth century by a generation sensitized by the modern movement towards concepts of space and massing rather than decorative detail, and this ability can already be seen in his early work. Hawksmoor's gift for creating buildings of immense force using a simplified architectural vocabulary would continue to invigorate many of his buildings. This is shown not just in his use of the classical orders, but also in his employment of the Gothic style, such as at All Souls College, Oxford, which metabolizes Gothic forms through Hawksmoor's aesthetic as successfully as his classical buildings do the orders.

EASTON NESTON AND HAWKSMOOR'S LATER CAREER

Near the end of his life Hawksmoor wrote to the Dean of Westminster, for whom he was building the west front of Westminster Abbey: 'let us have some inscriptions to inform posterity when this work was done, for I wish our progenitors had so obliged us.'[13] As we know, the frieze at Easton Neston dates

the house to 1702. Our story does not end at this date, however, as Hawksmoor would return to this early work, both to draw inspiration from it and to seek solace in it.

The decade after Easton Neston's completion would be the most productive of Hawksmoor's life. He would never again be the sole architect of a country house, but through his collaboration with Sir John Vanbrugh he would go further in creating houses of enormous grandeur suffused with interiors full of spatial surprises. But Vanbrugh brought his own visual sensibility to these projects, and though they are full of wonderful moments and a surplus of wit, they lack some of the monumental nobility of Easton Neston.

The building in Hawksmoor's career that, for me, most resembles Easton Neston, is his masterpiece, the mausoleum at Castle Howard, perhaps the most staggeringly moving building in Britain. That the mausoleum was Hawksmoor's last completed work means that these two projects bookend his career in a way that suggests the driving continuity of his artistic personality. Both were designed in a spirit of classical idealism. They look back to antique precedents, attempting to create spaces that, whilst not being governed totally by classical rules, nevertheless use an atmosphere of intense classical scholarship to create an image of permanence and gravitas. Both use a narrow intercolumniation, arguably out of keeping with strict classical rules, to bolster an emotive sense of muscular tautness and monumentality; the tight intercolumniation also makes these two buildings appear taller and therefore more severe. As at Easton Neston, a powerful contrast is set up between the noble gravity of the exterior and the floating lightness in the interior. After the gloomy Doric magnificence of the exterior, visible from miles around atop a windswept hill, the unexpectedly dazzling interior of the mausoleum is intense yet weightless, rising upwards on elegant Corinthian columns to a clerestory-illuminated dome. The same merging of contradictions between interior and exterior found at Easton Neston is still apparent at the end of his career. What Hawksmoor said in justification of the

> With two columns, ten pilasters and a coat of arms, Hawksmoor has designed an elevation besides which Chatsworth is pretentious, Castle Howard rhetorical and Belton almost banal…

ABOVE *The basement, with its double-pile plan, central corridor and solid vaults is – architecturally – a very different world from that above, suggesting that Hawksmoor inherited a basement that was already partly built when he started work on Easton Neston.*

Certainly the area of the vault below the main staircase has been strengthened after initial construction by the insertion of massive, beautifully built stone walls incorporating Roman-style arched openings that are very much in the manner of Hawksmoor.

mausoleum we might therefore quote as pertinent to Easton Neston: 'Its Grandeur will consist in the Completeness of the parts and the Strength and Beauty of the whole Composition and as Palladio observes I think we shall follow in this ffabrick: L'Utile – La Perpetuità – La Bellezza.'[14]

The publication of the first two volumes of *Vitruvius Britannicus* in 1715, which offered exemplary modern British architecture for admiration and emulation, has often been seen as a watershed in British architecture. It was traditionally portrayed as the defining moment at which the baroque freedom of architects such as Vanbrugh and Hawksmoor was attacked by the neo-Palladians. It was written by the Scottish architect Colen Campbell, who in 1715 designed the epoch-making Wanstead House, Essex, and would go on to build houses including Mereworth Castle, Kent (1720–5) and Houghton Hall, Norfolk (from 1722). In *Vitruvius Britannicus* Campbell praised Italian Renaissance architects and 'above all, the great Palladio, who has exceeded all that were gone before him, and surpas'd his Contemporaries, whose ingenious Labours will eclipse many, and rival most of the Ancients'.[15] This was contrasted to what had happened to Italian architecture after the Renaissance, with the emergence of the baroque: 'for the Italians can no more now relish the Antique Simplicity, but are entirely employed in capricious Ornaments, which must at last end in the Gothick ... How affected and licentious the Works of Bernini and Fontana? How Wildly Extravagent are the Designs of Boromini, who has endeavoured to debauch Mankind with his odd and chimerical Beauties ...'[16]

This has been seen as an attack not only on the Italian baroque, but on the English baroque that was inspired by it (often indirectly). However, the story is probably more complex, for Easton Neston is included in the first volume of *Vitruvius Britannicus* both in plan and in elevation, and both it and Hawksmoor are referred to in the text in a respectful manner: 'This is the Seat of the Lord Leimpster, in Northamptonshire ... And is the ingenious Invention of Mr. Hawksmore, to whom I am indebted for the Original Drawings of this House and many other valuable Pieces, for enriching this Work, which I could not in Gratitude conceal from the Publick: The Building was finish'd Anno 1713; with which I conclude the First Volume.'[17]

However, the house as depicted in *Vitruvius Britannicus* is far more elaborate than the one we know today. It probably represents a scheme by Hawksmoor intended to encourage Leominster's son, the 1st Earl of Pomfret, to build additions to his house. The house as depicted in the print is crowned by a cupola, rather in the style of the dome at Castle Howard. And the balustrade is surmounted by a row of classical-style statues. In this scheme the 'good for nothing' wings have been swept away, to be replaced by elaborate wings creating a courtyard, not dissimilar to the one at Blenheim Palace. All in all, we can see in the difference between these versions and the original designs the influence on

Hawksmoor of Vanbrugh's ideas on country house design. There is an increased staginess and a sense of heightened elaboration.

The fact that Hawksmoor returned to his early designs for Easton Neston later in life is indicative of how he saw his buildings. He was one of the first English architects to try to understand them within an environment or context. His plans for central Oxford, though not substantially completed, have nevertheless defined many of the characteristic spaces of the city. Other uncompleted plans show attempts to give context to other of his projects: an architectural space around St Paul's Cathedral; grand plans for Cambridge city centre; and a new parliament building and bridge at Westminster to complement his west front of Westminster Abbey.

Hawksmoor would return one last time to Easton Neston, in 1731, five years before his death. He was an old man by then, plagued by gout and disappointment. Lord Burlington, the leading figure of the neo-Palladian movement, had performed a coup on the architectural establishment, and Hawksmoor was to see his preferment passed over in favour of younger men with far less talent or experience. The English baroque, the style that Hawksmoor had pioneered, had fallen violently out of fashion. The new Palladian buildings lacked the spatial ingenuity and sheer force of their baroque counterparts. The architectural profession within which

LEFT ABOVE *The fire surround in the dining room, designed by William Kent in the early or mid-1730s.*
LEFT BELOW *Detail of the ceiling, showing a beautifully designed and executed scene of Venus and Adonis, attributed to Charles Stanley.*
OPPOSITE *During the mid-to-late 1730s the dining room was decorated in pioneering rococo manner by the leading stuccoist Charles Stanley. The walls, with their garlands, festoons, animal heads and huntsmen's accoutrements, such as muskets and horns, framing canvases showing hunting scenes, suggest how the food on the dining table had been acquired.*

Hawksmoor had been brought up had changed unrecognizably. Previously, it had been dominated by public buildings and projects completed on behalf of the Royal Office of Works. Indeed, Hawksmoor made his name on public projects for churches and universities. However, the eighteenth century was a period dominated by the building of country houses. It was a transformation that reflected the political changes happening in Britain at the time. Hawksmoor had been responsible for Easton Neston, one of the first private residences of the fledgling century to be built in a palatial style reflecting the new power held by the aristocracy. But one imagines that, unlike his debonair and cosmopolitan accomplice Sir John Vanbrugh, Hawksmoor was never completely comfortable in an aristocratic milieu. The Earl of Carlisle remained Hawksmoor's patron and supporter, but Hawksmoor was unable to convince any other of the great aristocrats of the day that he was the right man to be the architect of their house.

❝ The house and some of the grounds were bought ... by the fashion tycoon Leon Max. The contract was exchanged at 10 p.m. on 8 July 2005, thus ending the three-hundred-year tenure of Hawksmoor's Easton Neston by Fermor's descendants...

ABOVE *The Hesketh family outside the garden front in c.1930. The 1st Lord Hesketh with his daughters, Louise, left, and Flora.*

Nevertheless, Hawksmoor remained proud of his achievements, and looking back on Easton Neston, a house he had built thirty years previously, he wrote to Carlisle: 'The Body of ye House has some virtues, but is not quite finished, the Wings are good for nothing. I had the honour to be concerned in ye body of ye house, it is beautifully and strongly built with durable stone. The State and Convieniencys are as much as can well be in soe small a pavilion. One can hardly avoy'd loveing one's own children.'[18]

The sense of ownership expressed in those words is coloured by a movingly tender, albeit dispassionate, simplicity. The phrase 'loveing one's own children' satisfyingly echoes Hawksmoor's description of his work at Blenheim, where he compares himself to 'the loving nurse that almost thinks the child her own'.[19] The straightforwardness of a sentence such as 'it is beautifully and strongly built with durable stone' suggests something of the modest yet tough spirit with which Hawksmoor approached his buildings.

AFTER HAWKSMOOR

Hawksmoor died from 'Gout of the stomach' on 25 March 1736 at his home in Millbank, London. His biographer, having summed up the prodigious achievements of his career, added: 'And as his memory must always be dear to his country, so the loss of so great and valuable man ...'[20] However, it was not to be, and Hawksmoor's work drifted into relative obscurity. The English baroque architects are unusual in the history of architecture for being revered despite the fact that their style did not go on to influence future developments. For over a hundred years the Palladian style reigned supreme in Britain, with an almost unparalleled consistency. Early- to mid-nineteenth-century architects such as Sir John Soane and C.R. Cockerell were admirers of Hawksmoor, but it was not until the twentieth century that he was fully appreciated. Because it has never been open to the public, Easton Neston remains somewhat obscure and unknown in Hawksmoor's *oeuvre*, especially when compared to the much-beloved houses of Castle Howard and Blenheim Palace.

Until recently Easton Neston's history has been the story of Sir William Fermor's descendants. One of the most colourful of these was the 7th baronet, who commissioned a luxury steam yacht to go on a grand world tour. He married a San Francisco heiress on his travels, and also became an avid collector of Japanese art.

The last of Fermor's descendants to own Easton Neston was Lord Hesketh, who was Prime Minister John Major's chief whip in the House of Lords. The estate was costing him between £500,000 and £1.5 million a year to run, so he put the house and its 3300 acres of farmland on the market for £50 million to save his children the burden of its upkeep. The house and some of the grounds were bought at the bargain price of £15 million by the fashion tycoon Leon Max. The contract was exchanged at 10 p.m. on 8 July 2005, thus ending the 300-year tenure of Hawksmoor's Easton Neston by Fermor's descendants.

Max was born in Leningrad in 1954, the son of a Soviet playwright. Having worked briefly for the Kirov Ballet, he set off to New York's Fashion Institute of Technology, and used this as his base from which to start building a multi-million dollar fashion empire under the brand Max Studio. He now uses the wing that Hawksmoor designated 'good for nothing' as the headquarters of his European business.

Accustomed to living in houses designed by renowned architects, Max has described himself as a 'frustrated architect'. When based in California, he owned houses by the American Arts and Crafts architects Greene and Greene, and the Austrian-American Modernist Richard Neutra. On buying Easton Neston, Max told a journalist: 'I like the idea of being a country gentleman. I'm looking forward to shuffling to my atelier in my monogrammed slippers.'[21] And the informal company motto that has emerged is that you can't design an ugly piece of clothing while working in such a beautiful setting. Max is a lucky man. He owns and occupies a building of staggering importance that is central in the flowering of a distinctly English baroque style. It remains a sombre and magnificent tour de force ❖

WENTWORTH WOODHOUSE

Wentworth, South Yorkshire

18TH CENTURY

Political powerhouse

Wentworth Woodhouse, just a few miles south of Sheffield, was, in the late eighteenth century, one of the most important and powerful places on Earth. The family that had built the house in the first decades of the century and who lived in it were amongst the richest in Britain, with their vast house being not just the centre of a large and productive estate and a crucial part of the regional economy, but also part of the national – indeed international – scene. It was a key centre of the Whig political faction that had helped bring George I and the House of Hanover to the British throne in 1714, and that dominated British politics for most of the first half of the eighteenth century.

Wentworth Woodhouse, although built by the man who in 1746 became the 1st Marquess of Rockingham, is most fascinating because it was the home of the 2nd Marquess, who not only completed most of the interior of the house in the 1760s, but was also an inspirational politician who was twice prime minister. Indeed, from the mid-eighteenth century Wentworth Woodhouse was a veritable political and economic powerhouse, and the Rockingham Whigs and the Whig intellectuals who gathered there – such as Edmund Burke, Charles James Fox and the Duke of Portland – did much to forge modern Britain and champion political values still relevant today. Later members of the family who owned Wentworth Woodhouse, notably the 4th Earl Fitzwilliam, caused political waves in the early nineteenth century by being liberal almost to the point of radicalism. For example, he supported the notion of Roman Catholic emancipation in Ireland and questioned the policies that led to the Peterloo Massacre of August 1819, when a public meeting in Manchester pressing for a reform of parliamentary representation was broken up by yeomanry cavalry and fifteen people were killed.

Although the descendants of the 2nd Marquess were numbered amongst the most powerful and important in Britain, and the family home arguably the largest, most splendid and artistically breathtaking ever built in Britain, the origins of Wentworth Woodhouse are shrouded in mystery – even myth. The house was the result of an extraordinary and bitter feud between blood relations, which raged and boiled from the 1690s and expressed itself through architecture of ever-competing size and grandeur. Equally extraordinary is the fact that the mighty pile of Wentworth Woodhouse, which reached its existing and vast form in the 1780s, has – along with the enlightened and reforming 2nd Marquess – been largely forgotten. Wentworth Woodhouse is political architecture par excellence – its great size calculated not just to impress, but to entertain armies of people in a long campaign to win the hearts, minds and votes of the local electorate so that the family could take and hold Yorkshire for

PREVIOUS PAGES
The Palladian east front of the house, constructed from 1734–44, has a span of just over 600 feet and is one of the widest and most architecturally distinguished country house frontages in Britain.
LEFT ABOVE *Charles James Fox, a leading Whig and associate of the 2nd Marquess of Rockingham, who completed and rearranged many of the important interiors at Wentworth Woodhouse.*

LEFT BELOW *Charles Watson-Wentworth, the 2nd Marquess of Rockingham and leader of the 'Rockingham Whigs', who made Wentworth Woodhouse their political powerhouse.*
OPPOSITE *The Corinthian portico that dominates the east front. The Wentworth family motto emblazoned on the portico – 'Faith is my Glory' – was intended to proclaim the inflexible integrity and incorruptible virtue of Lord Malton and the Whig faction.*

the Whig interest. Far lesser buildings and lesser men remain household names from the eighteenth century, but the 2nd Marquess of Rockingham, and the house he inherited, embellished and of which he was such an ornament, have disappeared into relative obscurity. The reasons for this are perhaps obvious: Rockingham never fully realized his promise. The gods that had raised him high were ultimately against him. Both his periods in office were brief, and he died at the relatively young age of fifty-two, just fourteen weeks into his second term as prime minister and with so much more work still to do. Also, the house was long – and is again today – a most secret and private place, not open to the public.

The circumstances of my arrival could not have been more dramatic: I passed on to an obscure drive between gate piers and a sign saying 'Private, keep out'. On my left was a sorry group of low, alien-looking 1960s' institutional buildings, a legacy of one part of the more recent story of Wentworth Woodhouse. I made my way along the icy drive and on my right appeared, from behind a clump of trees, a large, stone-built and handsome classical building. Beautifully designed and detailed, it would be easy to take this for the main event. But so large is Wentworth Woodhouse, and so wealthy the family that built and occupied it for nearly 300 years, that this is just the stable block, built nearly fifty years after the main house was started. Beyond me, as I moved slowly forward, opened a vast, rolling scenery covered with virgin snow. A low and ethereal mist hung in the distant valley, so the landscape, and my vista, seemed uninterrupted, apparently stretching to infinity. Then suddenly, and with utmost drama, the huge form of Wentworth Woodhouse loomed into sight. It is truly gigantic, and many argue that its frontage of well over 600 feet makes it the widest country house in Britain. This is a matter of dispute, but it seems too large to measure with definitive accuracy, and whether it or Stowe in Buckinghamshire possesses Britain's widest country house elevation is among the many mysteries that shroud this remarkable house. Whatever the case, the Wentworth Woodhouse

frontage commands the landscape with incredible majesty, is ruthlessly symmetrical and possesses an astonishing solemnity. In its centre is a huge porticoed block of Roman gravity flanked by a series of wings that terminate with cubical towers, making it at once a superb theatrical backdrop and focus for distant vistas, and a superlative grandstand from which to survey the landscape.

The day I arrived the house could not have looked more beautiful or more other-worldly. Its tall, classical bulk rose out of a wide sweep of pristine snow so that, in a most magical way, I felt I was in St Petersburg, with the Yorkshire landscape looking like a raw and bleak stretch of north Russia in winter. I stood in the snow and contemplated this mighty creation. In the still winter morning, as the brittle and ethereal light from the low sun moved across the stone-built elevation, the house changed its character, its nature. It transformed from a forbidding black silhouette to a golden-hued palace of almost Mediterranean warmth. It was fantastic. It seemed a thing eternal, out of place and almost out of time: its composition full of variety and subtle movement, its parts all linked but of dramatically contrasting scales. It looked more like a little walled classical town, complete with bastions on its south side, than a house. But the incredible thing is that this eastern elevation – started in the mid-1730s – represents only part of Wentworth Woodhouse. Behind this elevation and the noble sequence of rooms it screens is another house, almost as large, that faces west. Stranger still, these two houses, structurally and artistically independent and almost entirely self-contained, were built by the same man, and in their start dates are separated by only a decade.

ROOTS OF GREATNESS

The story behind the creation of Wentworth Woodhouse is one of the oddest in the annals of British architecture. It is a tale that, with almost uncanny exactness, offers stunning portraits of both the age in which the house was built and the characters involved in what became, in a sense, a family feud conducted through architecture.

The story behind the creation of Wentworth Woodhouse is one of the oddest in the annals of British architecture. It is a story that, with almost uncanny exactness, offers stunning portraits both of the age in which the house was built and of the characters involved…

ABOVE *The west front of Wentworth Woodhouse, designed for Thomas Watson-Wentworth (later the 1st Marquess of Rockingham) in 1724 in an idiosyncratic Continental baroque manner.*

The outline of the story can be briefly given. There was a house on the site, beautified in the early seventeenth century and occupied by Thomas Wentworth, the 1st Earl of Strafford, a highly successful soldier, statesman and key adviser to King Charles I. But Strafford's talents and relationship with the king made him a target for Parliamentarians set on breaking royal power, so in 1641 he became trapped by intrigue, was impeached and forced to endure a lengthy show trial. The object of his political enemies was to remove him from the scene and, in the process, humiliate and weaken the king. Through legal skill, firm logical argument and oratory, Strafford at first thwarted his enemies' intentions. But it then became a bitter battle to the death, for if Strafford won, his would-be prosecutors could find themselves in danger.

During his rise to power, Strafford had made many enemies, and the vast personal wealth he had amassed made many suspicious of his motives. These circumstances, combined with much manipulation and savage lobbying, enabled parliament to pass a Bill of Attainder upon Strafford, which meant his execution as a traitor could be carried out without the legal 'burden of proof' of guilt, but only if the sentence was approved by the king himself. Charles had earlier pledged his support to Strafford, but now, under pressure, and fearful for the future of his throne and the personal safety of his family, was compelled to sign Strafford's death sentence. As a tearful Charles did so, he declared bitterly that 'My Lord of Strafford's condition is happier than mine.'[1] Strafford was duly beheaded and was, in many ways, the first major victim of the civil war that started the following year and effectively ended in January 1649 with the execution of the king who, as he addressed the crowd from the scaffold, clearly had Strafford on his mind, for he stated that he was being 'punished' by God with this 'unjust sentence' because of 'an unjust sentence that I suffered to take effect'.[2]

When Strafford was found guilty of treason his titles became void, but in 1662 his son William Wentworth had the Bill of Attainder reversed and regained the earldom to go with the Wentworth Woodhouse estate that he inherited. A monument commissioned by William, the 2nd Earl of Strafford, survives in the chancel of the old parish church in the village of Wentworth. It commemorates his wife, who died in 1685, and is a most fascinating work. It shows a curtain being parted to reveal a striking scene. Strafford, dressed in full armour, kneels and stares intently – lovingly – at an image of his kneeling wife, who has her eyes turned up towards God. It's a moving piece of work: Lord Strafford stares at the physical perfection of his wife, while she, in turn, stares towards the spiritual perfection of heaven. I contemplate the monument and wonder, for it shows the image of the man who made a momentous and fateful decision that was to lead to the bitter family feud and to the creation of three country houses of outstanding architectural interest. The 2nd Earl of Strafford, who was childless, decided, in defiance of tradition, convention and expectation, not to leave his house, land and fortune to his oldest and most direct male heir, but to the third son of his sister. So when Wentworth died in 1695, and the estate duly went to his nephew the Honourable Thomas Watson (later Watson-Wentworth), he unleashed a veritable storm of fury from his disappointed male heir Thomas Wentworth, who merely inherited the title Baron Raby.

LEFT ABOVE *The execution in 1641 of Lord Strafford, the owner of Wentworth Woodhouse, whom parliament declared guilty of treason.*
LEFT BELOW *The monument of 1685 in Wentworth church created to his wife by the 2nd Lord Strafford, the man who made a fateful decision that provoked the construction of three outstanding – and in*

many ways competing – country houses.
OPPOSITE *The courtyard of the vast stables at Wentworth Woodhouse, which were built during the 1770s to designs by John Carr for the 2nd Marquess of Rockingham – a man addicted to racing and gambling – and now forlorn and largely abandoned.*

The reason for Lord Strafford's action is not known. Perhaps the sudden and humiliating fall of his father had made him very close to his sister, whose younger son he wanted to present with an extraordinary and unexpected opportunity. Or perhaps he simply did not like Thomas Wentworth or his politics and didn't want the Wentworth Woodhouse riches and the power they could bring to fall into the hands of a man he thought unsound. We simply do not know, but what we do know is that the new Lord Raby was astonished, outraged and embittered in due proportions, and used all his talents to seek revenge. His character seems to have been alarming – Jonathan Swift called him 'infinitely proud and wholly illiterate',[3] and his talents were, as it happens, formidable. The posts he obtained were significant, and included ambassador to the court of Prussia from 1706 to 1711, and a commissioner in 1713 at the epoch-making negotiations that culminated with the Treaty of Utrecht, which ended the long War of the Spanish Succession and brought decades of peace, stability and prosperity to Britain. For his public

ABOVE *The baroque façade of Wentworth Castle, constructed from 1708 into the early 1720s for Lord Raby, the member of the Wentworth family made bitter by his failure to inherit the Wentworth Woodhouse estate. This grandiose design was intended to put the old house at* Wentworth Woodhouse firmly in the shade.

BELOW *A detail, carved around 1720, on the baroque front of Wentworth Castle. Lord Raby was a Tory and a Jacobite, so the keystone shows the Jacobite symbol of oak leaves sprouting from a decapitated tree trunk.*

achievements, Raby had been made the Earl of Strafford of the second creation – a title that would clearly have delighted him since he now had the rank that had once belonged to the family occupying Wentworth Woodhouse.

But despite all these achievements, the slight administered by the last Lord Strafford continued to rankle, and in 1708, while in Berlin, Raby had hatched a most cunning plan. He purchased a house, Stainborough, set on high land about five miles west of Wentworth, and then set about the secret purchase of Wentworth Woodhouse estate land. This was, in essence, a form of large-scale, early eighteenth-century turf war. Since Raby did not inherit Wentworth Woodhouse, he was determined to acquire as much of it as he could by purchase and, in every way possible, to overshadow and even supplant it. Key to this strategy was to build a grand new house, which he did from about 1708, in palatial Continental baroque style by no less a man than the French court architect, Jean von Bodt. And to make his intentions and claim to eminence clear to all, Raby renamed his house Wentworth Castle. He was to be the dominant and grand Wentworth in the region, as, he believed, was his birthright.

FIGHT FOR SUPREMACY

Lord Raby, as well as being single-minded in his determination to restore his family's position, was also deeply enmeshed in the politics of the age, and his allegiances can be read even in the mighty new house he constructed. His descent from the executed Lord Strafford, who had in essence died for King Charles I, seems to have helped bind Raby to the Stuart dynasty, and to the Tory view of rule through an autocratic monarchy in collaboration with a small and self-selected clique of aristocratic advisers. However, everything changed in 1714 when George I came to the throne and the House of Hanover was established as the ruling dynasty, largely through the aid of the Whigs. The Whigs' concept of rule was inspired by William and Mary's Bill of Rights of 1689, which limited the power of the sovereign and guaranteed the liberties of the subject and independence of parliament. Their belief in government through parliamentary democracy rather than through autocratic monarchy was in direct conflict with the beliefs of Tories such as Raby. So, within a few months, the political terrain changed dramatically for Lord Raby and his like. They were marginalized, denied access to power and to wealth-generating government posts. Thus was born the Jacobite cause – the desire among the politically dispossessed to bring back the Stuart dynasty, initially in the person of the ousted James II, and its form of monarchy.

Lord Raby, now with another source of grievance, could not resist enshrining his political and dynastic beliefs within the fabric of his new home. Although the exterior of the newly christened Wentworth Castle was completed by about 1713, the ornate baroque stone carving on the centre of the show-front was not executed until the 1720s. Most amusingly, Raby managed to embed among his swags and cherub heads a discreet Jacobite symbol that would have been recognized by fellow-travellers. Within the keystone above the ground-floor central door is the stump of a tree trunk from which oak leaves sprout. Charles II, when fleeing after defeat at Worcester in 1651, hid in the Boscobel oak, and since then the old Druid symbol of the oak had been appropriated by the Jacobites. This particular rendering, with its sprouts of young leaves, is evidently proclaiming that new life will spring from the stump that, in a most appropriate manner, represents the decapitated Charles I.[4]

Thomas Watson-Wentworth kept a low profile in his early seventeenth-century house at Wentworth Woodhouse, but his son, also named Thomas, declined to be overawed by his posturing cousin. At times things must have very difficult indeed for Watson-Wentworth, for he surely knew that, among other insults, Lord Raby in his coded correspondence about his surreptitious land purchases referred to the Wentworth Woodhouse household as 'the vermin'. Watson-Wentworth's response was to take up the architectural challenge, and in about 1724 he commissioned a large new house that would incorporate some elements of the old house and face west, confronting Raby's home in an emblematic gesture of defiance. The design he commissioned was, and remains, extraordinary. It is not agreed who designed the work, but it is in a wilful and idiosyncratic baroque style, and loaded with odd details that owe nothing to the English baroque school of Sir John Vanbrugh and Nicholas Hawksmoor (see pages 116–8), but, most surprisingly, much to the central European baroque tradition. The plan and interior of the new Wentworth Woodhouse must also have been intended as a riposte, but lack the punch of Raby's creation. Wentworth Castle possesses an astonishing first-floor picture gallery, almost certainly detailed in the early 1720s by James Gibbs[5] and completed in 1724, that runs the full width of the house and, with its screens of monolithic Carrara marble Corinthian columns, possesses the authentic presence of Renaissance Rome. Watson-Wentworth also created a long gallery in his house, but by comparison it is a relatively feeble effort. Also

far more impressive is the staircase at Wentworth Castle, furnished with superlative stucco ornament including, naturally, subtle sprigs of oak.

Perhaps it was the underwhelming nature of his architectural response to Wentworth Castle that prompted Watson-Wentworth to make an extraordinary decision. Or perhaps there were bigger things on his mind than local family rivalry, but in 1734 he initiated an action that was unprecedented in Britain's building history. Before his new house was completed, Watson-Wentworth started another, far larger house that was – astonishingly – set back-to-back with the 1720s house so that both were structurally, artistically and functionally self-contained and independent. The second house, facing east and with its towering Corinthian portico and vast frontage of around 616 feet, now defining the architecture of Wentworth Woodhouse, achieved several things. It proclaimed the new main orientation of the house: not looking towards Wentworth Castle but, in contemptuous manner, turning its back on it, and, when complete, its size and powerful architectural authority would turn the tables and put Wentworth Castle in the shade. But perhaps most important of all, the new Wentworth Woodhouse spoke a different architectural language, and this was a language that not only started to dominate British architecture in the early 1730s, but also carried a powerful and precise political message.

LEFT *Thomas Wentworth – Lord Raby – with his family in c.1732. Made the Earl of Strafford of the 'second creation', Raby was characterized as 'infinitely proud and wholly illiterate' and the great enemy of the family at Wentworth Woodhouse.*
OPPOSITE *The tapering pyramidal form of the Hoober Stand that rises from a triangular plan – forms that suggest a Masonic meaning. It was constructed in 1748 by the 1st Marquess of Rockingham, to designs by Henry Flitcroft, to celebrate the Hanoverian victory in 1746 over the Jacobites and Watson-Wentworth's elevation to marquess.*

The style came to be called Palladian, and the message it carried was patriotic. It reflected a quest to find a rational, national style of architecture that was appropriate for a Protestant, constitutional monarchy and distinct from the baroque architecture that had evolved and was associated with the Roman Catholic and autocratic monarchies of much of continental Europe. This quest was, of course, launched by Whig philosophers, politicians and architects who wanted to associate their political beliefs and social vision with an architecture that seemed to encapsulate the essence of the British, and in particular the English, character. The case was argued in 1712 by the Whig pundit Lord Shaftesbury, who wrote that 'an order of Beauty' that was 'rational' in its nature must inform the 'national taste' and so form the basis for a national style.[6]

Watson-Wentworth was of the Whig faction – indeed, had been a Member of Parliament since 1715 – had been created Baron Malton in 1728 and had major aims and aspirations for the Whig cause in Yorkshire (in 1733 he was created Lord Lieutenant of the West Riding), so it is easy to see why, with the Tory-tainted baroque style of his 1720s country house, he could feel disenchanted, even compromised. Quite simply, the timing of construction was unfortunate, the world of taste and architectural meaning changed dramatically in the mid-1720s, and the baroque Wentworth Woodhouse carried quite the wrong message for an up-and-coming Whig.

PALLADIAN DREAM

So, in circumstances we now know little about, some time between 1730 and 1734 Watson-Wentworth – now titled Lord Malton – commissioned local architect Ralph Tunnicliffe to design him the biggest and best Palladian house in the land. This was to be Whig architecture writ loud and large for all to see and understand, and would, in ambition and scale, blow away Lord Raby's troubling house on the distant hilltop.

But what exactly was Palladian architecture in the 1730s, and why was it seen as essentially English in character? To answer the second part of this question

means that a paradox must be unpicked. Palladian architecture was an architecture inspired by the north Italian mid-to-late sixteenth-century architect Andrea Palladio. Why, you might wonder, should this Italian architect's designs have been seen as providing a model for an English national style while the architecture of other eminent foreign architects was viewed as alien and inappropriate? This is a difficult question to answer, not least because it raises a number of issues about creative endeavour in the eighteenth century and about the contemporary perceptions of history and national character.

In simple terms, Palladio was admired in England because it had been given the imprimatur of fame by an architect who was, in early eighteenth-century England, viewed by many as the father of modern British architecture. That architect was Inigo Jones. He had been theatre designer and architect to the Stuart courts of James I and Charles I, but, strange as this may seem, in the second decade of the eighteenth century he was the darling of Whig designers. Colen Campbell, the house-architect to the Whig ascendancy, put the case succinctly in his pioneering and taste-forming publication *Vitruvius Britannicus*, which was dedicated to a prominent Whig, the 2nd Duke of Argyll. Campbell's book, the first volume of which was published in 1715, showed recently built British architecture that he believed displayed in due measure wealth and talent. Consequently, baroque designs executed for the great and wealthy were included – Campbell could not risk alienating powerful and potential clients – so Wentworth Castle and Easton Neston (see page 101) are included in the early volumes of the publication. But it was the newly completed Palladio-inspired designs, many by Campbell himself, that were given pre-eminence and intended to inspire and provide exemplary models that were be emulated to form the basis of a 'rational' national taste. Palladio was the model because it was thought that his architecture expressed immutable laws of beauty. Put simply, it was believed that the 'ancients' – the Greeks and to a lesser degree the Romans – had discovered, through observation of nature and

> A quest to find a rational, national style of architecture that was appropriate for a Protestant, constitutional monarchy...

ABOVE *An eighteenth-century view of Wanstead House, Essex, which had been designed by Colen Campbell in about 1715. It was the first great and profoundly influential Palladian country house of the eighteenth century. It provided, in a very direct manner, the model for the design of the east-facing Palladian house at Wentworth Woodhouse.*

through trial and error, the divine laws of beauty. They had seen that the essence of beauty lay in certain ratios and harmonically related and geometrically generated proportions, such as the golden section, and applied these to their art and architecture. It was the neo-Palladians' conviction in early eighteenth-century Britain that Palladio had rediscovered these immutable and divine laws of the ancients, codified them in a system of proportion and ratios, and applied them in the creation of an architecture that was bold in its harmonically related proportions and that – rooted in the perfection of nature – was utterly rational and reflected the timeless beauty of creation.[7]

Inigo Jones, when travelling in Italy in the very early seventeenth century with Lord Arundel, had apparently recognized the innate genius of Palladio's work, got hold of a copy of Palladio's *Quattro libri dell'architettura* of 1570 and, through observation and contemplation, evolved a theory of architecture that was later seen as essentially English.

On his return to England, Jones put his Palladio-inspired theory into practice, and in the process introduced Palladian architecture to England, notably with the Queen's House, Greenwich (1616–35), the Banqueting House, Whitehall (1619–22), the chapel at St James's Palace (1623–5), and the Piazza and St Paul's Church, Covent Garden (from the early 1630s). With these works, Jones had, it was argued, both displayed his own taste and genius and made the work of the sixteenth-century Italian Andrea Palladio the foundation of a British national architectural style that was, in the early eighteenth century, very different from the baroque architecture of the Roman Catholic courts of continental Europe. This point was made by Colen Campbell in the introduction to volume I of *Vitruvius Britannicus*, where he praised Palladio because his 'ingenious

Labours' had rivalled 'most of the Ancients' and attacked baroque architects because they had arrogantly abandoned the course of beauty that Palladio had outlined. Campbell accused them of endeavouring 'to debauch mankind' with their 'odd and chimerical beauties' – and nominated Jones the 'great master' who 'had outdone all that went before' and who proved that 'in most we equal and in some things surpass, our neighbours'.[8]

Campbell's veneration of Inigo Jones was underpinned by the Venetian architect Giacomo Leoni. He had issued the first full English translation of Palladio's *Four Books on Architecture* in separate volumes between 1715 and 1720, and then in 1726, in his translation of Leone Alberti's *Ten Books of Architecture*, not only joined in the attack on the wayward and wilful 'moderns' (as baroque architects were then generally called), but also echoed the adulatory and nationalistic sentiments of Campbell on Jones: 'The English nation needs no foreign example of perfection in the way of architecture. Inigo Jones, their illustrious countryman ... made in Italy so great a progress in his art, that he attained the first rank in it.'[9]

Among the works published in volume I of *Vitruvius Britannicus* are Campbell's designs for Wanstead House in Essex, which was designed in 1714–15. Wanstead is generally regarded as the first, and by far the most influential, Palladian country house design of the eighteenth century. It was commissioned by Sir Richard Child, who was a Member of Parliament and, according to the

LEFT ABOVE & BELOW *The Banqueting House, Whitehall, of 1619–22 and St Paul's Church, Covent Garden, of the early 1630s – both designed by Inigo Jones, and pioneering and inspirational examples of pure Italian Renaissance architecture, in the manner of Andrea Palladio, to be built in Britain. These buildings helped form a 'national' style and dominant* *architectural taste in early eighteenth-century England.* OPPOSITE *A view along the enfilade of rooms set behind the Palladian east front of Wentworth Woodhouse, looking north from the original dining room, across the marble floor of the Marble Hall, through the Statuary Room to the former State Bedroom, latterly the library.*

Complete Peerage, a Tory until 1715, after which date
he supported the Whigs, and was rewarded by being
created Viscount Castlemaine and then Earl Tylney.[10]
So Wanstead House was one of the earliest and
greatest expressions of the Whig association with
Palladian design. Volume I of *Vitruvius Britannicus*
contains two designs for Wanstead, including
elevations, plans and a sensational section through
the double-height cubical hall. The second of these
designs was executed. Volume III of *Vitruvius
Britannicus*, published in 1725, contains a single
plate of a third design for Wanstead, which is
essentially the house as built, but with tall, square-
plan terminal towers added to each end. It was this
design that caught the eye of Lord Malton. So the
local man Tunnicliffe was set the task of taking the
largest of the Wanstead designs and enlarging it yet
further as the basis of the new east-facing house at
Wentworth Woodhouse.

" Emulation of recognized
excellence was the very essence
of the Palladian school, which
viewed baroque invention and
originality with deep suspicion…

ABOVE *The Marble Hall in
1924. Measuring 60 feet
square and 40 feet high,
it is one of the most perfect
Palladian rooms in Britain
(much inspired by Inigo Jones's
Queen's House at Greenwich),
and one of the most
architecturally exciting. It was
started in the mid-1730s, but
not finally completed until the
mid-nineteenth century.*

For our age, which values artistic novelty and originality, it seems odd to copy an existing design or to see such an exercise as in any way creative. But emulation of recognized excellence was the very essence of the Palladian school, which viewed baroque invention and originality with deep suspicion. Since Palladio's architecture was based on the divine laws of the ancients, argued the Palladians, it should be regarded as the prototype of perfection, as should skilful designs produced by talented Palladio disciples, such as Inigo Jones and Colen Campbell. To do otherwise was to display ignorance or arrogance. In addition, of course, for Lord Malton, Campbell's Palladian design carried the right political message: it defined the house style of the dominant Whig party of which Malton was determined to be a great and vital ornament.

The design Tunnicliffe and Lord Malton produced between 1730 and 1734 is fascinating. In elevation, it emulates the six-columned Corinthian portico of Wanstead that sits, Roman-temple style, on a tall podium or 'rustic' storey. To each side of the portico the elevation of the tall, three-storey-high main block continues for the width of two windows. Then the elevations step back slightly and continue as two-storey compositions, with the tall *piano nobile* becoming the top storey. All is as Wanstead, except the lower flanking ranges at Wentworth Woodhouse are five windows wide rather than six. But now something most strange happens. It was traditional for large country houses to have subservient wings containing kitchens or lodgings, and these were usually set at right angles to the main block to form courts, or were set in front or behind the main block and connected by quadrant link buildings. Tunnicliffe's Wentworth Woodhouse has wings but, most extraordinarily, these wings are set on virtually the same plane as the main block, although with their details being strikingly smaller in scale. One can only suppose that this unusual arrangement was fixed upon because it gave the house a vast width of frontage and striking monumentality. No doubt Lord Malton not only wanted his house to be one of the biggest

in Britain, but also, when seen from head-on in particular, positively to look it. The wings, with central pediments and originally only two storeys high (a third storey and engaged columns were added in the mid-1780s by John Carr for the 2nd Marquess of Rockingham), are terminated by Wanstead-style towered pavilions.

The plan of Wentworth Woodhouse is much like Wanstead, but in one key respect strikingly different. Wanstead House, according to Campbell's published plans (the house itself was demolished in 1823), had sets of apartments opening off the double-height cubical hall – the great interior ornament of the house, inspired by Palladio's villas and most rationally expressed externally by what Campbell called the 'just portico'. The rooms forming the apartments had to a degree, and as was usual in country houses in Britain up to the mid-seventeenth century, to be entered by passing through one to get to the other. The development of the 'double-pile' plan in the 1650s, in which sets of rooms could be reached and individually accessed by means of a central spine corridor (see pages 81–4), had made country houses more convenient, but was not followed at Wanstead. Campbell and Sir Richard Child seem to have preferred pomp and parade above privacy and comfort, but at Wentworth Woodhouse a subtle compromise was reached. Lord Malton or Tunnicliffe decided upon apartments leading off the central hall to north and south, and the rooms forming these were furnished with aligned doors that, when all open, could offer a spectacular enfilade or vista along the entire length of the central block and provide a tremendous route of formal parade from hall to dining room or to state bedroom and adjoining closet. But, for the sake of convenience, a corridor and vestibule were also added to the west so that each of the staterooms could be entered separately and to provide a route for servants and servicing.

The hall at Wentworth Woodhouse, like the hall at Wanstead, was intended to shock and awe. The original staircase is off the corridor to the north of the hall, but in 1801 a new staircase was added, by

John Carr, in an apse to the west of the hall. Both routes of entry offer drama, but the original arrangement was more striking. From a fairly dark staircase of more or less conventional scale one would burst into a soaring volume flooded with light. The hall measures 60 feet square and is 40 feet high. Andrea Palladio, in his *Quattro libri*, offered a sequence of seven related proportions that were ideal for rooms. These included rooms that were square in plan and a cube in volume, rooms that were a square and a half or 3:2 in plan area, or that were 2:1 in plan area or a double-cube in volume.[11] The hall at Wentworth Woodhouse reflects this theory: its plan is square, and the relationship between its side to its height is the ratio of 3:2 if the basic unit of measure is taken as 20 feet. In volume, therefore, the hall is pure Palladio, but its detail is Inigo Jones, with the design of its plaster ceiling and its gallery echoing those in the Queen's House, Greenwich. So this mighty room evokes the work of the two great exemplars.

The hall took nearly a hundred years to complete and is the work of many men. It's now called the Marble Hall because the Ionic engaged columns that ornament its lower wall and help to support the gallery appear to be made of marble, but are in fact made of scagliola, an artificial marble made of plaster, pigments, glue and marble dust. The floor is indeed of marble, wonderfully detailed to reflect the design of the ceiling, but this was not completed until the mid-1850s, and certainly looks mid-nineteenth century in its details and execution. The neoclassical panels set between the engaged columns and the Greek Ionic capitals of the columns are probably the work of James Stuart, who in the mid-eighteenth century was one of the European pioneers of the discovery and application of Greek rather than Roman-derived classical details. And the neo-Greek marble panels above the two fireplaces in the hall, made by John Gibson, were not made or added until the early 1820s.

But perhaps the most striking thing is the most obvious – its size. To achieve an internally unsupported span of 60 feet was something of an

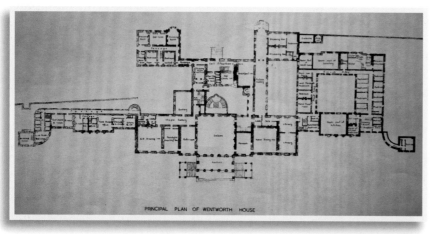

PRINCIPAL PLAN OF WENTWORTH HOUSE

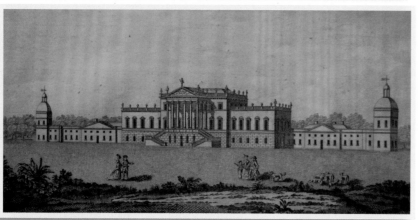

LEFT ABOVE *The first-floor plan with room uses as they were in the mid-1830s. North is to the right. Note the Marble Hall flanked by ranges of state rooms, all with their doors aligned to allow a dramatic vista through the house.* LEFT BELOW *The Tunnicliffe/ Flitcroft design of the early 1730s for the east front. Note that the wings were only two storeys high until heightened in the 1780s.* OPPOSITE *The Marble Hall.*

engineering marvel in the early eighteenth century. In the 1660s Sir Christopher Wren had made his reputation as an architect with the design of the roof of the Sheldonian Theatre in Oxford, an unprecedented internally unsupported span of 74 feet, which involved the construction of a series of timber trusses reinforced with wrought-iron bolts and straps, and the form of which was based on mathematical calculations. The ceiling was, in effect, suspended from the immensely strong roof trusses. Something similar was evidently achieved with the hall roof and ceiling at Wentworth Woodhouse. The arrangement of the staterooms to the north and south of the hall differ, so although the façade of the east-facing house is ruthlessly symmetrical, its plan is not, but varies to accommodate differing functional requirements. To the south are three staterooms in a row – originally the Great Supping Room, a drawing room that also served as an ante-room, leading to the dining room, the largest of the three and, in Palladian manner, square in plan. To the north are four rooms, originally an ante-room, a square-plan drawing room or presence chamber, the state bedroom and, to its west, a large closet.

On the second floor of the centre block were additional bedroom apartments; in the north wing were the kitchen, pantries, storerooms and servants' hall; while in the south wing were minor bedrooms and offices for estate staff and steward. On the ground floor of the central block were, as became usual in great Palladian houses, comfortable rooms of domestic scale that were used by the family on a more daily basis and when not entertaining in state in the rooms above. So the floor area of the Marble Hall is echoed below by the Pillared Hall, a large space defined by rows of Tuscan columns that, with its stone floor and robust detailing, has something of the feel of an exterior piazza. Off the Pillared Hall to left and right were rows of rooms, smaller than those above, intended to function as more intimate dining and withdrawing rooms.

Below the ground floor an extensive, vastly strong vaulted basement was created, containing wine cellars, a huge water cistern – entered via a robust but ornamental Venetian door, suggesting that it might also have been used by the family for bathing – storage rooms and a broad groin-vaulted north–south route to be used by servants carrying food from the kitchen to the main dining rooms, or moving between north and south wings. In the heyday of Wentworth Woodhouse, when the house was occupied by the family and its guests, there would have been well over a hundred servants present, and these vaults – almost industrial in their scale and sublime brick-vaulted construction – would have buzzed with life and activity.

The connection between this east-facing house and the earlier south-facing house is one of the oddest things about Wentworth Woodhouse because, in essence, there is no considered connection. There is a series of courts, built of good-quality red brick, like the body of the baroque house, with the court to the west of the kitchen being a wonderful affair, its ground floor arcaded like an urban piazza. Its lead rainwater heads bear the date 1743. The main internal link between the two houses is the Long Gallery in the baroque house, which was updated and probably extended in the 1740s to the east to link to the corridor vestibule in the Palladian house.

The plan of the Palladian house and the basic organization of its main rooms were almost certainly resolved by Tunnicliffe and his client, but at some point in the mid-1730s the design team changed. Malton was made an earl in 1734, and soon after he appears to have consulted the Palladian doyen of the age, the Earl of Burlington, about the design of the east-facing house at Wentworth Woodhouse. It is not known what took place when the designs were discussed, but following the meeting, one of Burlington's architectural protégés – the London-based Henry Flitcroft – was drafted in, and replaced Tunnicliffe after he died in 1736. Presumably Flitcroft was appointed to ensure that the detailing of the house had an up-to-date metropolitan grandeur and Palladian correctness.

Light is thrown on the construction of the Palladian house, the purpose and meaning of its

Malton entertained on such a lavish scale for political reasons. He was out to win the affection – and thus, he hoped, the votes – of the local population in a bid to gain and hold South Yorkshire for the Whigs...

PREVIOUS PAGES *The Palladian east front of Wentworth Woodhouse was completed in 1744. The centre block was inspired by the 1715 designs for Wanstead House. The lower wings contained the kitchen (right) and steward's room and minor bedrooms (left).*

The terminal towers were inspired by a later design for Wanstead.
ABOVE *The Pillared Hall in the ground floor or 'rustic' storey is set below the Marble Hall and functioned as the robust entrance hall for everyday use.*

vast size – and on the personality and character of its creator – by an extraordinary document now lodged in the City of Sheffield archives. In the middle of an early eighteenth-century account book are nine pages, written in a bold and clear hand, by Malton. Essentially, it is a journal, written over a number of years, that documents and reflects upon key events in the building and life of the house, incorporating building costs and quantities of food consumed, all interspaced with personal anecdote. Why Malton kept this spasmodic journal in such a strange manner is not known. The gems of information and insights it offers are priceless. They are also written in strange order. For example, on the top of one page Malton noted that the 'Expense in building to Lady Day [25 March] 1733 [was] about £27,000' (£2.3 million today) and then recorded that in January 1732, when the baroque west-facing house was nearing completion, 'I gave a large entertainment to all my tenants in the neighbourhood & their wives & some neighbouring gentlemen also came ... the number of guests was about one thousand' and 'two hundred and twenty five dishes were served' including 'viz: of beef 43, of Pork 30, Venison pastys 24, Turkeys 15, Geese 21 ... Apple and Mince pies 16 ... Boar's Heads 4 ...' To prevent confusion 'all invited had tickets sent them with the name of the Rooms they were to repair to ... men by themselves and women by themselves.'[12] This 'entertainment' was before the custom of seating men and women alternately, a polite development of the 1780s based on the idea that men should, in gallant manner, help women to their food and drink.[13] And, of course, all were to be 'seated according to their rank'.

Malton entertained on such a lavish scale for political reasons. He was out to win the affection – and thus, he hoped, the votes – of the local population in a bid to gain and hold South Yorkshire for the Whigs. And this, of course, explains the vast size of Wentworth Woodhouse. Its mighty dimensions were not just to express family wealth, pride and position, but were also entirely practical. If a house dominated the land, exuded power, voters would be impressed and – more to the point – if huge and vote-winning entertainments were to be given, the house had to be big to accommodate guests and to provide sleeping quarters for those who had travelled far – and of course for their servants. It's now hard to estimate, but it's reasonable to assume that an event like this could result in two or three hundred people sleeping within the house for a night or two. The 1720s' baroque house could not accommodate such numbers, so at one level Malton had a most practical reason for building the Palladian house and thus increasing his capacity to entertain in style. Were such large-scale entertainments worthwhile politically? Almost certainly, given that the number of eligible voters in the region in the late 1730s and early 1740s was around 15,000 and that many were not located in towns (which could more easily be controlled) but in the countryside. So they had to be wooed most vigorously and, given the relatively small number of voters, it was possible to entertain and influence virtually all of them with a series of such lavish receptions.[14]

Another entry in the account book covers expenditure on the house, with the total spent by 23 May 1736 being £36,484. 4s. 3d. (about £3 million today). An entry for 1737 states: 'New parlor and drawing room below stairs were finished, furnished and used, the Great Hall and portico begun, the Cellars, Rustic storey … and the Great Hall erected to the height of the first windows.' The parlour and drawing rooms might refer to rooms in the rustic storey of the Palladian house, but since this was

evidently still a construction site and these rooms were 'furnished and used', it is more probable that they were in the baroque house. 'I compute,' added Malton, 'the expenses of these nineteen months to New Year's Day 1737/8 including carriage, materials & furniture to be five thousand pounds' with the total 'expenses to New Year's Day 1738: £41,500 [about £3 million today].'

In 1738 'The Great Hall was built and covered in', the 'Supping Room finished' and the 'place for staircase erected'; and 'In the year 1739 The great Portico was built, which considering the size of the Stones, the quantity of Carving etc was the greatest piece of Building I had ever done in one year.' Having described the completion of the house's mightiest architectural ornament, the feature that dominated the landscape and best expressed the material power of the family, Lord Malton fell into a reflective mood, provoked by a great sadness: 'This unfortunate year I lost my Dear Eldest son William, Lord Higham, for whom I hoped to have prepared these Conveniencys. I had laid out in the whole as near as I can compute about fifty six thousand Pounds [£4.8 million today].' Having, with his mighty porticoed palace, made his mark on the land in no uncertain terms with the aim of proclaiming worldly power, wealth and aspirations, Lord Malton now reflected in most philosophical manner upon the transient nature of all earthly things: 'God prevent our being attached to the Honour, Grandeur or State of this world above what we ought, and Bless my now Dear only Son Charles to a long and

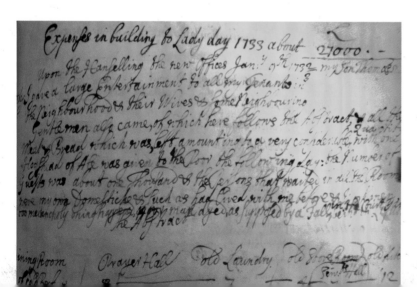

LEFT Part of a page from Lord Malton's journal, bound within an account book, that notes the costs of building Wentworth Woodhouse, dates when elements were completed, and anecdotes and reflections on the great enterprise. Here he notes that up to Lady Day 1733 the project had cost £27,000 – and at that date the works were less than half complete.

OPPOSITE The staircase, built in 1801 to designs by John Carr, that links the Pillared Hall and rustic storey to the Marble Hall and first-floor piano nobile.

Christian life & to the Enjoyment of these so as to be
fit at leaving them to enjoy Everlasting Glory.'
Charles did survive into manhood and, indeed,
became one of the most admirable Englishmen of
his age. It was at this time, in 1739, that Lord Raby –
the family rival and initial catalyst for the ever-
escalating building campaign at Wentworth
Woodhouse – died, still in utter political isolation.
But Raby's death did nothing to reduce the progress
of Lord Malton's works, which now had a seemingly
unstoppable impetus.

During 1741–2 the north wing was erected, and
carpenters' work on the ceilings of the Great Hall,
dining room and portico was completed, and a coat
of rough plaster laid on. By New Year's Day 1744
the total building cost had reached £70,000 (about
£6 million today). In 1744 Westmorland slates were
brought to cover the main roof, and in 1745 Malton

ABOVE *The Great Dining Room
at the southern end of the first-
floor enfilade was decorated in
high Palladian style in the mid-
to-late 1730s by Henry
Flitcroft, from which time the
plaster ceiling and pedimented
door surrounds date. The room
was then altered into a drawing
room and embellished in the*
*early 1760s in restrained rococo
manner by the 2nd Marquess
to provide a setting for the
painting he had commissioned
from George Stubbs of his
very successful racehorse
Whistlejacket – shown far
right in this 1924 photograph.
The painting is now in the
National Gallery.*

recorded that he 'finished off the ceilings of the Great Dining Room next to the Portico, paved many rooms below and fitted several bed chambers and the Butler's room. Steward's Parlour, Hall, etc, set up a new Billiard table & built several walls of modern contrivance with stoved and Gilt frames &c,' and last, and perhaps most important, 'Covered the Great Hall'. The following year, 1746, Lord Malton states that the majority of the house was finished, that he 'bought some marble chimney pieces, but as the materials of timber &c were not very great I compute this years expense to about £2,000 [about £173,000 today]'. Malton also records that 'the Rebellion the latter part of last year was an expense of some Thousand Pounds to me'.

The last note is an almost casual reference to a defining event in the history of the Wentworth family and of its palatial seat. The rebellion was, of course, the last serious Jacobite attempt to seize the throne of Britain. After an invasion of England as far south as Derby by an army of Scottish Highlanders and Irish and French units led by Prince Charles Edward Stuart, the Jacobite cause ended in disaster, with bloody defeat in April 1746 at Culloden. But early Jacobite successes, and the invasion, had initially and most seriously alarmed the House of Hanover and its Whig supporters. As the Jacobite army passed Wentworth on its march south to London, Lord Malton's newly finished palace suddenly found itself in the front line. It became a military centre of Whig resistance and a rallying place for militia units gathering in readiness to attack the Highlanders. Lord Malton must have funded the supply of these militias, and while the park was turned into a military camp, Charles – Lord Malton's only surviving son and merely fifteen years of age – disobeyed his father and made his way to Carlisle to join George II's son, the Duke of Cumberland, who was organizing the Hanoverian riposte to the Jacobites. In the event, neither Charles nor the Yorkshire-based Whig militia were required. The Jacobite army lost its nerve, retreated north, was finally confronted and destroyed by an army of tough British regulars returned from Flanders, and the Jacobite cause was irredeemably lost.

CELEBRATION OF VICTORY

In 1747, to celebrate the triumph of the House of Hanover, the Whigs and the Protestant cause – and, indeed, his own political and perhaps actual survival – Lord Malton erected a tall monument on a hill overlooking Wentworth Woodhouse. The monument, called the Hoober Stand, is somewhat peculiar-looking. Its tapering pyramidal form rises from a triangular plan and is truncated at its apex to form a viewing platform. It was designed by Henry Flitcroft, and it is possible that its idiosyncratic appearance possessed symbolism that appeared appropriate at the time, perhaps to do with Freemasonry, which was then popular amongst the upper echelons of society, making much use of triangles and pyramids in its imagery. Perhaps the Jacob's ladder-like internal spiral staircase would have been seen as representing man's journey from the dark material world to the elevated spiritual realm of light, with high-climbing initiates here rewarded with a celestial view of the giant's palace of Wentworth Woodhouse. Indeed, the pyramidal monument, topped with a hexagonal lantern, can be seen as the equivalent of the Masonic pyramid crowned with an all-seeing eye.[15]

If the form of the monument is mysterious, its message is most explicit and emblazoned for all to see above the door leading to the viewing platform: 'This Pyramidal Building was Erected ... in Grateful Respect to the Preserver of our Religion, Laws and Libertys, King George the Second, who by the blessing of God having subdued a most unnatural Rebellion in Britain Anno 1746, Maintains the Balance of Power and Settles a just and honourable Peace in Europe. 1748.' The monument, the inscription also records, was erected 'by his Majesty's most Dutyfull Subject, Thomas Marquess of Rockingham'. Lord Malton's reward for unquestioning loyalty to the House of Hanover was to be created the 1st Marquess of Rockingham in 1746.

THE HOUSE IN RECENT TIMES

I first went to Wentworth Woodhouse nearly twenty years ago, when the future of the house hung in the balance, the potential victim of an utterly changing world. Who in the 1990s could use a house with just over 300 rooms when its reason for existence and the traditional source of its financial support had long been removed?

I returned again in late 2010 when imminent danger had passed and a quest was afoot to find a new use that would help finance the house's future. A close inspection of Wentworth Woodhouse

revealed many things, both good and bad. The house is, in many ways, the epitome of eighteenth-century English civilization – the product of exquisite taste and a breathtaking window into the politics, economy and society of the age. Although big in size, Wentworth Woodhouse is far from bland: its details, both in the baroque west-facing house and in the Palladian house, are of the highest quality, both in conception and execution, and full of variety and vitality.

I walked through the central door in the ground floor of the eastern house into the Pillared Hall. All was orderly and empty. The rooms to the south are well preserved, those at the far end – drawing room and ante-room – finely panelled and with Palladian decoration in the manner of the late 1730s. But before these rooms are reached the visitor, walking from the Pillared Hall, enters the Painted Drawing Room. It is most remarkable. Canvasses fitted snugly to its walls show the triumph of the five senses, each rendered in a charming allegorical manner. For example, 'Touch' is expressed by a pair of lovers touching hands, and 'Smell' by two young women smelling flowers, with all actions mimicked and amplified by cavorting putti. This decorative scheme, rendered in playful French rococo taste and perhaps designed by Jean François Clermont, was executed in the 1760s, as indeed was much of the interior of the main rooms in the Palladian house.

The 1st Marquess of Rockingham had died in December 1750 when his great project was still incomplete. His twenty-year-old son, the

LEFT ABOVE *The fireplace in the vaulted room south of the Marble Hall. Originally a drawing room, it was converted in the late eighteenth century into a repository of full-length family portraits by Van Dyck and became famed as one of the great country house treasure rooms of Britain.*

LEFT BELOW *A detail from the ground-floor Painted Drawing Room, which shows the triumph of the five senses, painted in around 1760, probably by Jean François Clermont. This detail shows 'Smell', with two women sniffing flowers.*

OPPOSITE *Detail of the marble fireplace in the Van Dyck Room, probably dating from the 1730s, a particularly fine example of a standard Palladian design showing a pair of caryatids or terms as delicately carved Grecian maidens.*

remarkable 2nd Marquess, took over and in the process enlivened the by then slightly dated heavy Palladian style. The extent to which the 2nd Marquess brought the interior scheme up to date is revealed by a stroll along the first-floor enfilade. Flitcroft's original open-well oak staircase survives (although seemingly much altered and rebuilt in the late nineteenth century), but I ascend from the Pillared Hall to the Marble Hall above by means of the elegant stone-built imperial staircase of 1801–3. Important parts of the Marble Hall were executed for the 2nd Marquess, notably the wall panels and, arguably, the Ionic capitals by James Stuart in the 1760s, that reflect the emerging taste for Greek and authentically antique-inspired neoclassicism.

The sequence of staterooms leading south from the Marble Hall were either completed or subtly but significantly changed by the 2nd Marquess, and their uses were revised. I walked through them, picking out the details designed and fitted by Flitcroft before 1750 for the 1st Marquess, and those installed during the later 1760s and 1770s for the 2nd Marquess. The quest is fascinating and informative. From the start the rooms were intended to possess variety, achieved through the application of differing Palladian proportions, volumes and details combined with elements derived more directly from Rome, or that were intended to be allegorical or heraldic. The first room I entered, south of the Marble Hall, the 1st Marquess's Great Supping Room, is mostly Flitcroft – the plaster ceiling modelled on designs by Inigo Jones, and the massive marble fireplace (perhaps moved here from elsewhere in the house) sports a pair of griffins, mythological beasts that feature in the Wentworth/Rockingham coat of arms. The 2nd Marquess made this room into an ante-drawing room. The next room going south, a drawing room, appears to be largely Flitcroft. It has a splendid coffered and vaulted ceiling of tremendous Roman authority, based loosely on the dome of the Pantheon in Rome and perhaps inspired by the similar but larger-scale ceiling that William Kent had created from the mid-1730s at the inspirational Palladian Holkham Hall in Norfolk. This room also

contains a tremendous fire surround, no doubt by Flitcroft too, that incorporates a pair of caryatids in the form of delicately carved Grecian maidens.

South of the drawing rooms was the original Great Dining Room. This is now one of the best rooms in the house. Its original function is enshrined within the surviving Flitcroft decorative elements – the marble fire surround features a grape-festooned head of Bacchus, the god of wine, and scenes showing cherubs trampling grapes. And above the pedimented doors are gilded images of Flora, goddess of fertility, with ears of corn, and a Bacchante peering through a grape-loaded vine. These are, of course, all images of conviviality and revelry, of drink and of plenty – all appropriate for a well-appointed dining room. But the 2nd Marquess changed the room's function and its scheme of decoration. As well as being an utterly political creature and an increasingly eminent Whig leader, the 2nd Marquess was also a fanatical fancier of horseflesh and a dedicated gambling man. This led him in the late 1760s to commission John Carr to design a stable block of epic size and most noble form, and in the early 1760s to commission George Stubbs to paint a large and sensational portrait of one of Rockingham's best-loved and successful race horses, Whistlejacket, that in one race alone in 1759 had won a purse of £2,000 (about £150,000 today). There were fortunes to be made – and lost – in eighteenth-century racing. The 2nd Marquess decided to hang the Stubbs' painting in this room in about 1762, and seems to have redecorated the walls around it. The theme is Roman-inspired neoclassicism, with numerous portrait busts of classical figures, but all executed with a fashionable rococo flourish.

The staterooms to the north of the Marble Hall were also completed or changed in detail and use by the 2nd Marquess, with a new dining room created in the centre of the run of rooms, its volume and wall (although not door) decoration being virtually identical to that in the former dining room, now the Whistlejacket Room. At the northern end of the sequence the state bedroom, with a fine coffered and vaulted ceiling similar to that in the south

> The 2nd Marquess commissioned George Stubbs to paint a large and sensational portrait of one of Rockingham's best-loved and successful race horses, Whistlejacket, that in one race alone in 1759 had won a purse of £2,000…

ABOVE *Palladian details from the original Great Dining Room and latterly the Whistlejacket Room. Being a room dedicated to food, drink and conviviality, the decorations include images of cherubs pressing grapes to make wine (top left), the face of a bacchante staring through a grape-loaded vine (lower left) and the face of Bacchus – the god of wine – in the centre of the lintel above the fireplace opening (top right).*

range, and with a marble fireplace decorated delightfully with carvings of informally arranged local flowers, was made into a library.

The 2nd Marquess used Wentworth, even more than his father had, as a nationally vital Whig power base and rallying ground. Enormous as the house was, in the mid-1780s he added upper floors to the north and south wings, increasing the building's capacity to lodge in reasonable style and comfort those attending political gatherings. But in his political convictions the 2nd Marquess was significantly unlike his father. Both were committed Whigs of course, but while the 1st Marquess was an unquestioning supporter of the House of Hanover, his son was far more astute and critical. The 2nd Marquess perceived in George III, who came to the throne in 1760, a wayward and autocratic propensity that threatened, if fanned by the power-eager Tories, a slide back towards a form of arbitrary monarchy largely ungoverned by parliamentary democracy. In 1762 Rockingham resolved to challenge the Hanoverian king. In protest against George III's political policies – which favoured Tories such as Lord Bute, threatened the long-established Whig ascendancy and promised to destabilize and divide Britain – Rockingham most provocatively resigned his post of Lord of the Bedchamber. George, in petulant response, almost immediately removed Rockingham from the office of Lord Lieutenant of the West Riding of Yorkshire, Lord Lieutenant of the City and County of York, and Vice-Admiral of the North. And so the fight was joined between two visions of Britain – one reactionary, conservative and autocratic, the other progressive, liberal and determined in its desire to forge a more egalitarian nation fit for the increasingly technological and scientific modern world.

Rockingham had a year in the mid-1760s as prime minister to pursue his policies, and during this time repealed the Stamp Act that had long caused ire in the American colonies because, as a direct tax from the British parliament, it represented for the Americans the evil of taxation without representation. But having made this enlightened move, Rockingham's government also passed the Declaratory Act, which affirmed the power of the British parliament to legislate for the colonies 'in all cases whatsoever'. Not surprisingly, perhaps, Rockingham's government pulled itself apart within a year due to internal dissent. Then, for the next sixteen years, Rockingham watched, from opposition, as George III and his incompetent government proceeded first to provoke the American colonists to armed rebellion, and then to mismanage and finally lose the resulting war in the most humiliating and damaging of circumstances. Rockingham, who had called for American independence as early as 1778,[16] returned to power in 1782 in time to formally, and as decently as possible, end the American war that was already lost. But after only fourteen weeks in office, he died in a most untimely manner.

THE LAST GREAT CHANGES

The 2nd Marquess of Rockingham had married in 1752 but had no children, so on his death his house and estates – although not his title – were inherited by a nephew, the 4th Earl Fitzwilliam. His own lands combined with those of Wentworth

LEFT ABOVE *The coffer-vaulted State Bedroom, decorated in the late 1730s and later turned into the library, photographed in 1924.*
LEFT BELOW *Detail of the 1730s' marble fireplace in the former State Bedroom, showing informal renderings of local flowers.*
OPPOSITE *The Rockingham Monument, conceived in the*

early 1780s by the 4th Earl Fitzwilliam to commemorate the life, ethics and political achievements of the 2nd Marquess of Rockingham. Designed by John Carr and completed in 1788, the monument acts as the focus of an intensely political landscape and as a splendid eye-stopper when viewed from the east front of the house.

Woodhouse made the 4th Earl one of the richest men in Britain – a wealth that was soon greatly increased when extensive coalmining started on the earl's Yorkshire estates in the very late eighteenth century. As well as being tremendously wealthy, the 4th Earl was also a leading and most liberal Whig politician – and, in 1782, a very grateful man. Soon after acquiring Wentworth Woodhouse he pondered upon an appropriate token of thanks, and in 1783 commissioned the 2nd Marquess's architect, John Carr, to design a monument that would celebrate Rockingham's virtues both as a politician and a man. The monument, a tall, domed and colonnaded temple started in 1788, is a splendid eye-stopping garden ornament when seen from the east-facing Palladian house. Built on high land it also offers a splendid location from which to contemplate the house and the park, the latter, like everything about Wentworth Woodhouse, vast in size, and in this case defined by a wall over nine miles in circumference. Inside the monument

ABOVE *The Statuary Room, immediately north of the Marble Hall, was conceived by the 2nd Marquess and finally executed in the late eighteenth century by the 4th Earl Fitzwilliam. This photographs shows the room in 1924. The statuary has now been dispersed, with just a few of the Ionic column plinths remaining in situ to act as sad memorials of what was.*

is a domed and delicately decorated chamber within which sit eight busts of 'British Worthies' and eminent Whigs, including Charles James Fox, Edmund Burke and the Duke of Portland, with at its centre a marble statue of the 2nd Marquess. He stares at the distant house and holds up his right hand towards it, as if in benediction. On the base supporting the statue are texts that record Rockingham's titles, achievements, virtues, constancy, political creed and one that – penned by Burke – also explains the meaning of the monument. Burke admired the 6th Earl, whose liberal Whig beliefs and boldness of action made him the natural successor to the 2nd Marquess, but nevertheless used the monument to remind the Fitzwilliams of the political policies and responsibilities they had inherited. On the east side of the pedestal Burke's warning is emblazoned: 'Let [Rockingham's] successors who daily Behold this monument, consider that it was not built to Entertain the Eye, But to instruct the mind. Let them Reflect, that their conduct will make it their Glory, or their Reproach …. Remember, Resemble, Persevere.'

The Rockingham monument was the last major work in the Wentworth Woodhouse park, which, from the Hoober Stand of the 1740s, had become a most political landscape, where nation-defining events were commemorated. Structures include the Keppel Column, commissioned by the 2nd Marquess in the 1770s, which celebrates the acquittal of Admiral Keppel, a leading Rockingham Whig, following a politically motivated court martial.

The 4th Earl Fitzwilliam was unable to follow in the political footsteps of his uncle. He defended the right of public assembly for political protest and condemned the illegal military intervention that provoked the Peterloo Massacre of 1819 as a step towards military dictatorship, a stance that was brave, popular and led to him losing – as his uncle had before him – the office of Lord Lieutenant of the West Riding.

But by the 1820s times had changed for the worse for the Whigs. The party had split in the 1790s, largely as a result of conflicting views over the French Revolution. Some saw it as bloodthirsty chaos, while other more radical members perceived it as a necessary evil.

As for Wentworth Woodhouse, the 4th Earl employed Humphry Repton in the 1790s to landscape the park in a fashionably informal manner, but inside the house did little but make it a trifle more romantic and picturesque. The library – the world of learning and reflection – was extended, the ante-room to the north of the Marble Hall was transformed into a Statuary Room in which marble sculptures, most commissioned by the 2nd Marquess, were gathered together on pedestals and columns rising from a scagliola floor intended to look like porphyry and marble. This room, like the adjoining Marble Hall itself, was calculated to have the feeling of an outdoor space, as if a small piazza, and in an amusingly disconcerting way confuse inside with outside. Finally, the 4th Earl converted the vaulted drawing room to the south of the Marble Hall into the Van Dyck Room, an idea he may have inherited from the 2nd Marquess, in which were located the eight full-length family portraits and a portrait of Archbishop Laud painted by Van Dyck in the 1630s. The 4th Earl probably also created the strange little room at the top of the south tower, whose walls are studded with marble and plaster panels showing classical schemes, including the Grecian gods reposing on Olympus. Presumably this elevated room was where the Fitzwilliams, as gods in their own domain, came to survey their beautiful lands and the workmen toiling in the park and distant fields.

When the 4th Earl Fitzwilliam died in 1833 political power and aspirations moved from Wentworth Woodhouse. But money did not. Even if the family played a far lesser role in the politics of the nation, it remained one of the wealthiest in Britain. But by the mid-twentieth century, following crippling death duties, the nationalization of the Fitzwilliam mines in 1947 and devastating mining works that destablized the building, the mighty house stood on the edge of oblivion – a despoiled leviathan with no use and no future.

DECAY AND RESURRECTION

The house I walked around in late 2010 shows only too clearly the depredations of the last seventy years or so, as well as the efforts made during the last decade to halt decay and bring Wentworth Woodhouse back to life. Most of the house and grounds were occupied by the army during the Second World War, with the Fitzwilliam family retreating to rooms in the west portion. The 7th Earl died in February 1943, and the 8th Earl, after distinguished war service, was killed in an aeroplane crash in France in 1948. Between those two events a decision was made that was to have disastrous consequences for Wentworth Woodhouse. In September 1945 Manny Shinwell, then Minister for Fuel in the new Labour government, used wartime powers still in operation to requisition Wentworth Woodhouse park and strip off its surface for open-cast mining. Many were shocked by this government action, not least because the surface coal in the area was known to be

of very poor quality and hardly worth the winning.

Despite protests from the president of the Yorkshire branch of the National Union of Miners, who pointed out that 'Wentworth is the beauty spot of Rotherham and Barnsley districts, the garden and spacious grounds having been enjoyed by our mining folk for very many years',[17] and from the Fitzwilliam family, the open-cast mining started, and Shinwell decreed that it would proceed up to the very doors of the baroque west-facing house. With hindsight, this seems to have been nothing more than vengeful class warfare. For generations the house and its estate had been the very heart and economic soul of the region – most local families had worked for the Fitzwilliams in one way or another, and to a degree the park had been their recreation. Now all was being destroyed in a most brutal and speedy manner.

The nationalization of the Fitzwilliam collieries a few months after the start of the open-cast mining meant that not only was the setting of their house being ruined, but also that the source of much of their wealth, and their role as major local industrialists and employers, came to an abrupt end. The prospects of the family in their traditional heartland – and in their vast and now beleaguered house – were bleak indeed. Their immediate response in 1947 was to let the Palladian portion of the house, the stables and riding school to the West Riding County Education Authority as a training college for female physical exercise teachers. This use was organized by Lady Mabel,

LEFT *The delicate, late eighteenth-century fireplace survives in the Statuary Room, with one bas-relief portrait – embedded in the wall and classed legally as part of the fabric of the house – still in situ.*
OPPOSITE *The room at the top of the south tower, decorated in* *the late eighteenth century, with images including the Grecian gods in Olympus. It is where the family must surely have sat as gods in their own domain, surveying the garden and park below them. Now an air of dereliction hangs over it.*

a local councillor and the socialist sister of the 7th Earl, so the new facility was named Lady Mabel College. Never surely could such a palace have been given over to such an unlikely use. Strapping girls exercised in the Marble Hall, played hockey on the ornamental lawns and lodged in the wings, with the old kitchen and much of the interior of the north wing being destroyed and replaced by a new kitchen, serving area and communal dining rooms. Meanwhile, the 9th Earl Fitzwilliam, who inherited in 1948, co-inhabited the house and park with the PE girls and occupied about forty rooms in the baroque house. He lived the life of a somewhat eccentric bachelor, and would sit in the bay window of the Long Gallery, sipping brandy and watching the lunar landscape and towering slag-heaps move slowly but remorselessly towards his house.

Inevitably, a number of sales of contents took place, and so began the dismantling and dispersal of an interior that collectively was one of the greatest works of art in the country and a monument to a high point in national taste. A six-day sale in July 1949 'of a large portion of the contents of Wentworth Woodhouse' included 2005 lots, ranging from groups of eighteenth-century chairs and desks by Chippendale to batches of eighteenth-century muskets.[18]

The 9th Earl died in 1952 and, to make matters worse, the inheritance was bitterly disputed between two brothers, with their partisan and muddling mother declaring that one of her sons was illegitimate. Finally, Thomas became the 10th Earl, with his brother Toby being compensated with an annual allowance. The new earl lived at Milton Hall near Peterborough rather than at Wentworth Woodhouse, so the house fell more deeply into gloom, despite the abandonment of open-cast mining and the house's Grade I listing in 1952 as a building of architectural and historic importance. When the 10th Earl died in 1979 without a male heir the title became extinct and the Fitzwilliam occupation of Wentworth Woodhouse – although for years only token – effectively came to an end. Most of the family's highly prized heirlooms, including the Van Dyck portraits, passed to Lady

Juliet Tadgell, the daughter of the 8th Earl, who still possesses the majority of them, while the estate passed to Lady Hastings, the step-daughter of the 10th Earl. In the same year Lady Mabel College closed, and the lease of the entire house was taken over by Sheffield City Polytechnic. It remained in occupation until 1986, then, after three years of abandonment, the vast and decaying house was sold by the Fitzwilliam family to Wensley Haydon-Baillie, a man who seemed willing and able to repair and occupy it. Covenants limiting future uses were attached to the sale, as were about 100 acres of garden, with the rest of the surrounding land and most of the garden buildings remaining in Fitzwilliam ownership. But Haydon-Baillie ran into financial difficulties, and in 1998 the deeply troubled Wentworth Woodhouse, its multitude of gutters and roofs leaking and its hundreds of rooms utterly empty, was repossessed by a bank.

In 1999 a new saviour appeared in the person of Clifford Newbold who, with his wife and three sons, has spent the last decade gradually repairing and stabilizing the house, and they now live in the baroque west-facing portion. Currently, as the Newbold's architect reveals, plans are being prepared that will, it is hoped, bring new life to the house, make it self-supporting and give it a viable future. These plans, which include opening the main staterooms as a country house museum, have yet to be revealed in detail or tested by the planning system and listed building legislation, or against the covenants. But before work can proceed the structural stability of the house has to be determined. The mining works around the house have disturbed water levels, and cracks have appeared in the fabric. The seriousness of these cracks, to what extent they are the direct result of mining and are still active, and who should take financial responsibility for the expensive repairs, have still to be fully discussed and agreed.

Wentworth Woodhouse now is a most strange and haunted place. The baroque house is occupied, but the far larger Palladian house is still empty and echoing, some rooms gently tilting, with plaster ceilings cracked from structural movement. The

The world turns and changes around it, but in some almost magic way Wentworth Woodhouse seems frozen in time…

once-grand furniture is long gone, Stubbs' *Whistlejacket* replaced by a now-faded photographic copy, and the north and south wings forlorn and decaying. There is a sublime yet tragic atmosphere about it. The long-term future of this house – without doubt one of the greatest Georgian houses ever built in Britain – is still in doubt. If the current proposal is found not to work, then what?

I leave the house at dusk, a sprinkling of snow on the lawn, and look back at the Palladian front. With its portico and parapet statues silhouetted against the evening sky, and lights on in some of its richly ornamented rooms, it looks stupendous. The world turns and changes around it, but in some almost magic way Wentworth Woodhouse seems frozen in time. Yes, at the moment, the house endures, and while it does, there is hope. It is movingly beautiful and also a fantastic document that says so much about the age when Britain was ruled from country houses like this, with Wentworth Woodhouse being the most tremendous powerhouse of them all ❖

CLANDEBOYE HOUSE

Bangor, County Down,
Northern Ireland

19ᵀᴴ CENTURY

Architecture of empire

❖

MY ARRIVAL AT CLANDEBOYE HOUSE IN County Down brings back strong and starkly contrasting memories. It's a house I've known for well over thirty years, having first visited in the mid-1970s, when the recent Troubles cast a dark and terrible shadow over the land. Then the short journey from Belfast to the house was almost apocalyptic. Sandbagged blockhouses at the airport, vigilant British soldiers patrolling back-to-back through the deserted streets of the city, numerous vehicle checkpoints and swathes of dereliction. But now things are very different. Belfast has come back to life, with the Troubles – although far from resolved – seemingly now a memory from another nightmarish world. And also, this time I arrive at Clandeboye by train. That might seem a rather insignificant difference, but it is not. The station I arrive at – Helen's Bay – is an architectural outrider of the house I've come to see, and also a direct expression of the bold architectural vision and aspirations of the man who made Clandeboye one of the most fascinating houses in Britain.

Frederick Hamilton-Temple-Blackwood became Baron Dufferin and Clandeboye in 1841, and in 1888 was raised in the peerage as the 1st Marquess of Dufferin and Ava. Between these two dates Lord Dufferin lived the most extraordinary life, moving from a champion of the starving poor in Ireland and lord-in-waiting to the young Queen Victoria in 1849, to intrepid explorer of the North Atlantic and Egypt during the 1850s, to Governor General of the nascent Dominion of Canada from 1872 to 1878,

ambassador to the Russian Empire in 1879, to the Ottoman Empire in 1881, and from 1884 to 1888 achieving the pinnacle of imperial administration as Viceroy of India. And Lord Dufferin's ancestral home, Clandeboye House, is in a sense his autobiography in masonry and mortar – the story of his life, his dreams and achievements – told through the vast number of objects ('curios' as he termed them) that he collected during his decades of travel and power, and through the inspired, and at times fantastical, alterations he proposed and made to the house.

There is no other house in Britain like Clandeboye – a monument to a man whose life was like a Victorian fairy tale of adventure, and a monument to the golden age of the largest and most far-flung empire the world has ever seen. Clandeboye House and estate was, like the empire itself, an epic creation – but, unlike the empire, it endures still, a vignette of a now almost-forgotten age and little altered since Lord Dufferin died in 1902. Clandeboye House would, no doubt, be generally acknowledged as one of the wonders of Ireland if open to the public and better known. But the inner life of the house remains discreet, hidden, if not entirely secret. This is the world I enter when I step from the train at Helen's Bay station.

The land into which the railway line from Belfast penetrates was, in the 1860s, owned by

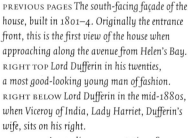

PREVIOUS PAGES *The south-facing façade of the house, built in 1801–4. Originally the entrance front, this is the first view of the house when approaching along the avenue from Helen's Bay.*
RIGHT TOP *Lord Dufferin in his twenties, a most good-looking young man of fashion.*
RIGHT BELOW *Lord Dufferin in the mid-1880s, when Viceroy of India, Lady Harriet, Dufferin's wife, sits on his right.*
OPPOSITE *A grandiose representation of the Dufferin and Clandeboye coat of arms embellishing the bridge at Helen's Bay station, constructed in 1863.*

Lord Dufferin. At that time he hoped to develop Helen's Bay as an idyllic seaside town with exemplary architecture. This was perhaps the most ambitious expression of Dufferin's architectural passion and of his lifelong need to make money – a commodity that for Dufferin, like so many nineteenth-century Irish landowners, was always in short supply. The visionary town did not grow as he had envisaged, and money did not roll in, but in 1863 Helen's Bay got its station, complete with ornamental buildings built by Dufferin. These included the main station building, incorporating his lordship's own private waiting room, and a turret-encrusted bridge. All was designed for Dufferin by the talented Gothic Revival architect Benjamin Ferrey. From this station Dufferin could progress, by private avenue, to nearby Helen's Bay or to Clandeboye House, lying just over two miles distant. I pass from the platform down to the avenue, as Lord Dufferin would have done as he descended via a private staircase to his waiting horse-drawn carriage. All is now overgrown and the buildings somewhat decayed, but the original grandeur is still apparent. Seen from below, the bridge appears as a mighty medieval city gate, towered and stone-vaulted, its arch embellished at its centre with the huge stone-carved and flamboyant coat of arms of the Dufferins of Clandeboye. I walk below the bridge, towards Clandeboye House, and feel that I am indeed entering a portal to a hidden world, to a lost and forgotten age when men such as Lord Dufferin could find themselves virtual rulers of millions of people in far-distant lands when Great Britain was the arbiter of a large portion of the Earth.

As I walk the deathly quiet and overgrown avenue, I can't help but ponder the ironies of the world that I am entering. Here, for a brief moment in the late nineteenth century, was, in a sense, the heart of Britain's empire. Here was the ancient home of the man who, for four years in the 1880s, ruled – as a semi-autonomous representative of the monarch – the most valuable of Britain's imperial possessions. Yet Dufferin's estate of Clandeboye stood in a land that was itself a controversial and contested part of the empire – indeed, arguably, Ireland was England's first and oldest imperial possession. Dufferin was himself just as much Scottish and English as Irish, yet there he was in the 1880s, the key administrator of Britain's empire in India, whose home stood in a country that was, for many of its native inhabitants, itself a victim of imperial exploitation and domination. Dufferin was only too familiar with those agitating for Home Rule, land reform and political independence for Ireland, so for a viceroy he had an almost unique perspective on the increasing number of Indian subjects who in the 1880s were pressing for Home Rule for India. The Clandeboye estate was an enchanted domain in Lord Dufferin's time, a place of repose and fantasist escape, yet it was also, from time to time, unsettled by the bustle and fury of external political events in Ireland and the empire, by rebellion, war, death and destruction.

THE HOUSE

The first glimpse of Clandeboye House, approaching from the avenue, offers a distant view of a long, low, two-storey building set on slightly rising open ground beyond clumps of trees and a swathe of grass with, on my right, a sheet of water and a small bridge. The house took its present external form in the first few years of the nineteenth century, but at its heart incorporates the bones of a smaller seventeenth- and eighteenth-century house. The man responsible for the rebuilding was James Blackwood, 2nd Baron Dufferin and Clandeboye – the great-uncle of the 1st Marquess. The architect Blackwood commissioned was Robert Woodgate, an Englishman who had been trained in the London office of the brilliantly inventive – indeed idiosyncratic – architect Sir John Soane, for whom Woodgate eventually acted as clerk of works. Woodgate's design, constructed between 1801 and 1804, appears unexceptional externally and lacks the abstracted and minimal classical detail perfected by Soane. The façade is rendered with Roman cement, with details picked out in a mellow stone. I see a corner of the house, so get a slightly diagonal view of an elevation with its centre emphasized by a

> **As I walk the deathly quiet and overgrown avenue, I can't help but ponder the ironies of the world that I am entering. Here, for a brief moment in the late nineteenth century, was, in a sense, the heart of Britain's empire…**

ABOVE *Clandeboye House, seen across the lake from the east. The two-storey curved bay marks the saloon. The drawing room is on the left and the dining room on the right.*

three-window-wide eaves pediment, below which is set a single-storey portico formed with handsome and conventional Roman Doric columns. This low-key portico was clearly intended by Woodgate to mark the primary entrance to the house. I continue walking parallel to this entrance elevation and see, set at right angles to it, a façade incorporating a generous two-storey segmental bay at its centre. The largeness of the windows of these elevations – and their formality – makes clear that behind them are grouped the major reception rooms and bedrooms of the house.

The rebuilding date of the house is significant. The Irish insurrection of 1798, when Irishmen – including Protestants as well as Roman Catholics – took up arms in a bid to rip the country from the grip of English rule, was quickly put down. But the shock of the event provoked the British government into dramatic and speedy action. The insurrection had been undertaken with French aid, as had another abortive insurrection of December 1796, when French troops had attempted to land in Bantry Bay to assist Irish patriots in capturing Cork and then march on Dublin. In 1798 Britain was locked in war with Revolutionary France – a land proclaiming liberty and equality for all – and a French invasion of England was a distinct and terrifying possibility. It was clear to the English that political stability had to be established in Ireland as quickly as possible, not only to reduce the danger of Ireland providing a vulnerable 'back door' for a French invasion, but also because a very large proportion of the British army and Royal Navy was made up of Irishmen – indeed, by around 1810 an estimated 40 per cent of Britain's Napoleonic army was Irish-born.[1] If these soldiers believed their homeland to be on the verge of independence and questioned the nature and legitimacy of their loyalty and allegiance to the British Crown, then for the English, mutiny and all manner of frightful possibilities loomed like spectres in the shadows. Action had to be taken fast, and the speedy solution chosen was to decrease rather than increase Ireland's sense of freedom, self-determination and ability for independent action. In 1800 the Act of Union was passed, becoming law on 1 January 1801. This involved the Irish government in Dublin voting itself out of existence and, instead, established direct rule – and control – from Westminster, making Ireland little more than an English province. Pushing this legislation through the Irish parliament at speed required much negotiation and many and varied forms of persuasion for those with

valuable and virtually hereditary parliamentary seats attached to landholdings. These included the Blackwoods, who had been baronets since 1763. In 1800 they were created Barons Dufferin and Clandeboye in the peerage of Ireland, one of the many Act of Union peerages created in that year.[2]

The Act of Union had numerous immediate and far-reaching consequences, many of which were to reverberate through Ireland and mainland Britain for generations to come. One of the consequences was, perhaps paradoxically, to provoke an increase in country house building in Ireland. As Mark Bence-Jones, the distinguished Anglo-Irish architectural historian explains, 'the popular belief that half the Irish nobility and gentry disappeared to England after the Union is not true'. Rather, as Bence-Jones points out, the upper echelons of Irish society did tend to desert Dublin when it was no longer the seat of government in Ireland, but instead of decamping to England, most spent more time on their Irish estates, where they enlarged existing houses or built new ones. In addition, many families found money was suddenly available for building because those that had lost valuable parliamentary boroughs through the Union were compensated by the British government.[3] In general terms, this is precisely what happened at Clandeboye. In the year following the Act of Union the existing house was engulfed within an ambitious new building that provided a large amount of fashionable, comfortable and convenient new accommodation.

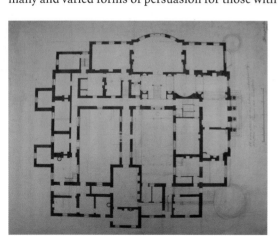

LEFT Ground-floor plan of the house drawn by Woodgate in c.1801 and as built. At the top, east, are from left to right: dining room, saloon and drawing room all served by a corridor-gallery. To the right, south, is the original entrance hall, now the library. To the north is service accommodation, and bottom, west, is the original scullery and large kitchen connected by the service corridor to the dining room. OPPOSITE Looking east through the former scullery and kitchen and along the stairs in the service corridor – all transformed in magical manner by Lord Dufferin around 1869 to form a new entrance vestibule and double-height hall as part of a processional route from a new west entrance door to the gallery and main rooms in the eastern portion of the house.

The Blackwoods were typical of the Protestant
ascendancy families that dominated social, political
and economic life in much of Ireland, and
particularly in Ulster. They settled in Ulster in the
early seventeenth century – probably during the
1620s – having arrived from Scotland. It seems they
received no grant of land or other inducement from
the English authorities, but were originally tenants
of the powerful Hamilton family. By 1688, though,
they had become landowners in their own right,
'having bought the freehold of Ballyleidy [as until
the 1840s the Clandeboye estate was called] and
other Hamilton townlands sold to pay the debts of
the second lord Clanbrasil'.[4]

Through advantageous marriage alliances
and sagacious hard work the Blackwoods gradually
built up a large estate in Ulster with, at its heart,
the estate of Ballyleidy. One of the most important
marriage alliances was with the Hamilton family
itself. The Hamiltons, based at Killyleagh Castle,
County Down, had possessed the title of Viscount
Clandeboye since 1622 (the name itself an evocation
of the ancient O'Neill family, which was once a
power in the region as the Lords of Clann Aodh
Buide or Clandeboye), with the 2nd Viscount
created the Earl of Clanbrassil in 1647. It seems
clear that the Blackwoods hoped to assimilate
with the Hamiltons, to assume their titles and
ancient pedigree and prestige – even, in a sense,
their identity.

Frederick, Lord Dufferin's father – Price
Blackwood, the 4th Baron Dufferin and Clandeboye
– inherited the title in 1839, after years of service
as an officer in the Royal Navy. Due to his father's
absence, Frederick, who was born in 1826, was
brought up largely by his mother, Helen. Of Irish
and Scottish parents, she was a woman of strong
character and – for the age – of marked individuality
and independence of mind. She was born Helen
Selina Sheridan in England in 1807, the
granddaughter of the Irish playwright and theatre-
owner Richard Brinsley Sheridan. During her
lifetime, Helen established a reputation as a poet,
playwright, composer and songwriter, as well as

ABOVE *Lord Dufferin's mother,
Helen, in the 1840s.*
OPPOSITE *Killyleagh Castle,
County Down, the ancestral
home of Lord Dufferin's wife,
Harriet.*

being acknowledged as a witty society beauty.

Helen had tremendous ambition for her son. She wanted him to rise and be a leader of men, preferably within the structure of the Irish or, better still, the English peerage. Frederick's father was an Irish baron, the lowest rank of hereditary peerage, but Helen was determined that Frederick would, through his talents and achievements, rise higher and become a power in the land. While Helen and young Frederick lived together – in Clandeboye House during the summer and in Long Ditton, west London during the rest of the year – strong bonds formed between them. The first half of the nineteenth century was an age of strong, sometimes maudlin, sentimentality, when all doted on their 'home sweet home' and sons were encouraged to love their mothers with an almost religious veneration. This seems to have been the case in Clandeboye, but with an almost obsessive intensity. But Helen's love for her son did not stand in the way of his education and early introduction into the world of power. It was important that Frederick should receive the training to rule, and make

essential connections at an early age, so in the mid-1830s he was sent to one of Britain's premier public schools, Eton College, near the royal castle at Windsor. Despite being an only child from a pampered matriarchal home, Frederick seems to have flourished at Eton, where he was nicknamed 'the orator' because of his precocious ability as a public speaker. No doubt he was confident and educationally in advance of his fellows due to the careful and inspiring tutelage he had received from his ambitious and intelligent mother. But Frederick did suffer a sadness at Eton. It was here, in 1841, that Frederick saw his father, Price, Lord Dufferin, for the last time. Soon afterwards Price Temple-Blackwood died in strange and suggestive circumstances. He took a morphine overdose while on a steamship travelling across the Irish Sea. It can only be assumed that he had been in great pain for some period of time, the result of an ailment that is now unknown. So, at the age of only fifteen, Frederick became the 5th Baron Dufferin and Clandeboye.

A few years later, fulfilling his mother's plan to give him the education essential for a putative member of the ruling elite, Lord Dufferin went to Christ Church, Oxford, the university's then-grandest college, with a reputation for grooming high-flying aristocratic statesmen and politicians. Lord Dufferin, by nature sensible and modest, seems to have been alarmed by the undergraduate life he led in Canterbury Quad, the portion of the college reserved for lords and well-connected gentlemen. Dufferin wrote to his mother, 'We dine at a table by ourselves, raised on a dais at the top of the hall, our gowns are made of silk and a gold tassel is put on the cap [indicating their fathers were peers], all others are interdicted from keeping servants and horses; we are not even expected to do so much in our college examinations; in short there is no circumstance in which we are not given the advantage, consequently we are tempted to think that there must be some intrinsic merit in ourselves to deserve such attention and begin to look with contempt upon those our fellow students, who are not treated with like respect.'[5]

The Great Famine

But the world of exclusive privilege at Oxford was not destined to last long. In 1847 Lord Dufferin felt compelled to re-enter the painful and brutal real world. He journeyed to Ireland in an attempt to understand the fullness of the catastrophe that had fallen upon the country and, in some small way, to help. In 1845 Ireland suffered a famine that was to define the nation and provoke a diaspora that would, in turn, define many emerging nations around the world – notably the United States and British territories in North America and Australia – as they absorbed tens of thousands of hard-pressed and often embittered Irish peasants and destitute rural families. Dufferin was determined not to spare himself, and went to Skibbereen in the southwest of Ireland to observe the worst of the famine. Like his mother, Dufferin expressed himself directly and easily through writing, and instantly penned and published in 1847 a *Narrative of a Journey from Oxford to Skibbereen During the Year of the Irish Famine*. The

pamphlet was intended both to confirm the horrors of the famine that – to Dufferin's amazement – many complacent, ignorant and distant English doubted, and to serve as a call to action. As Dufferin put it: 'Within two days journey from the richest and most thriving country in the world [is] found a town plunged in the lowest depths of misery and desolation.' Dufferin pulled no punches and his text must have shocked many: 'The scenes we have witnessed [are] equal to any [horror] that has been recorded in history ... famine, typhus fever [and] dysentery are sweeping away the whole population ... dead bodies [lay] putrifying, in the midst of the sick remnant of their families, none strong enough to remove them, until the rats and decay made it difficult to recognize they had been human beings.' When Dufferin and his party attempted to distribute bread, a dangerous riot ensued, so they were forced 'to throw it out of the window', which provoked 'fighting [and] screaming' as the crowd, 'with an insatiable expression' of hunger, swayed 'to and fro ... as it rushed in the direction of some morsel'. This was powerful journalism, almost sensationalist – an eye-witness account from an informed correspondent, seemingly objective yet impassioned and calculated to impress, to pierce the heart. Helen must have been impressed by a son's novice effort to use his pen to rouse the public to take action in the face of such a calamity.

The immediate cause of the famine was a blight that destroyed three successive crops of potatoes, long the staple diet of the working people of

LEFT ABOVE *The sixteenth-century Great Hall at Christ Church, Oxford, where Lord Dufferin was an undergraduate in the 1840s.*
LEFT BELOW *Illustration from the 1840s, showing famine victims in Ireland.*
OPPOSITE *The hall at Clandeboye, created in the late* 1860s *out of the original kitchen, looking west through the entrance vestibule to the front door. On the walls of the hall is a collection of arms from India, and Egyptian stone fragments from Deir el-Bahri. On the floor is the skin of a tiger shot by Dufferin in India in the 1880s.*

Ireland; and in the six years after 1845, the population fell by up to 25 per cent, with around a million dying from starvation and disease, and another million emigrating in a desperate attempt to find life and sustenance overseas. The wider cause was the long-established abject poverty of much of Ireland, where landlords – many absent – grabbed what they could in rents and made few wealth-generating improvements to their estates. The census of 1841 revealed that half of the families in Ulster fell into the poorest category, which meant that they lived on the very edge of subsistence.

Lord Dufferin's response to the horrors he had witnessed was not just to pen a piece of journalistic outrage in an attempt to get the authorities to act, but – much to his credit – to act himself. He returned to Oxford, campaigned among his fellow undergraduates and wrote in a letter to his mother that 'the news we have brought back has made a great impression upon the men here. They are squeezing money from every possible sponge.'[6] Eventually, Dufferin was able to contribute £1000 (about £60,000 today) to the Relief Fund. This was, of course, little more than a gesture, but a great deal more than was done by Lord John Russell, the Liberal prime minister from June 1846 to February 1852, whose administration merely uttered its laissez-faire opinion that 'Irish property must support Irish poverty'.[7] The bankrupt and breathtakingly thoughtless nature of this attitude is really self-evident. The general mismanagement of 'Irish property' by the small minority of Anglo-Irish families that owned a vast amount of the land was to a significant degree responsible for the poverty of the people and the plight that now overtook them. In these circumstances, how could 'Irish property'-owning interests alone solve the immediate catastrophe of famine that was the result of generations of poverty? In fact many, in an attempt to deal with the problem by cutting rents, merely went bankrupt, had to sell their lands and houses, in the process creating more chaos and unemployment.

Lord Dufferin, who had inherited control of 18,000 acres in Ulster when he came of age in 1847,

seems to have been aware that, in the dreadful circumstances of the famine and with his new legal responsibilities, he should return as soon as possible to Ireland to manage his estate and take what action he could to aid his hard-pressed tenants. He terminated his studies in Oxford and, without taking a degree, returned to Clandeboye. He journeyed through his estate to take stock, and in 1848 wrote to his mother that 'a more melancholy and saddening employment can scarcely be conceived'.[8] He reduced tenants' rents and set up work-creation projects on his land, including the formation of two large lakes and islands in front of Clandeboye House – an effort that not only gave unemployed tenants some paid work, but beautified the immediate setting of the house. At the time Lord Dufferin's own financial situation was far from satisfactory – indeed, it was somewhat alarming – so his rent reductions and the capital costs of estate improvements were actions he could not really afford. In 1847 he had debts totalling £29,261 (about £1.7 million today), and although the income from his estates was around £18,000 per annum, a large number of annuities reduced this to just over £4615.[9] Dufferin was living way beyond his means and something had to be done.

LORD-IN-WAITING TO VICTORIA
One of the things that he did was, it seems, to indulge in lavish escapism. The pressing problem of offering some aid to his desperate tenants was, for Lord Dufferin, offset by parallel activities that now, by contrast, seem utterly bizarre. In 1849, fresh from witnessing the agonies of the famished and impoverished Irish peasants and tenants, he accepted Lord John Russell's patronage and was appointed a lord-in-waiting to Queen Victoria. This post, no doubt the result of Lady Dufferin's ambitious lobbying on her son's behalf, involved much courtiership at various royal palaces, and allowed Dufferin to forge a strong relationship with the young and newly married queen. Lord Dufferin was to become part of her intimate entourage and, while the Irish poor starved in their tens of thousands and while in England working men

> **❝** Victoria was evidently delighted by Dufferin's company and appearance. When he was first suggested for the post, the young queen playfully demurred, suggesting that he was 'much too good looking and captivating'…

ABOVE LEFT *Some of the artefacts in the entrance vestibule, including, on the left, a temple bell from Burma, curling stones from Canada and a model of Dufferin's schooner, The Foam.*

ABOVE RIGHT *A rhinoceros head sits on top of a 4000-year-old Egyptian altar from Mentuhotep II's temple and tomb at Deir el-Bahri, excavated by Dufferin in 1859–60.*

campaigned for social and political reform and for the vote through the Chartist movement, he amused the queen at court and accompanied her on expeditions to grand country houses. Victoria was evidently delighted by Dufferin's company and appearance. When he was first suggested for the post, the young queen playfully demurred, suggesting that he was 'much too good looking and captivating', and when he did become part of her court, Victoria 'would point and giggle and tease him about his long poetic hair'.[10]

Lord Dufferin kept a journal during his time as a lord-in-waiting, and this reveals much about court life, his character and his relationship with the queen. Volumes of the journal, typed and bound, are kept in the library at Clandeboye House. I browsed through them and found myself entering the long-lost world of the young Victoria who, in 1849, was happily married to Prince Albert, only thirty years of age and still girl-like in her love of fun and games, of country house visiting and hosting dinner parties.

All, of course, was to change dramatically in 1861, when Albert died and Victoria was plunged into deep gloom and perpetual mourning.

In his journal for 1849 Lord Dufferin recorded that on 17 November he was at Windsor Castle with the queen and court when the Duke of Wellington came for dinner, during which he sat next to the Duchess of Kent and then 'played at patience with her and ye Duke'. The following day Dufferin went 'to chapel with ye Queen', was joined once again by the duke for dinner and then 'at ye Queen's table played with ivory letters' – clearly some early form of Scrabble because Dufferin was mortified when he 'mispelt [sic] my word'.

Despite the escapism and elevated social rounds of the royal court, Dufferin could not entirely escape his money worries. A journal entry dated London, 15 March 1850, states that he 'played tennis' and was 'offered £1,000 to be re-payed [sic] at 5 per cent by £100 a year instalments'. While brooding on this offer, Dufferin went to 'Dinner at ye palace ... sat next to the Duchess of Kent [and] when sitting at ye Queen's table ... they all burst out laughing at my melancholy face.'[11] Poor Lord Dufferin! Even when sitting with the queen, he couldn't stop fretting over money.

The increasingly intimate relationship that grew between Victoria and Dufferin gave him the queen's ear. He might well have used his position to attempt to persuade her to bring pressure on her government to offer direct aid to the Irish famine victims. There is, however, no record that he did, and no royal action to suggest that Victoria had indeed been nobbled by the decorative Dufferin.

A FANTASTICAL REBUILDING SCHEME
As well as living within the elevated and rarefied atmosphere of the royal court, Lord Dufferin also escaped into architectural fantasy of the highest order. Despite his debts, in 1848 he commissioned William Burn, one of Britain's most fashionable country house architects to draw up a lavish scheme for remodelling Clandeboye House in the then-fashionable Jacobethan style. Dufferin knew he could not afford the work but, presumably, just toying with the idea implied he had

LEFT ABOVE & BELOW *Queen Victoria and family in the mid nineteenth century with the Duke of Wellington at Windsor Castle. It was at this time that Lord Dufferin (left) was a lord-in-waiting. His relationship with the queen became close and long-lasting.*
OPPOSITE *The ascending 'procession route' in Clandeboye House, leading east from the entrance and hall to the heart of the house. The Burmese Buddha, surveying all who enter the house, is a recent acquisition.*

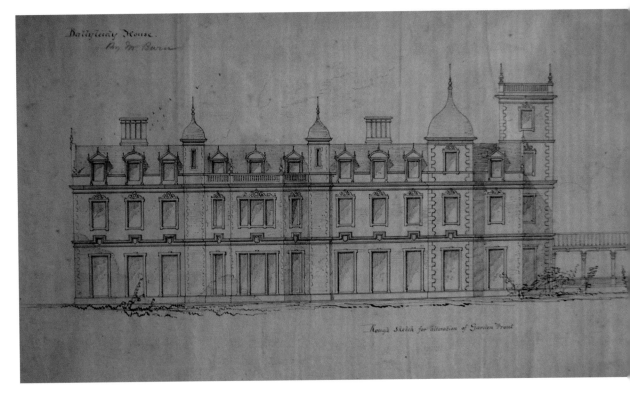

the means to rebuild in the manner and style of his far richer English and Scottish peers. The Burn scheme involved a substantial reworking and rebuilding of Clandeboye to create a Jacobethan confection. Nothing happened, and Dufferin seems to have entered a world of even more fantastic escapism. He appears to have virtually given up all ambition of a worthwhile public life and decided, despite his mounting debts, to enjoy himself. While the nation was rocked by the mismanagement and grim casualties of the Crimean War, Lord Dufferin was absorbed by thoughts of foreign travel. The war, between Britain, France and the Ottoman Empire on one hand and Russia on the other, started in October 1853, and in 1854 Dufferin was involved in a minor way as an attaché for peace talks with Russia. But for him this seems to have taken second place to planning his big adventure. In 1856, just as the Crimean War ground to a bloody and humiliating end for all involved, Dufferin set sail on a four-month journey. Despite his debts, he had acquired a handsome schooner named *The Foam*, and, with his doughty crew, cruised the beautiful,

"Lord Dufferin and 'thirty souls', as he put it in his journal – including his mother Helen – along with a small menagerie comprising three dogs, one jackdaw, two parrots, one goat and one sheep – set sail from Portsmouth … and headed for Alexandria in Egypt…

ABOVE William Burn's scheme of 1848 for re-cladding the east elevation of Clandeboye House in a rather pallid neo-Jacobean style.
OVERLEAF The corridor-gallery, looking south, is one of the most successful spaces created by Woodgate in 1801–4. The staircase, also by Woodgate, is embellished with a pair of spiralling narwhal tusks, presumably collected by Dufferin during his journey of 1856 to the Arctic.

remote and dangerous waters of the North Atlantic and Arctic. One more expression of escapism? Perhaps. But during the adventure, he kept a journal and took daguerreotypes, and when he returned he wrote it up. His book, *Letters from High Latitudes*, was a best seller, and Dufferin immediately gained a reputation as an intrepid traveller and, what is more, during his visits to such remote regions as Iceland, he was perceived – and acted – as Britain's formal emissary. He clearly loved the role and was evidently rather good at it. Also, it seems that during these travels Lord Dufferin started to collect exotic items, such as a polar bear skin and narwhal tusks, that were to become the core of his collection at Clandeboye House.

The experience of heroic travel and the acclaim his book received were in many ways the making of the young man. Lord Dufferin gained confidence and reputation, but still did not get engaged with national events. In May 1857, mutiny broke out among Sepoy regiments in India and spread with alarming speed. Many British were killed, and the imperial grip on India was seriously challenged in turn, as the insurrection was quelled, because many Indians were killed, often as part of a policy of revenge and terror. By July 1858 the insurrection was as good as over and the wave of panic that rattled Britain was past. But within this epic and tragic tale, Lord Dufferin – the future Viceroy of India – played no part, indeed seems to have had little interest. He spent his time in Ireland and England socialising, shooting and planning his next adventure. In September 1858, even before the insurrection in India was officially over, he set sail again, this time heading east through the Mediterranean. Lord Dufferin and 'thirty souls', as he put it in his journal – including his mother Helen – along with a small menagerie comprising three dogs, one jackdaw, two parrots, one goat and one sheep – set sail from Portsmouth aboard the steam yacht *Erminia* and headed for Alexandria in Egypt. They arrived in late December and pottered about, seeing the sights and making the social round. For example, Lord Dufferin recorded in his journal that on 17 December 'my mother went to dine with the Sultana. She was much amused'.[12] After Christmas the party steamed down the Nile. This was a journey that was, in certain key respects, to change Lord Dufferin's life and to define the future of Clandeboye House.

ADVENTURES IN EGYPT

Since Napoleon Bonaparte's invasion of Egypt in 1798 and Horatio Nelson's epic victory over the French fleet in Aboukir Bay near Alexandria in the same year, the culture and architecture of ancient Egypt had become better known and inspired a mania for exploration, collecting artefacts, and even a fashion for Egyptian-style architecture. In this context it was not surprising that the inquisitive Lord Dufferin should make his way towards the great temples of ancient Thebes, part of the riverside city of Luxor. But he wanted to be more than just a tourist. He landed on the West Bank of the Nile at Luxor – the land of the dead of ancient Thebes – and made his way to the then very fragmentary and mysterious remains of mortuary temples and tombs.

At Deir el-Bahri, nestling below hills just to the east of what was to become known as the Valley of the Kings, Dufferin decided to fund the excavation of an ancient site. He purchased permission to dig from the Egyptian authorities, located a young English archaeologist named Cyril C. Graham in Cairo, and embarked upon a most extraordinary enterprise. The site he had chosen to explore turned out to be the 4000-year-old mortuary temple and tomb of the eleventh-dynasty Mentuhotep II, the first pharaoh of the Egyptian Middle Kingdom. The remains were fragmentary but it emerged that the structure was organized around an east–west axis and consisted of a causeway and ramps leading to a succession of raised and colonnaded terraces terminating, at the east end, with a tomb and shrine cut into the sacred hill. The temple was clearly conceived as a route or journey, from large and open courts at its east end – arguably representing the world of man and the living – to the world of death, rebirth and the gods within the elevated, shady and secreted hypostyle hall and shrine at its west end.

Lord Dufferin's team soon excavated a number of objects of spectacular interest, including a vast granite altar weighing several tons and bearing the eighteen names and titles of Mentuhotep II and images of offerings, and in the centre entwined lotus and papyrus stems and flowers flanked by kneeling Nile gods. These were spells to sustain and ease the passage of the soul of the pharaoh through the underworld and to ensure his survival on his way to rebirth. Dufferin's team also excavated a portion of one of the columns bearing an image of the god Horus as a falcon, the name of the pharaoh and a proclamation that he would live forever; a fragment of an offering table showing creatures of sacrifice – a heron, geese and a trussed ox – and the inscription that these were all for the god Ra Horus; and the lower legs and feet of a larger-than-life standing statue that a hieroglyphic inscription reveals to be that of Mentuhotep II.

But Lord Dufferin's greatest find, artistically and in terms of power and presentation, was a seated limestone statue (34 inches high) of Amun, the great god of Thebes. In his left hand he grasps an *ankh*, the token of life, on his girdle is the token of the goddess Isis, and on his face is a benign but penetrating gaze. After some trials and tribulations Lord Dufferin managed, in the early 1860s, to get all these major finds carried to Clandeboye. This was done with the full agreement of the Egyptian authorities, who regarded the objects as Dufferin's legitimate property since he had purchased the right to dig and spent his own money on the excavation.[13]

Later discoveries about Lord Dufferin's objects, and about the temple and tomb of Mentuhotep II, have proved particularly fascinating. In the very late nineteenth century, excavations of the site took place immediately to the north of Mentuhotep's temple, and here was uncovered the sensational mortuary temple of Hatshepsut, which, though long buried and partly collapsed, was revealed to be one of the architecturally most significant and best preserved of its kind in Egypt. It now seems incredible that Lord Dufferin dug only yards away from this temple without knowing of its existence, for all was obscured. Hatshepsut's temple was constructed nearly 500 years after that of Mentuhotep II, but with its precise east–west orientation, causeway, ramps leading up to colonnaded terraces, and shrine at the west end, is now acknowledged to be an enlarged copy of Mentuhotep's temple. The origin and nature of Lord

LEFT ABOVE *View of Deir el-Bahri taken by J.P. Sebah around 1890 on the West Bank of the Nile at Luxor. This shows the site of Mentuhotep II's mortuary temple and tomb much as Dufferin would have known it in 1859.*
LEFT BELOW *Detail of an offering table, from the temple* of Mentuhotep II and now in the hall at Clandeboye House, showing creatures, including a heron and a trussed ox, to be sacrificed for the ancient Egyptian sun god, Ra Horus. OPPOSITE *Head of a Buddhist celestial brought back in 1886 by Lord Dufferin from Mandalay.*

Dufferin's Amun has also been revealed by later
scholars. It seems the statue shows the eighteenth-
dynasty pharaoh Amunhotep in the form of the god
Amun. The discovery of Amunhotep's image in
Mentuhotep's temple is odd but explained by the
fact that Hatshepsut, when constructing her
mortuary temple, cleared away the 200-year-old
temple of Amunhotep that stood on the site she
wanted, but preserved its statues by placing them in
the nearby temple of Mentuhotep.

Lord Dufferin returned from Egypt a wiser man
enriched with objects, insights and perceptions that
were to greatly influence the remodelling of
Clandeboye. But before this took place, Dufferin's
experiences in the Middle East obtained for him a
post that, arguably, launched him fair and square
on his sparkling career as diplomat, imperial
administrator and arbiter. In 1860 the British
government appointed him its representative on
the Five Powers commission that met at Damascus
in Syria and was charged with investigating the

> **When Lord Dufferin returned
> to Clandeboye he found his
> extraordinary homage to his
> mother – Helen's Tower –
> nearly complete…**

ABOVE *Helen's Tower, located
on high land on the Clandeboye
estate, was designed in 1850 by
William Burn and completed
by Lord Dufferin in 1861 in
honour of his mother.*

massacre of Maronites by Druses. It was noted that Lord Dufferin behaved with impeccable fairness and compassion, and displayed great diplomatic skill. He had, in a sense, found his career.

HELEN'S TOWER – A TRIBUTE
FROM SON TO MOTHER

When Dufferin returned to Clandeboye he found his extraordinary homage to his mother – Helen's Tower – nearly complete. Designed by William Burn ten years earlier in the manner of a sixteenth-century Scottish tower house, the finishing touches were made in 1861 when a number of brass panels were installed in an upper-level reading room fitted with oak panels, Tudor Gothic detail and window seats. Two of the brass panels were engraved with poems proclaiming the eternal love between mother and son. One shone, as if lettered on burnished gold, with a poem that had been written by Helen in 1847 to commemorate Lord Dufferin's twenty-first birthday. Entitled *Fiat Lux* (Let there be light), Helen's poem starts by asking, 'How shall I bless thee?' and then reflects that 'Human love is all too poor in passionate words: The heart aches with a sense above all language that lips afford. Therefore a symbol shall express my love – a thing not rare nor strange, but yet eternal, measureless, knowing no shadow and no change … light.' In reply Lord Dufferin commissioned the leading English poet of the day, Alfred, Lord Tennyson, to put his filial emotions into words. Duly the sonorous lord produced a punchy little poem:

> Helen's Tower, here I stand,
> Dominant over sea and land.
> Son's love built me, and I hold,
> Mother's love in lettered gold.
> Would my granite girth were strong
> as either love, to last as long.

Rarely in Romantic Victorian architecture was such an exact and explicit demonstration made of the endless love felt between an adoring parent and devoted child. Given the nature of this close relationship between mother and son, what happened next was either peculiar or, perhaps, inevitable. In 1862 Lord Dufferin married Harriet Rowan-Hamilton, a cousin and a member of the Hamilton clan of Killyleagh Castle. Subsequently, Dufferin added, by royal licence, Hamilton to his surname and formally ended a long-running and petty dispute between the two families over the ownership of Killyleagh Castle.

TWO WEDDINGS AND A FUNERAL

A contemporary watercolour of a key moment at the wedding hangs to this day in the gallery of Clandeboye House. It shows the couple – Harriet, the new Lady Dufferin, veiled and in her pure white wedding dress, with Lord Dufferin by her side – entering the very same gallery after their wedding at Killyleagh. Throngs of schoolgirls throw flower petals below the feet of the couple as they walk towards the staircase ornamented with the tall, spiralling narwhal tusks that Lord Dufferin acquired in the Arctic in 1856 and that still grace the gallery. This is the start of the wedding reception, all the numerous guests appear happy – as indeed they should. But one very important person was not among their number – Lord Dufferin's mother! Exactly why she was absent no one knows. There are many possible reasons. She was ill; she was in some way jealous of the bride; she felt abandoned; or, perhaps, it was because Helen had become closely involved with a man seventeen years her junior and an acquaintance of her son. For years Lord Gifford had courted Helen and she, out of propriety, had rejected his offers of marriage. But in 1862 things came to a head when Lord Gifford was seriously injured. Out of pity, she explained, so that she could comfort and nurse Gifford openly and in a manner she thought respectable, Helen agreed to marriage. So on 13 October 1862, ten days before her son's planned marriage to a woman seventeen years his junior, Helen married a man who was seventeen years *her* junior. It must be assumed that Helen was absent from her son's wedding because she was on her honeymoon, nursing a new husband who turned out to be terminally ill. Within two weeks of their marriage, Gifford was dead.

How Lord Dufferin took this most unconventional marriage and its tragic conclusion is unknown, but it seems that the deep and mutual love between mother and son survived. This is in part confirmed by a melancholy document that remains, lodged in lofty isolation, in the library of Clandeboye House. It is Helen's 'death journal', which she started in January 1867, when she knew she was dying of breast cancer and had only a few, increasingly painful, months left to live. The journal was written for her son and to be read after her death. As Helen explained: 'My dearly loved and loving son, I shall keep this little journal of my thoughts and innermost feelings for you as some things to speak to you when I am no longer with you.' In the following, densely written pages, Helen does indeed record her thoughts, her feelings, her sorrows and her suffering: 'You know well that I should ask not to be separated from you in Death,

whom I have loved so infinitely beyond any other created being. But He [God] has been so merciful to me. I have you to comfort and support me through my last trial.'[14] And Helen sought to justify her behaviour to her cherished son. She admitted that 'after you' she had 'dearly loved' not Lord Dufferin's long-dead father, but 'my poor, affectionate faithful Gifford'. What could Lord Dufferin have made of these 'innermost feelings' when he eventually read the journal? This is high drama on a minuscule scale, the small, leather-bound journal still quakes with emotion and shocks with revelations, some veiled, some explicit and raw. The last entry Helen made is dated Friday, 15 March 1867: 'last night I could hardly refrain from praying that this time of trial may not be greatly prolonged. But what am I that I presume to choose times and seasons for God's judgement and mercy.' I stare at these stoic words in the journal and notice that one of the letters is smudged by water, perhaps by a teardrop? Less than three months later Helen was dead.

During this period of emotional turmoil – between Helen's marriage in October 1862 and her death in June 1867 – Lord Dufferin veered between pondering in public on Ireland's politically fraught economic problems and throwing himself into highly personal and fantastical projects for rebuilding Clandeboye House. His personal

LEFT ABOVE *A watercolour showing Lord Dufferin leading his bride, Harriet, into Clandeboye House after their wedding in October 1862. The couple walk from the entrance hall (now the library) into the gallery, a space that remains little changed: for example, the narwhal tusks shown in the distance in the watercolour are still in situ.*
LEFT BELOW *Harriet in the mid-1880s, when wife of the Viceroy of India.*
OPPOSITE *The fireplace in the Tudor Gothic library of c.1860 in Helen's Tower.*

observations of suffering during the famine led him to bleakly conclude that the country contained too many people for the available agricultural land, and in 1867, in *Irish Emigration and the Tenure of Land in Ireland*,[15] he argued the case for emigration as a solution to unemployment, poverty and famine. Naturally this proposed policy to export the nation's poor raised many issues, both ethical and practical, and became increasingly unpopular with Irish Nationalists and the Roman Catholic Church. An alternative solution to the problem of famine and political unrest was not to enforce emigration, but to make significant amounts of land available to the poor in the hope that they could then fend for themselves more effectively. This suggestion, of course, horrified Ireland's landowning community, who realized that such a policy must ultimately eat away at their assets and, in defence of his property and of the rights of Irish landowners, Dufferin once again took up his pen and in 1868 published *Mr. Mill's Plan for the Pacification of Ireland Examined by Lord Dufferin*.[16] John Stuart Mill's plan, as Dufferin

ABOVE *Detail from the last page of Helen's death journal of 1867. Dying painfully from breast cancer, she leaves intimate messages, offering love and advice to her son Lord Dufferin. In the left-hand margin is a smudge, caused perhaps by a falling tear.*

BELOW *A design of the late 1860s produced for Lord Dufferin by Lynn for a huge, Scottish-style neo-medieval house on a virgin site at Grey Point, Belfast Lough.*

characterized it, consisted of 'landed estates of all proprietors' being 'brought to a forced sale, their price fixed at the discretion of parliamentary commissioners' and the 'vacated property ... handed over to that section of the Irish agricultural class who may happen to be in occupation of farms at the moment the Act receives Royal Assent.'[17] As Dufferin made clear, this would, for many, mean an injustice and the end of the great Irish estates and the contribution they made to the economy of the land. To his mind, giving rights of ownership to tenants would solve nothing. Indeed it would, he argued, make matters worse by in effect substituting 'a crowd of needy landlords for the present more affluent proprietors' and make life worse for the labouring class, for smaller landlords would be less forgiving than the 'affluent' great estates.

MORE ARCHITECTURAL ESCAPISM AND LAND REFORM

Lord Dufferin's escape into an intensely private architectural wonderland – in such stark contrast to his public utterances on major political and social issues – continued in most dramatic manner in the mid-1860s, when, having dropped Burn, he commissioned the then much-admired, English-based Gothic Revival architect Benjamin Ferrey to produce a scheme for remodelling Clandeboye House. Ferrey, no doubt working closely with Dufferin, envisaged recladding the existing house and extending it with a high-roofed tower and crow-step gables to produce a medieval and sixteenth-century-style Scottish castle. Although Ferrey did design and execute Helen's Bay station, nothing came of his scheme for Clandeboye House, which was hardly surprising since Lord Dufferin simply could not afford such projects. At this time he was slipping deeper into debt and becoming ever more embroiled in arguments over land reform and tenants' rights. Despite Lord Dufferin's affiliations with the Liberal party, his opinions about the 'Irish Question' were not heeded by William Ewart Gladstone when he won the 1868 general election. Within two years, the First Irish Land Act was drafted and passed through both houses of

parliament. It was a weak and compromised piece of legislation, but did, for the first time, increase – in principle at least – the rights of tenants in Ireland. It offered protection, compensation to tenants if evicted for reasons other than non-payment of rent, and made government money available – at very good terms – to those tenants wishing to buy the land they worked, but only if their landlords agreed to sell. Although weak, the Act did challenge existing laissez-faire legislation and the absolute rights of property and of landlords. Lord Dufferin opposed not just the Act, but the thinking and ultimate intentions behind it. This isolated him from Gladstone and from the Liberal party, so it was at this time, in the very early 1870s, that Dufferin realized he had no future in party politics and that, if he wanted public office, it would have to be in the realm of diplomacy and imperial administration.

While locked in these debates, Dufferin, despite his debts, continued to spend money on architecture. He was clearly addicted to building, and lived through the imagination and the construction of castles in the air. In the late 1860s, after the termination of his relationship with Benjamin Ferrey, Dufferin turned to the Belfast architect William Henry Lynn. By the end of the decade Lynn had produced a lavish folio of detailed designs – plans, sections, elevations, perspectives – that suggest Lord Dufferin was well and truly detached from reality. Under Dufferin's guidance and inspiration, Lynn produced a scheme for rebuilding Clandeboye, with the Woodgate house reclad in French Renaissance manner, towered and pinnacled and with a vast Scottish baronial tower rising on the site of the original entrance hall. Almost simultaneously, Lynn designed a new house for Dufferin, at Grey Point on Belfast Lough near Helen's Bay, that was conceived as a small medieval town with towers, a series of mighty gates, battlemented walls, bastions and courts.

Needless to say, nothing of these fantasies was realized, but that is not to say that nothing happened at Clandeboye House. Records are now scarce and obscure, but it would seem that, even while Dufferin was consulting with Lynn about these grandiose building plans, he was – with the Belfast building contractor Mr Henry – making relatively modest and presumably temporary alterations to the house, effectively acting as his own architect. These revolved around a most interesting decision Lord Dufferin made in the late 1860s. He would turn the house back to front.

The 1804 Woodgate house had its main entrance in the centre of the south elevation, and this was approached via drives from the south and southwest. Lord Dufferin decided to turn the entrance hall into a library and make the main entry, from the west, into the back, or service portion, of the house. This meant that the entry drive would come from the north, offering – rather awkwardly – the stables, walled garden and service range of the house as the first sights to arriving visitors. This strategy also meant that the Woodgate scullery,

vaulted kitchen and service corridor – rising up from west to east to the dining room behind the east elevation – had to be transformed into a sequence of entry halls and a corridor-gallery. The clear advantages of this curious scheme were first, that it would be economic in realization, for it involved utilizing the existing plan and making only modest physical alterations, and second, that for minimal outlay Lord Dufferin acquired a series of new reception rooms and a lot of extra room and wall space for the display of his rapidly increasing collection of objects. All well and good, but there might have been a little more inspiration behind Lord Dufferin's scheme than is generally recognized or acknowledged, more meaning and intention than merely the creation of gallery space on the cheap.

EGYPT IN IRELAND

Standing at the new main entrance, placed asymmetrically in the low, long, largely blank and unbecoming wall forming the west elevation of the house, it is possible, with a little imagination, to see the whole thing differently. Surely Lord Dufferin, when sketching out his alterations in the late 1860s, was thinking of his tomb-exploring days in Egypt a decade earlier. The anonymous and blank west wall is reminiscent of the outer walls of tombs and many temples that Dufferin would have known and that give little away about the wonders secreted inside. And when you open the simple main west door at Clandeboye it is, in a sense, like breaking the seal

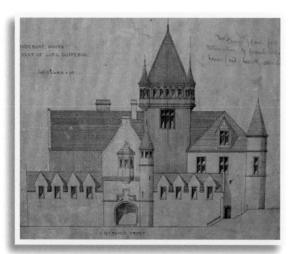

LEFT ABOVE *Benjamin Ferrey's design of the mid 1860s for remodelling and extending Clandeboye House in medieval and sixteenth-century manner.* LEFT BELOW *Henry Lynn's scheme for transforming Clandeboye House into a* medieval fairy-tale castle. OPPOSITE *The library, probably created during the 1870s, within the original entrance hall. Extended to form a near double-cube volume, the library in now the convivial heart of the house.*

on an Egyptian tomb. The door opens to reveal treasures and – more significant – the plan and route into and through the house seems inspired by the plan of mortuary temples and tombs like that of Mentuhotep II – Lord Dufferin's own discovery. Brilliantly, Dufferin turned the rising ground level of Woodgate's house to great advantage to create a route that ascends from ground level to entrance vestibule, to tall, baronial entrance hall, and then ascends again, via steps and landings in a long corridor-gallery, to the main reception rooms. All echoes the ramps, terraces, corridors, shrines and halls in Egyptian temples, especially those at Deir el-Bahri, as they rise from the low and open world of man to the dark, narrow, constrained and exclusive world of the gods. So Dufferin turned kitchen and service corridor into a processional route, leading from entrance door to the heart of the house via a tall hall or gallery, much as the ascending passage in the Great Pyramid in Giza passes through a tall gallery before arriving at the dark and mysterious double-cube volume that contains the sarcophagus-like ark or coffer and that appears to be the Holy of Holies of the pyramid.

Was Dufferin, in this economic scheme of transformation, truly evoking memories of Egypt? This speculation is supported by the fact that he created rooms off the central processional route, the equivalent of the shrines and treasuries in Egyptian temples – indeed, one of these rooms became his museum and the repository of some of his own treasures. But, more tellingly, Dufferin disposed his Egyptian antiquities along the processional route and, most dramatically, placed his statue of Amun to serve as the focus and visual termination of the ever-ascending journey from the front door to the heart of the house. As in an Egyptian temple, Amun was placed high up at the end of the route, to survey with its perceptive gaze all who entered the house and who ascended the processional route. Indeed, the analogy can be continued. The statue of Amun, sold in a house sale in 1937, so sadly removed, can be seen as a portal, a point of initiation past which only favoured friends and guests could proceed.[18]

Those who passed the scrutiny of Amun turned

right, then left, as if passing through a labyrinth, and found themselves in the wide gallery of the Woodgate house. The gallery runs parallel to the dining room, saloon and drawing room behind the east façade with, to its west, the noble imperial staircase of 1804. At the end of the gallery was the original entrance hall transformed by Dufferin, seemingly in around 1869, into a library. This is the ultimate point of arrival for favoured guests – a beautiful room, lustrous with the mellow leather and gilded spines of books stacked in shelves that rise virtually from floor to ceiling on all four walls. It's a place of the intellect, of learning, of meditation and repose. It is, in a sense, the Holy of Holies of Lord Dufferin's remodelled Clandeboye, the treasure room and the end of the journey through the magical interior world of the house. And, perhaps not by chance, Dufferin moved and rebuilt inner walls when he changed the room from entrance hall to library. He made the tall room longer, more into the volume of a mystic double-cube – the 2:1:1 proportion found at the heart of the Great Pyramid and that is the form of many shrines in Egyptian temples.

Frustratingly, Lord Dufferin's intentions were not documented, or if they were, the records are destroyed or currently mislaid. There are simply a number of intriguing and enigmatic comments and references. Lord Dufferin never realized any significant aspects of Lynn's proposals of the late 1860s for rebuilding Clandeboye, but the two men remained in regular contact for the next twenty years or more, forever discussing architectural matters at home and abroad. Among preserved transcripts of letters between the two men are several references to the works undertaken in the late 1860s. For example, on 13 July 1887 Dufferin wrote to Lynn about the earlier works that resulted in the 'present connexion between the hall and the gallery'.[19] Dufferin was clearly referring to the area where the statue of Amum once stood, and where the passage cranks to form the junction between the corridor from the entrance hall and the gallery in the Woodgate house. Evidently, Lynn did not approve of the way this junction was handled – therefore confirming that he was not involved and that it was

The original entrance hall … is the ultimate point of arrival for favoured guests – a beautiful room, lustrous with the mellow leather and gilded spines of books … It's a place of the intellect, of learning, of meditation and repose. It is, in a sense, the Holy of Holies of Lord Dufferin's remodelled Clandeboye…

ABOVE *The ascending corridor-gallery in Clandeboye House in the 1890s, when the exquisite statue of Amun, which had been excavated by Dufferin's team at Deir el-Bahri, still occupied its commanding position at the top of the staircase. The processional route and sequence of halls created by Dufferin seem to have been inspired by ancient Egyptian precedent.*

the work of Dufferin and Mr Henry, the Belfast contractor. This view was confirmed by Mark Bence-Jones, who, in his 1970 article in *Country Life*, refers to Lord Dufferin's letters to Lynn of 1887 and 1888 about a proposed grand new hall for Clandeboye, and concludes that Dufferin was finally obliged to make do 'with the halls which he had formed out of the old scullery and kitchen many years before'.[20]

Lynn would, no doubt, have preferred a grand and conventional staircase rising straight and direct from corridor to hall rather than the circuitous and mysterious affair concocted by Dufferin and Henry. Dufferin admitted in his letter to Lynn that the existing winding junction between corridor and gallery that 'you observed one day with just professional scorn' was 'the joint outcome of poor old Henry's and my own ingenuity'. With great modesty, and without offering any explanation for its form, Dufferin admitted the junction was not very 'dignified' but, he argued, 'possessed certain quaint characteristics'.[21]

These alterations were all that Dufferin was to do at Clandeboye for over twenty years because from 1872 until the mid-1890s he and his wife Harriet lived almost exclusively abroad, executing various diplomatic and ambassadorial posts. This retreat from the travails of private life in Ireland into the subsidized realm of public office came none too soon for Dufferin. In 1872 he had debts of £300,000 (about £14 million today) and the rental revenue from his Irish estates was in steady decline – indeed, his lands seem to have been leaking money, and there was little he could do to put things right. As he observed ruefully in 1874, 'Irish estates are like a sponge, and an Irish landowner is never so rich as when he is rid of his property.'[22] And this, during the late 1870s, is to a degree what Dufferin did.

DEBTS AND LAND SALES

From the 1860s Lord Dufferin borrowed money from the only people who had money to lend – Belfast manufacturers and industrialists making

fortunes from linen and ship-building. In September 1864 Andrew Mulholland, the head of a family of prosperous Belfast linen manufacturers, provided Dufferin with a mortgage of £21,000 (about £1 million today) secured against land. In 1864 Lord Dufferin received two further mortgages from Mulholland, totalling £13,000, in 1866 another £10,000, and in 1868 £20,000. By this time the Mulholland mortgages represented 40 per cent of Lord Dufferin's debts with, in 1872, the interest payments on these debts alone coming to just over £6561 for the year. The loans were made on very short terms, so by the mid-1870s, as Dr A.T. Harrison puts it, 'Dufferin was insolvent. He could no longer continue borrowing having reached the position where his future loans would be paying not just interest charges but the actual capital sums of existing debts' leading to 'the ludicrous position' where 'Dufferin would be borrowing money from Mulholland to pay back … interest and capital sums related to earlier Mulholland loans'. Dufferin's only way out of this financial mire was to sell all, or at least a major part, of his estate to turn revenue-raising assets into ready capital to pay off his creditors.

Duly, the estate sales started in 1875 and lasted until 1880. Initially, Lord Dufferin wanted to apply a condition to the sale to ensure that the disposal of his land did not dilute the power of Ulster's traditional landowning class. As Harrison explains, 'at first Dufferin wanted to restrict the sales to established gentlemen' but as the 'harsh economic

LEFT *The royal standard of the North Down Militia and Lacey-made smooth-bore percussion muskets of the 1830s ornament the entrance vestibule. The standard, dating from about 1801, proclaims loyalty to 'King and country'.*

OPPOSITE *The handsome staircase off the gallery dates from 1801–4, but the large bay window is an addition of the 1880s or 1890s. To the left and right of the staircase are Burmese state beds brought from Mandalay.*

THE PEERLESS PEER.
OR, JOHN BULL DIOGENES LOOKING FOR ANOTHER DUFFERIN.

reality of his position sank in, he had to countenance the purchase of his property by men of business and industry like Mulholland'.[23] Thus did part of Dufferin's ancestral land pass to Ulster's nouveau-riche entrepreneurs, including, of course, the Mulhollands. Despite Dufferin's eventual willingness to sell to anyone with money, the process of raising the required capital proved tough indeed. He even at one point accepted the need to sell Clandeboye House itself and its demesne. This proved not to be necessary, but by the end of this deeply troubling period Lord Dufferin's land ownership in Ulster had been reduced from the 18,000 acres he inherited to just over 6000 acres – essentially the park and estate around Clandeboye House. The result of this capitalization of assets was to settle debts, but it also, of course, dramatically reduced Lord Dufferin's income from rents. He had gained breathing space but was by no means out of the woods.

ABOVE Lord Dufferin's term as Governor General of Canada, from 1872 to 1878, was widely regarded as a great success – both by Canadians of most persuasions and by the British public. This cartoon, published on his return to Britain, shows Dufferin and his family, sorrowful at leaving Canada, being welcomed home by an approving John Bull, who is busy looking for a man 'worthy to be his successor'.

OVERLEAF Looking east, across the park towards the lake, from the large bay window in the saloon – a serene, beautiful and light-filled room.

It was during this difficult period, and just before the land sale was finally accepted as the only possible means of financial salvation, that Lord Dufferin – recently elevated in the peerage to an earl – secured his first really major public appointment. Due to political patronage (and no doubt to Dufferin's close relationship with Queen Victoria), he was in 1872 appointed Governor General of Canada. This was an important, high-profile appointment because Canada was only five years old as a nation and was suffering serious teething troubles. Great diplomatic skills would be needed to deal with a whole range of problems and to help meld the disparate North American British colonies into a dominion with a sense of unity, identity and destiny. The appointment, which brought him a generous income of around £10,000 per annum (about £460,000 today) plus expenses, also allowed Dufferin to escape the immediate worries of the Clandeboye estate, including fears that he would be shamed by being unable to sustain his accustomed lifestyle. Being made Governor General offered Dufferin a most useful role and was his social and financial salvation.

One of the major challenges facing Dufferin, as he contemplated the birth of this new imperial nation, was the hostility of a large section of the United States population to the presence of the British Empire on North American soil, who wanted the vast tracts and resources of Canada to be annexed for the enjoyment of US citizens. The nascent United States had tried to seize Britain's North American colonies during the distraction of the Napoleonic War, and provoked the war of 1812 that ended inconclusively in 1814 with no territory gained permanently by either side but with certain borders in the far west under dispute. Then, in 1866, after the American Civil War, regiments of Fenian or Nationalist Irishmen – in large part veterans of the fighting between the states – formed themselves into the Irish Republican Army and launched a series of surreptitious 'invasions' from the United States of the British colonies. These incursions were small in scale and petered out by 1871 after US

intervention, but had been intended to put pressure on the British to pull out of Ireland. Lord Dufferin had to deal with the aftermath of these disturbances as well as tackling the other great challenge – the integration of the French Canadians with their culturally very different English, Protestant Irish and Scottish fellow countrymen.

Also, when Lord Dufferin arrived in 1872, the whiff of internal rebellion lingered in the air and there was mounting pressure within British Columbia in the west to pull out of the dominion and go it alone. The rebellion revolved around the Métis, a mixed-race community formed by the intermarriage of French Canadians and Native American tribes. In the late 1860s one of the leaders of the French-speaking Métis, Louis Riel, had become involved in an armed protest against perceived discrimination that concluded with the execution of Thomas Scott, a Protestant Ulsterman (whose parents by chance were among Dufferin's tenants) who had held Riel and his companions in contempt. It emerged that the shot that killed the Ulsterman had been fired by Riel himself, and by the time Dufferin arrived in Canada, Riel had been arrested, tried, found guilty of murder and was awaiting execution. But the case was far from straightforward. Much of the French-Canadian community and many native tribes supported Riel, while much of the Anglo and Protestant population wanted him punished. Thus Dufferin found himself locked in a conundrum – if he reprieved Riel he would alienate one part of the population, and if he confirmed execution he would alienate the other part. In the end, with diplomatic skill and displaying something of the wisdom of Solomon, Dufferin confirmed that Riel should be punished, but commuted his sentence to imprisonment because Riel had helped the dominion in its resistance to Fenian invasion. In fact, Riel sought exile in the United States, where he lived for some years.

Dufferin's diplomatic skills and delicacy displayed in the Riel case, his mastery of French, sense of style and generosity as a host greatly impressed French Canadians, and did much to reconcile them to British imperial rule. Lord

Dufferin's skill in creating and sustaining harmonious relations between French-Canadian Métis and the other elements of the nation is revealed by the events that unfolded when, long after Dufferin had left, Riel returned to Canada. He became involved in the North-West Rebellion to secure Métis rights, was again arrested and in 1885 charged with high treason. With no official on hand possessed of Dufferin's astuteness, Riel was executed and turned into a divisive folk hero of the Métis and other French Canadians exasperated by British imperial rule.

As well as his positive work among the French-Canadian population, Dufferin also displayed compassion and tact towards Native American tribes, encouraging them in 1874 to 'take a patriotic pride in those characteristics of your past history [which] will add colour and interest to your existence as a distinct nationality'[24] and arguing that

their title to land ownership be recognized and treaties honoured. This made the relationship between European settlers and Native American tribes far more placid in Canada than was usual south of the border in the United States, where land greed and contempt for native rights and culture regularly led to treaties being broken and bloodshed and massacre. Indeed, Canada, when Dufferin was Governor General, had to undertake delicate negotiations with various native tribes who sought refuge in its territory from predatory and vengeful US troops. This was particularly the case in the late summer of 1876, when thousands of Sioux (Lakota) and Cheyenne under Sitting Bull took sanctuary in Canada after killing General Custer and nearly 270 of his command during the defence of their village on the Little Big Horn river in Montana.

Lord Dufferin did much to ensure the peaceful integration of the different factions, religions, races and cultures that formed the Dominion of Canada and helped secure its future as a nation and as an imperial possession for generations to come. He also, being a man addicted to architecture, tried to use his position as Governor General to realize in Canada some of the grand projects that he could not afford for himself in Ireland. In consultation with Lynn, he restored the ancient walls of Quebec, attempted to add grandiose (and not altogether archaeologically correct) city gates, and proposed the reconstruction of the Chateau St Louis. But, as in Ireland, money was a problem and most of the schemes remained unrealized.

LEFT *A terracotta statue of Lord Dufferin, garbed in the robes and uniform of Viceroy of India, that stands in the entrance hall.* OPPOSITE *Pompeian-style detail from the marriage bedroom created by Lord Dufferin in 1862 for his bride.*

When Lord Dufferin left Canada in 1878 his term as Governor General was generally regarded as a great success. During his six years in office, he had, according to his own account book, entertained – through dinners, lunches, balls and 'theatricals' – 35,838 people.[25] This is an astonishing number, but presumably a necessary action to win the hearts, minds and loyalty of many in the new nation. Some criticized him for the expenditure of public money this lavish round of entertainment cost. Others, such as his friend the Duke of Argyll, feared that such largesse would inevitably eat into Dufferin's own very limited private funds, and in the late 1870s warned him that he faced 'ruination' if he continued in his lavish lifestyle, and begged him not to be too 'Irish' and 'Sheridanish' in his reckless generosity and disregard for money.

Lord Dufferin's generosity, along with his intrepid determination to explore the nation and meet people, was without doubt one of the main reasons for the affection he'd inflamed within the hearts of many Canadians. As the *Northern Whig* of 2 May 1878 put it, Lord Dufferin's 'six years of Canadian Viceroyalty will always be regarded as a brilliant episode in the history of the Dominion. It has given great satisfaction among the colonists of all races and creeds.' Dufferin was, observed the newspaper, 'not a mere official without much sympathy for the people [but] mixed with the colonists [and] entered into the spirit of their laborious lives'.

Lord Dufferin returned only briefly to Clandeboye, but did so loaded with Native American artefacts, including an eighteenth-century Cree quill belt, snowshoes and an 'Octopus' bag dated 1873 (a gift from the Ojibwa), for display in his new entrance hall. Then, in 1879, he was sent as ambassador to imperial Russia, a most useful posting for anyone interested in gaining insights into the continuing intrigues between Russia and British India as they competed to establish and control spheres of interest and borders in the disputed 'buffer' state of Afghanistan and along the North-West Frontier with India. Lord Dufferin returned from St Petersburg with, among other trophies, the skins of two infant bears that he'd shot and had stuffed and mounted to serve as snarling gate guardians along his processional route at Clandeboye.

In 1881 he was appointed ambassador to the Ottoman Empire, and thus put in a position to arm himself with more insights useful for imperial diplomacy – and to collect more artefacts for Clandeboye. Clearly, Dufferin was being groomed for high public office, but much depended on political patronage and support. Benjamin Disraeli, who had appointed him to Russia, died in 1881, and Dufferin had long been estranged from his successor, William Gladstone, over the latter's proposals for the reform of land ownership and tenancies in Ireland. Dufferin, enlightened when it came to imperial policies abroad, remained a dogged opponent of land reform in Ireland and the increase in tenants' rights, which he saw as a system that would ultimately and among other perceived evils rob great estates of the revenue-earning farmland that was essential to support house, family and ornamental park. If the battle was lost then for Dufferin, the end of the Irish country house, and the life it engendered and supported, had finally arrived.

In the early 1880s the Irish Land War continued to rage between traditional landlords, such as Dufferin, and reformers fighting for 'the three Fs' – fair rent, fixity of tenure and the free sale of land – a struggle supported by Gladstone's Second Land Act of 1881.

VICEROY OF INDIA

While the historic struggle between the great estates and their tenants and would-be freeholders took its course, Lord Dufferin once again looked east – thanks to Gladstone, who had become prime minister in 1880. Despite their differences over the issue of land reform, Gladstone approved Dufferin's appointment in 1884 as Viceroy of India. This was the premier administrative job in the British Empire. The viceroy was the representative of the Queen Empress in Britain's richest possession, was to all practical extents and purposes the ruler on a daily basis of millions of people, and the arbiter of the largest, most populous and wealthiest imperial possession the world had ever seen.

> Lord Dufferin's 'six years of Canadian Viceroyalty will always be regarded as a brilliant episode in the history of the Dominion. It has given great satisfaction among the colonists of all races and creeds.'

ABOVE *A photogragh taken in the 1890s showing the entrance vestibule, hall and ascending staircase leading up to the figure of Amun. It seems that little has changed (see page 185) because the pair of small Russian bears and the arms are still there, but the timber Egyptian mummy case and the large stuffed bear have long gone.*

Among the papers lodged in the libraries at Clandeboye is a folder initially disarming in its modesty but that, as closer inspection reveals, still burns with subdued, almost strange, emotion. The folder contains letters to Lord Dufferin from Queen Victoria. They are written in a scrawling hand and, although in the third person conventional for royal letters addressed to subjects, are surprisingly intimate. I looked at one written just as Lord Dufferin was taking up his position as viceroy. Dated 11 November 1884, it states: 'The queen waited till the last moment before he left for India to send Lord and Lady Dufferin an earnest "Godspeed" and every possible good-wish for their welfare and success in their new and very responsible position in her great Empire of which she is proud to be the Empress.' Then, after this private but essentially official message, Victoria unburdened her emotions and convoluted self-pity on her old friend. She had clearly not yet got over the death of her husband some twenty years earlier, and seemed still rocking with the shock, sorrow and unfairness of her painful bereavement. 'The queen must now,' wrote Victoria, 'thank Lord Dufferin for his extremely kind letter which, as well as with her lonely life, deprived more and more of friends and help, high and low, near and dear, is truly felt.' Evidently warming to the task of portraying herself as an innocent and wronged victim of misfortune, Victoria confided to Dufferin the pleasure she experienced when 'she sees that people feel for her and are sorry for her!' and reminded him that the 'balm for an often bleeding heart of true sympathy is not to be told'.[26] The letter is of course tragic, but also extraordinary since the emotional fragility and vulnerability it reveals were being suffered by the Queen Empress of the British Empire at its peak, probably – in terms of wealth and global influence – the most powerful woman who had ever lived.

Lord Dufferin's job in India was, in simple terms, to keep the peace, to bring a sense of stability to a highly volatile land and to use his diplomatic skills to ensure good relations between the disparate peoples of the subcontinent and Great Britain. He was, instructed Lord Kimberley, Secretary of State for India, to take the political heat out of the debate that was raging between arch imperialists and those – British as well as Indian – who favoured a form of Indian self-government. Dufferin was to exercise a largely administrative role, avoid political games-manship and keep the lid on the cauldron. Given these aims, it is extraordinary how things turned out.

AFGHANISTAN AND FEARS OF RUSSIAN INVASION

First, Lord Dufferin – while helping to cement relations with Afghanistan in the wake of the Second Anglo-Afghan War – found himself embroiled in what looked for a while like a major Russian incursion into Afghanistan, even into the North-West Frontier region of India. The Second Anglo-Afghan War ended in September 1880 with Britain in control of Afghan foreign policy, and thus the dominant external power in this vital buffer state between India and tsarist Russia. Dufferin was charged with responsibility for controlling the pro-British Afghan ruler installed in

LEFT ABOVE A 'viceregal group' in 1885 – Lord Dufferin in the centre, Lady Dufferin to his left, with, on his far right, daughter Lady Helen holding a monkey, while Lord William Beresford holds its tail.
LEFT BELOW Lord Dufferin and his party arrive in Rangoon in early 1886 on a tour of inspection soon after the annexation of Burma by British India.
OPPOSITE The attire of a high-status Burmese lady, acquired by the Dufferins in 1886 and now displayed at Clandeboye.

September 1880 – Emir Abdur Rahman Khan – and with ensuring that the Russians made no headway in the country. This proved to be far from easy, and events came to a climax in 1885, when a Russian invasion of Afghanistan was expected. One tragic consequence of this anticipation and resulting panic was the demolition in Herat of the beautiful fifteenth-century Musalla complex of Muslim madrasahs and tombs by Rahman's forces and British military engineers to create a clear field of fire for artillery because it was feared a Russian invasion force was about to appear. The force never emerged and one of the greatest architectural jewels of Central Asia was left in utter ruins.

THE ANNEXATION OF BURMA

The other great political and military event during Dufferin's viceroyalty was the annexation in late 1885 of the sovereign state of Burma. The Burmese, pugnacious, territorially acquisitive and often ruthless in their rule, had long been a thorn in the northeast side of British India and a challenge to its domination of the region. Two Burmese wars had

ABOVE TOP *Abdur Rahman Khan, the Afghan ruler (centre, with Dufferin on his left) during a state visit to India in 1885.*
ABOVE *The Burmese King Theebaw and his wife Queen Supayalat, sitting on their throne-like state bed shortly before being deposed by the British.*

been fought from the 1820s, defeats inflicted by British forces, Burmese territories, including Rangoon, had been seized and held, and treaties made. But the Burmese remained aggressive, treaties were broken and in November 1885 the British decided to solve their Burmese problem once and for all by toppling its king and absorbing the state into the British Empire. The business was risky – the Burmese were not a contemptible military power and had mauled British forces in the past; the logistics were tricky; and world opinion might take a very dim view of what could be seen as nothing other than an imperialist adventure. But the possible gains were great. India's border would be secured, and valuable natural resources – particularly timber – acquired, as would the vast wealth of Burma's royal family. In the event, the campaign was quick and brutally effective. Within little more than a fortnight, British forces had destroyed the Burmese army, taken the old capital of Ava and the great royal city and palace of Mandalay, and dethroned King Theebaw and his wife Queen Supayalat. And then, after military victory, began the dismantling of the Burmese kingdom. As was traditional at the time – and as had happened when British forces defeated Tipu Sultan and the Muslim kingdom of Mysore at Srirangapatna in south India in 1799 – the contents of the royal palaces and state treasuries were appropriated by the conquering power. Some treasures were taken as private trophies by eminent individuals, others dispatched as gifts, but most were catalogued and systematically auctioned to raise money to help pay for the campaign. Was this looting or simply part of the established system of warfare in which the spoils go to the victor? From the nineteenth-century viewpoint, Britain's conduct in Burma was not exceptional, nor particularly shocking.

Early in 1886 Lord and Lady Dufferin made the journey to Rangoon and then on to Mandalay to see the newly conquered nation. As ever, Lord Dufferin was highly inquisitive. He commissioned photographs of buildings, places and people, and, given his predilections, he collected avidly – cannons, costumes, Buddhist images, ceremonial

beds and umbrellas – to fill his new halls at Clandeboye and to help turn his Irish home into an all-embracing biography of his life, travels, interests and achievements.

When Dufferin returned to his viceregal palace in Calcutta he found a letter waiting from Victoria, the Queen Empress of India. The letter, preserved amongst his papers in Clandeboye, is dated 1 January 1886 from Osborne, and in it Victoria, writing as usual in the third person, congratulates Dufferin for the admirable way 'the Burman affair has been carried out and settled'. Victoria then reveals that, although regarded popularly as the black-clad widow of Windsor lost in perpetual mourning, she was not immune to the sparkling and girlish delights of jewels. 'The Queen-Empress hopes,' she continued, 'the Viceroy will not think her *greedy* when she asks if some Burman jewels will be sent her, as she received a bag with some pearls etc. from Oude when that was annexed, and from Lahore, when the Punjab became ours, the celebrated Kohinoor, splendid pearls, emeralds and uncut rubies.' Dufferin clearly bore the request in mind, for his journal records that on 26 March 1886 he 'amused' himself 'by examining and unpacking a large box of ex-king Theebaw's jewels which had been sent from Burmah for transportation to her Majesty the Queen, and the Prince and Princess of Wales. For the Queen there were Theebaw's principal crown, three large emeralds and a necklace with a diamond peacock ornament, for the Prince of Wales two beautifully carved elephant tusks and for the Princess of Wales a gold figure of Buddha.'

Lord Dufferin's reign as viceroy ended in 1888, but not before he had at last enjoyed a crucial role in the realization of a large-scale and palatial building of the sort he had long hoped to build at Clandeboye. Simla (now Shimla), north of Delhi and high in the Himalayas, had long been the British summer capital because of its cool and pleasant climate. The viceregal residence the Dufferins inherited, a modest bungalow called Peterhoff in ironic reference to the Russian imperial palaces of St Petersburg, offered Lord Dufferin a splendid opportunity. Peterhoff was self-evidently below the dignity of a viceroy of India and, argued Dufferin, had to be rebuilt in grander style. What resulted was the one great and large-scale building project that he ever achieved. His direct involvement in the design and execution of the new viceregal lodge remains uncertain. The architect is recorded as Henry Irwin of the Public Works Department, but the Jacobean and slightly Scottish baronial style – sensibly enhanced by picturesque tiers of verandas in the Shimla manner – and the fact that Dufferin consulted Lynn about the design suggests very strongly that the ultimate architect of the viceregal lodge was the viceroy himself. It was completed in 1887, so Lord Dufferin had only one season to fully enjoy his palace. With its halls, galleries, ornate panelled walls and processional route, it was surely what – in his imagination at least – Dufferin wanted for Clandeboye.

While exchanging letters with Lynn about the design of the viceregal lodge, Dufferin was also in constant contact about plans for Clandeboye. Now,

though, the scheme was not to rebuild on a large scale but to transform the existing building through major alterations and additions. On 13 July 1887 Lord Dufferin wrote from Simla to request Lynn to 'go some day to Clandeboye and see whether you could make any suggestion for improving the entrance, and for adding a good big hall'. These works were needed, explained Dufferin, because 'when I come home from India I shall have a great number of curios from all parts of the world to add to my present collection, and the present hall is already too small for what it contains'.[27] It seems that the plan was to sweep away Woodgate's service quarters forming the north and west ranges of the house, to keep the front door on the west – where Dufferin had placed it in 1869 – but replace Dufferin's 'temporary' conversion of scullery, kitchen and service corridor into entrance hall and processional route with a large new entrance hall, staircase, gallery 130 feet long, and dining room. In addition, the exterior of the house was to be clad in sixteenth-century French Renaissance manner.

Lynn produced a detailed set of plans in 1887, an estimate of £10,000 (£600,000 today) for the works and sent them to Dufferin in India. The viceroy's response was telling and final. He wrote to Lynn from Calcutta on 3 January 1888, thanking him for his latest designs but lamenting that 'Alas! With them has come the estimate which goes into far more money than I could dream of spending. I would therefore propose to confine myself to the bow window in the drawing room [and] a window

LEFT ABOVE *The viceregal lodge in Shimla soon after its completion in 1887. It seems that Lord Dufferin provided the architectural inspiration.*
LEFT BELOW *The viceroy's house, Calcutta, a splendid classical palace conceived in the* 1790s. *This photograph appears to show Lord Dufferin leaving, or arriving, in state.*
OPPOSITE *The south end of the dining room at Clandeboye House, little changed since it was completed in 1804 to Woodgate's designs.*

in the present hall, and the little bit of wood-work connected with it.'[28] And that, after all the glorious architectural dreams, was effectively that. A single south-facing canted bay was added to the drawing room, the single window at the south end of the gallery was replaced with a pair of windows clad externally and most optimistically, if somewhat tragically, with Renaissance-style columns that serve as mute harbingers of what could have been. During the 1890s there were other minute tinkerings after it was finally accepted that the temporary 1869 scheme was in fact here to stay. Some Gothic detail and a 'quaint' Elizabethan-style door were added in the main hall[29] and, as late as September 1901 according to Lord Dufferin's journal, the 'dome light' was 'placed' in the 'outer hall', which turned out to be 'a tremendous difficult operation on account of its great bulk and weight'.

DUFFERIN'S INDIAN LEGACY

Lord Dufferin's achievements as viceroy were not so glowing, nor so generally recognized or commended, as were his achievements as Governor General of Canada. But they were substantial. He had indeed managed to keep the peace within the most important part of Britain's empire; the stabilization of Afghanistan and of the border with tsarist Russia had been achieved in satisfactory manner; and the extent and wealth of British India had been greatly expanded (and its security assured) by the speedy acquisition of Burma and its valuable natural resources. But others took, and continue to take, a less sanguine view. Dr A.T. Harrison, who edited the *Dufferin Papers* at the Public Record Office of Northern Ireland, offers a most interesting perspective, made possible after the passing of over 120 years. He points out that Lord Dufferin's instructions, and inclination, not to be drawn into internal Indian politics, combined with a preference for the company of aristocratic, essentially feudal Indian princes and senior military men rather than for educated or politically active Indians caused him to be alienated from those people arguing for autonomy, for elements of self-government and even – like many of Dufferin's Irish countrymen –

for independence from the British Empire and for self-rule. As Harrison explains, this attitude led Dufferin 'into conflict with educated, native India, which came to regard him as maintaining the stranglehold of Anglo-Indian officialdom on the Indian government and administration'. Also, points out Harrison, 'educated India ... became alienated from Dufferin by the annexation of Upper Burma, and his strengthening of India's military defences in the North West to meet the Russian threat. Both these developments were viewed by native political activists as imperial sabre-rattlings which plundered India's feeble finances.' No doubt as a consequence of Dufferin's actions and attitudes, Indian political organization accelerated during his viceroyalty, with the first meeting of the All India Congress taking place in 1885. Harrison observes that the process of alienation worked both ways: 'Dufferin was proud and aristocratic in a paternalistic Whig manner, and he found educated India's newspaper attacks upon his administration slighting and offensive, from both a personal and political standpoint. He also viewed the sending of Indian nationalist envoys to Britain – where they spoke on radical electoral platforms and condemned his policies – with extreme disfavour.'

The PRONI notes also, critically, help to explain his behaviour in India by placing it in the wider context: 'Dufferin's alienation from educated or nationalist India was intensified by the Irish Home Rule crisis of 1886. As a member of the Irish Protestant landowning ascendancy ... Dufferin was strongly opposed to Home Rule, and he began to view Indian nationalists as "Home Rulers" on the Irish model.' However, he kept his views private, despite his growing anti-nationalist convictions, until very nearly the end of his Indian reign. 'On 30 November 1888, at a St Andrew's Day dinner in Calcutta, a few weeks before leaving India, he delivered a withering speech attacking the pretensions of educated and nationalist India. India's population, he claimed, was deeply divided by race, religion and social development, and the Westernized, educated, native gentlemen represented a 'microscopic minority' of that

" Lord Dufferin's achievements as viceroy were not so glowing, nor so generally recognized or commended, as were his achievements as Governor General of Canada. But they were substantial…

ABOVE *Lord Dufferin contemplates the tigers he has shot while on a hunt in India.*

population, alien to the broad mass of the peasantry.'[30] Harrison suggests that Lord Dufferin had a very specific reason for making this speech. He wanted to divide the moderates from the extremists in the educated native camp, for he realized that the British administration in India had to win moderate educated Indian support, thus one of his last dispatches from the subcontinent proposed to the Secretary of State for India that the Indian legislative councils should be reformed and Indian representation increased.

THE PROGRESSIVE IMPERIALIST
Lord Dufferin's perception of empire was, and remains, wonderfully complex, subtle and, arguably, paradoxical. In essence, he held what can be characterized as a liberal and progressive view of empire (which might seem a contradiction in terms) in which Britain's technically advanced, democratic and Christian civilization was seen to represent a peak of human achievement – both materially and

spiritually – that granted enlightenment to less developed societies. The possession of conquered nations, the exploitation of their national resources and the appropriation of their treasures was justified ethically and morally by the 'manifest' superiority of Western Christian society and by the introduction to conquered people – in theory at least – of equality before the law, education, modern medicine and nebulous concepts of fair play and sportsmanship.

But this enlightened view of imperialism did not

embrace consistency and was, sadly, almost inevitably tainted by hypocrisy, false notions of superiority and the racism that conquering people tend to feel for the subjugated. Lord Dufferin seems to have been free of the worst of these vices, but, for example, in Canada he accepted that the desire for eventual 'independence' was natural among its hardy 'colonists' of European extraction, while simultaneously, in his homeland of Ireland, he opposed Home Rule. In India he wrestled to give expression to the desires of millions of rural and urban poor who had no voice, while being irritated by educated Indians whom he perceived as an awkward Asiatic equivalent to Irish Republican patriots and Nationalists. In Canada he had stoutly opposed the machinations of United States factions that argued for the annexation of Canada because such an action would be a frightful infringement of national and democratic rights while, as Viceroy of India, he had been actively involved in 1885 in the annexation by British India of the sovereign nation of Burma. These complexities and contradictions are, of course, the very essence of nineteenth-century imperialism and nationalism. If nothing else, Dufferin, the humane and progressive imperialist, was very much a child of his age.

When Lord and Lady Dufferin returned to Clandeboye from India in 1888 their arrival must have been spectacular. They would have been loaded with 'curios' from India, Afghanistan and Burma, and crates must have been arriving for weeks, if not months, afterwards, each packed

LEFT ABOVE *The head of a tiger skin on the hall floor in Clandeboye, one of a pair and perhaps the very tigers shown freshly killed on page 227.*
LEFT BELOW *A group of items on the library mantelshelf, including a Buddhist head from Gandhara, Afghanistan, perhaps one of those collected for the viceroy by John Lockwood Kipling.*

OPPOSITE *Indian weapons on display in Clandeboye, including, on the left, a fearsome 'katara' dagger, its blade embellished with a scene from a tiger hunt, and demonstrating that the most deadly item can possess a poetic if sinister beauty.*

with its own particular treasures. Up on the walls of the house went dozens of paintings of Indian maharajas and other grandees (most presents from the sitters themselves), and arrays of Indian weapons (swords, armour, fierce 'Katara' daggers, tiger-claw 'thieftakers', helmets, matchlock 'Toradar' muskets and home-made jezails from the North-West Frontier). And on the floors went the skins of tigers Lord Dufferin had shot, and elephant-foot baskets. In the Museum Room, along with Egyptian artefacts acquired in the 1850s and 1880s, went Burmese Buddhist mementoes and fragments of 1600-year-old Greco-Buddhist sacred art from the ancient Gandhara kingdom that straddled the border of Afghanistan and India, some of which had been acquired and sent to Lord Dufferin by Rudyard Kipling's father, John Lockwood Kipling.

CALAMITY

But even now Lord Dufferin, aged sixty-two, didn't linger long in Clandeboye. In the year of his return from India – 1888 – he was rewarded for his services by being made a marquess (he added Ava to his title out of pride, it must be assumed, for his role in the annexation of Burma), and from 1888 until 1891 served in Rome as ambassador to Italy, and from 1892 until 1896 in Paris as ambassador to France. Then, finally, he returned to Clandeboye to savour his extraordinary creation, every inch of its curio-encrusted interior evoking vivid memories of his travels and achievements abroad. But Lord Dufferin was not to enjoy a pleasant or restful retirement. In 1897 he was asked by a businessman named Whitaker Wright to become chairman of the London Globe Finance Corporation. Dufferin agreed and invested heavily in the company that, in 1900, failed in most spectacular manner. Not only was he humiliated and financially bruised but, as chairman, felt responsible for those who had also invested in the company, so compensated some from his private funds. At almost the same time his eldest son was killed in the Boer War. It seems Lord Dufferin lost his will to live. He became ill and took to his bed at Clandeboye, where he died on 12 February 1902.

He was buried in the grounds within a *campo santo* (cemetery) he had created years earlier for family burials. Here he was laid, not facing east as in most Christian burials, but lying north–south, like some early Egyptian pharaohs, whose funeral images face the northern hemisphere constellations from which they believed they had come and to which they would return.

Clandeboye was in a parlous financial state, but the viceroy's second son, Terence, a career diplomat who succeeded to the title, married a rich New York girl and presumably brought some much-needed financial stability into the family. On his death in 1918, the title and estate went to a younger brother, Frederick, whose son Basil turned out to be something of a prodigy. Basil was an exceptionally bright scholar at Eton, and belonged to a glittering group at Oxford that included the future economist Roy Harrod, the future Lord Pakenham and the oddball young poet and adventurer John Betjeman. Basil married a rich Guinness girl, launched himself upon a brilliant political career, held various offices, but after the Second World War started, turned down an offer of a place in Churchill's coalition government, preferring to enter the army. He served in various theatres but, with a tragic irony suggesting the dark humour of the gods, Basil was killed in a Japanese ambush in March 1945 while on a covert mission in Burma. The place of his death was near Ava, the ancient city that his grandfather had chosen as a token of achievement when made a marquess in 1888. Basil was succeeded by his son Sheridan, whose wife, the painter Lindy Guinness – the Marchioness of Dufferin and Ava – now owns Clandeboye following her husband's death in 1988.

THE FUTURE

The present Marchioness of Dufferin and Ava has a deep and emotional commitment to Clandeboye and to the legacy of the 1st Marquess. She is determined to keep the house and estate going. And the future is bright. The house, its contents and the grounds are in excellent condition, the stables are used for money-raising events, and the walled gardens as an

" Anyone who wants to understand nineteenth-century history and the complex British notion of empire, with its highlights and its shadows, need do little more than visit Clandeboye…

arboretum committed, with advice from Kew Gardens, to growing trees for planting in Ireland. In addition, Lady Dufferin has a vision that she is determined to realize. In the nineteenth century the world came, in a sense, to Clandeboye. Now the position must be reversed, and the house and estate serve the larger world. Clandeboye must not be just a repository of objects, history and memory, but also a living place that plays a creative role in the contemporary world – a centre of learning and study, a focus that can unite academic institutions in Ireland, India, Canada and in all the countries touched by Lord Dufferin during his extraordinary life. As Lady Dufferin says, anyone who wants to understand nineteenth-century history and the complex British notion of empire, with its highlights and its shadows, need do little more than visit Clandeboye, contemplate its contents and study its vast and unique archive of documents. To govern the future, it is essential to know the past, and this is a knowledge that Clandeboye possesses in abundance and can pass on to all interested in learning the lessons of history ❖

MARSHCOURT

Stockbridge, Hampshire

—

20TH

CENTURY

—

Very English
Modernism

❖

The arrival at Marshcourt in Hampshire is amongst the oddest and most engineered I have encountered in the realms of British country houses. It is conceived to surprise, to delight, to entertain – which is hardly surprising since the man behind its creation in the first decade of the twentieth century was Edwin Lutyens, arguably the wittiest of English architects. The approach from Stockbridge is quintessentially English. I drive past a simple war memorial (also by Lutyens) and the remains of a medieval chapel (painted a most Italian ochre), then along a gently rising tree-lined road. Soon, on my left, is a drive, also tree lined, that curves intriguingly into a deep cutting. Nothing more is to be seen. I move slowly along the drive, into the cutting that continues to curve with its sides growing higher, feeling like Alice entering Wonderland, or perhaps Never Never Land. Then I suddenly curve on to the level with the surrounding ground, and two large buildings of curious design and construction come into view. I am obliged to turn 45 degrees and drive between them. Ahead is another straight, tree-lined and lawn-flanked drive. I pass along it and gradually, at its far end, make out a wide, low building glowing a dull white in the evening sun. This is Marshcourt, completed in 1904, and considered by many to be Lutyens' finest house of all. It is the last of his great cycle of Arts and Crafts, Gothic or Elizabethan-inspired houses – utterly modern in their sense of space and light, in their regard for comfort and convenience; highly functional machines in which to live life, yet also touched with the power of visual poetry, rich in ornament, deeply imbued with a sense of history, beautifully constructed and very site specific in their use of local and traditional materials, and wonderfully rich in witty details and idiosyncratic references. Of all these Arts and Crafts houses, Marshcourt – with its huge Elizabethan-style windows that let light flood inside, its open-plan interior inspired by the great halls and chambers of late medieval houses, and its pure chalk 'clunch' facing that makes it look almost like the early white-box architecture of Modernists such as Le Corbusier – best suggests the direction that modern architecture could have developed in twentieth-century England if all had not been usurped by the ruthless, history-hating functionalism of the continental 'International style'. Marshcourt proclaims a world to come,

PREVIOUS PAGES *The entrance front of Marshcourt, completed in 1904, appears symmetrical, beetle-browed and, in theatrical manner, screens the dramatic landscape beyond from arriving visitors.*
LEFT ABOVE & BELOW *The pair of buildings, of curious design and construction, that* frame the straight entrance drive to Marshcourt.
OPPOSITE *The tall bay windows on the southwest corner of the garden front, lighting the Great Hall and drawing room. The bold sculptural nature of the design is striking, as is the walling of white chalk blocks or 'clunch'.*

in which modern architecture was evolutionary not revolutionary, in which contemporary design built upon rather than rejected history, used old with new, and combined pioneering materials, such as steel-reinforced concrete, with traditional and local materials, such as the chalk, brick and flint used by Lutyens to clad Marshcourt. But while a harbinger of things to come, when completed Marshcourt was – despite its visual power and splendour – soon revealed to be a monument to the past. It represented a false dawn. The world changed around it, so its portents and promise went unrewarded and ultimately unrealized.

THE MARRIAGE GIFT

In 1897, when Edwin Lutyens became engaged to Emily Lytton, he could not afford to offer her much financially. At this stage in his career, despite showing considerable talent, he was far from established, with most of his great projects – such as the Viceroy's House in New Delhi – decades away. So as an engagement present, Edwin gave Emily a green leather casket. Inside, the casket was divided into compartments, each compartment containing a different precious object: a Bible, a pipe-stopper, a heart and an anchor. The casket remains in the Lutyens family today, as does its most treasured piece of cargo – a miniature roll of plans for a white house, with a red-tile roof and a plan formed of the interlocking initials they shared – EL. One day, promised the young Edwin Lutyens, he would build such a house for them and it would be their family home. They never would live in this dream home, but Lutyens did build it. Although not for himself, it was built only a few years later. It was Marshcourt.

The story of the building of Marshcourt and its first owner-commissioner is the story of the last great flourishing of the British country house before the First World War. It is a story of Victorian social mobility, the rise of the money markets and a reminder of their inherent instability. Built between 1901 and 1904 to designs by Lutyens, the up-and-coming architect of the age (with later additions also by him in the 1920s), the house seems to embody the mood of a nation at play. The years of its building spelt the dawn of the Edwardian era. During these years, Britain was moving on – finally – from the state of national mourning that had typified the late years of Victoria's reign. It was the age of the Galsworthian house party, a ballooning middle class, the first motor cars and early aviation. Britain was waking up and speeding up; propelling itself into the new century, with a new (albeit middle-aged) king, and a new optimism. This, we now see, was the golden age of the British Empire – the glory before the storm that would break in 1914 and change the world forever.

At Marshcourt you can see this playful optimism and confidence around every corner. The house is Lutyens at his best, not only the largest, latest and most fully realized example of his experiments with the Arts and Crafts Tudor/Elizabethan style, but also the glory of his most productive and creative period as a country house architect. In the ten years between 1897 and 1907, Lutyens' office was a frenzy of activity that saw the design of Orchards (1897), Goddards (1898), Tigbourne Court (1899) – all in Surrey; Deanery Garden, Berkshire (1899); Grey Walls, East Lothian (1900); Homewood, Hertfordshire (1901); Little Thakeham, Sussex (1902); and Monkton House, Sussex (1902). Nashdom in Buckinghamshire was started in 1905, and Heathcote in Yorkshire in 1906, but by the time Lutyens designed these last two, he and the tastes of the times had changed. Unlike the earlier houses, largely asymmetrical, freeform and Gothic vernacular in spirit, Nashdom and Heathcote are classical – Heathcote particularly so, for it is inspired by the Renaissance classicism of Michele Sanmicheli and Andrea Palladio.

Lutyens' ability to almost mass-produce country houses without losing his original and individual touch – and his willingness to abandon Arts and Crafts Gothic for a vigorous and inventive classicism – displays his creative genius, his personal ambition and, more prosaically, his need to support his new wife and family in some style. Consequently, by the first decade of the twentieth century, Lutyens was Britain's premier country house architect.

“ Britain was waking up and speeding up; propelling itself into the new century, with a new (albeit middle-aged) king, and a new optimism. This, we now see, was the golden age of the British Empire – the glory before the storm that would break in 1914 and change the world forever…

ABOVE LEFT *Sir Edwin Lutyens at work on his drawing board.*
ABOVE TOP RIGHT *Goddards, Surrey, completed to Lutyens' design in 1898.*
ABOVE BOTTOM RIGHT *Little Thakeham, Sussex, a Lutyens design of 1902.*

HERBERT JOHNSON

Marshcourt was not a country house in the traditional sense of the word. The country house in Britain had, by usual custom, been financed by the land on which it stood. This meant that the size and grandeur of the house had almost always been linked to the income its estate could provide, whether by rents, farming or mineral mining. Of course there was potential for the occasional courtly or imperial appointment, or a particularly beneficial dowry, or money from trade or the professions, but on the whole, the great country houses of Britain had always fed off the land they presided over.

With Marshcourt, as with most of the country houses Lutyens built, this was not the case. The money that paid for the building of Marshcourt had been made in the City of London – on the expanding and increasingly volatile stock markets. In consequence, the house, rather than being the central 'head office' of a working estate, was a place in which to withdraw, away from the bustle of the

City. The model for this kind of country house had its roots in the villas of ancient Rome. For the wealthy nobles of that city, the country was the arena of pleasure, of *otium* – sports, flirting and free time – while the metropolis itself, and the forum in particular, was the arena of business or *negotium*, literally non-pleasure. The one was endured to create space for the other.

For Herbert Johnson, who commissioned Lutyens to design Marshcourt, this was certainly the kind of house he wanted: somewhere to escape to during weekends and holidays to pursue what he most enjoyed – fishing and hunting. The railway had even made its way to Stockbridge, allowing Johnson to be that newest of things, a commuter, should he choose to be.

Johnson – Johnnie to his friends – is, historically speaking, quite an elusive figure. He was not a marquess, earl or knight of the realm, yet his life seems to embody the spirit of the times he lived through. In his early years he had lived the Victorian dream. He was born in Brighton on 24 January 1856, his family moving to South Africa while he was still young because his father, the Reverend Henry Isaac Johnson, had secured the job of principal at the Grey Institute in Port Elizabeth. In the late 1860s, Johnnie moved back to England with his mother because of her poor health. Once in England, Johnnie, who had always showed a remarkable talent for figures, won a mathematics scholarship to attend Cheltenham School, his elder brother having won

the scholarship for classics. Later, when Johnnie's father was planning to move back to England to be reunited with his family, the headmaster at Cheltenham offered him a job there on account of the intellect and learning of his sons.

His father made good progress in his career, later becoming headmaster of the influential Royal Institution School in Liverpool during its final years until it closed in 1892. Johnnie, meanwhile, was offered another scholarship – this time to attend The Royal Military Academy, Woolwich. He never took up the offer, but instead left home at a young age for London in search of fortune. He became a clerk in a firm of stockbrokers, his natural aptitude for numbers standing him in good stead for a profession on the Stock Exchange.

In the 1880s, the stock market was ballooning in size year-on-year and there were fortunes to be made (or lost) at a rate perhaps faster than ever

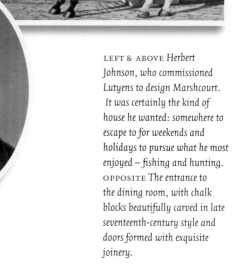

LEFT & ABOVE *Herbert Johnson, who commissioned Lutyens to design Marshcourt. It was certainly the kind of house he wanted: somewhere to escape to for weekends and holidays to pursue what he most enjoyed – fishing and hunting.*
OPPOSITE *The entrance to the dining room, with chalk blocks beautifully carved in late seventeenth-century style and doors formed with exquisite joinery.*

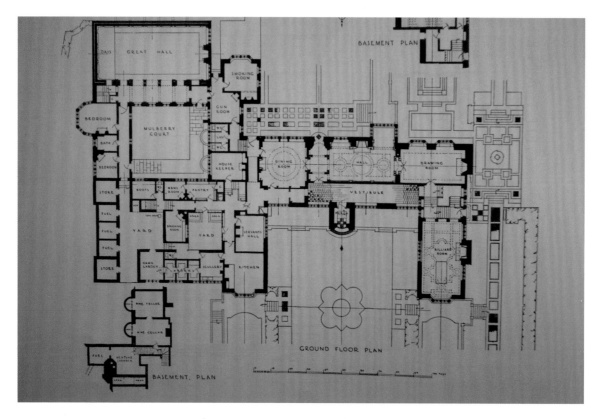

before. It offered a new kind of social mobility, and it seemed to work particularly well for Herbert Johnson. Beginning as a clerk, he quickly became a stockjobber and a partner in Wedd Jefferson when George Wedd and Harry Jefferson established the firm in 1885. They dealt in government stocks and other fixed-interest returns, known as the gilt-edge market or simply 'the funds'.[1] Being a partner in a stockjobbers meant that you received no salary, only a cut of the profit or loss. Fortunately, the firm would become one of the most influential stockjobbers in the city.

Today the Stock Exchange conjures up an image of impersonal computer screens, toxic debt and collapsed hedge funds, but it was a place with strange rules of engagement in the late nineteenth century. The men wore top hats, ties and pinstriped suits. All trading was conducted face to face, with most of the money being made in the morning between 9.30 and 10.00. The stockjobber was essentially a wholesaler of stocks, a middleman between stockbrokers, who would buy up shares

❝ In the 1880s, the stock market was ballooning in size year-on-year and there were fortunes to be made (or lost) at a rate perhaps faster than ever before. It offered a new kind of social mobility, and it seemed to work particularly well for Herbert Johnson.

ABOVE *The ground-floor plan of Marshcourt. North is to the bottom. South of the entrance porch and of the long thin entrance hall or vestibule is the sequence of formal rooms, with (from left to right) the square-plan dining room, the hall – with its mighty projecting bay, and the drawing room. These rooms, together with the billiard room in the northwest wing, were built for entertainment and conviviality. To the east is the service portion of the house, with, on the southeast corner, the ballroom (referred to here as the Great Hall) that was added in 1924–6.*

and hold them until selling them on, hopefully at a profit. Some were harsh on the stockjobber, saying he was essentially a bookie. But for better or worse, the stockjobber was making his mark on contemporary society. In 1893 the *Western Mail* published a short column that offered a recipe for the making of 'a modern English gentleman: ... Wash a large, red stockjobber, brush and trim, baste all over with money; arrange in luxurious West End house, surround with puff-paste; then serve up hot. Will keep for months.'[2]

The stockjobber was a caricature of 'modern' English society at the turn of the twentieth century. But he was also 'modern' in the sense that he was a relatively new phenomenon, proliferating into the upper classes, pockets bulging with banknotes.

Johnnie achieved notoriety for his talents – being a jobber required flair – and for designing and publishing a kind of ready reckoner that calculated losses and gains by volume of shares, buying price and selling price. With the help of these tables, Johnson could calculate losses and profits at unmatched speed. His firm flourished, and so did his personal finances. By 1910, Wedd Jefferson's six partners – of which Johnnie was one – were dealing with securities valued at around £1 billion (about £6 billion today).[3] By 1900, through his work and also his personal investments in South American railways and Greek government stock,[4] Johnnie had amassed a fortune of over £500,000 – roughly equivalent to £29 million in today's money.

When the Marshcourt estate was auctioned at 2 p.m. on Friday, 10 February 1893, Herbert Johnson knew he was bidding for one of the best stretches of chalk-stream fishing in the country. The sales brochures stressed the estate's 'Excellent fishing rights, forming the unsold portion of the Houghton Club water, extending for nearly two miles on the celebrated river Test, one of the finest trout, grayling and eel streams in England with two eel weirs, fish rearing ponds, &c... with good Partridge, Snipe and Wildfowl shooting'.[5] It had previously belonged to Dr T.C. Wickham of Winchester, a famous name in late nineteenth-century 'sport'. He was a pioneer of dry fly fishing, maker of the 'Wickham's Fancy' fly,

and founder of the Houghton Fly Fishing Club, which was as legendary as it was exclusive. Johnson had almost certainly been a member.

Having secured an estate in an unrivalled position, Johnson did not rush into building a new house on it. Instead, for many years, he made do with the existing farmhouse on the site. But when, in around 1899, he decided to build, he knew exactly who was the best man for the job: Edwin Lutyens.

Since its launch in 1897, the weekly magazine *Country Life* had championed all things country – hunting, rural crafts, fishing, duck ponds – and even featured a debutante of the week. Inevitably, just like those today who listen to the rural exploits of *The Archers*, most of its audience were city-dwelling professionals. It portrayed a life that was perhaps disappearing, or perhaps had never existed. Yet among its pages the magazine championed the work of one contemporary architect in particular – the young and ambitious Edwin Lutyens. Not only were almost all of his country houses featured in the magazine's pages, but *Country Life*'s owner, Edward Hudson, had commissioned his own Lutyens house, Deanery Gardens, which was completed in 1899. A friendship was formed, and over the years Hudson would commission Lutyens to build him a further two houses: Lindisfarne Castle, Northumberland, in 1902 and Plumpton Place, Sussex, in 1928. Even the new *Country Life* offices on Tavistock Street in Covent Garden were designed by Lutyens in 1904, as a pioneering example of what he playfully called his 'Wrenaissance' style, wittily playing with classicism and convention in a thoroughly modern way.

Not only was Hudson himself responsible for giving Lutyens a host of commissions, but many readers of the magazine also became Lutyens' clients, having been similarly enthused about the work of this new architect appearing in the pages of *Country Life*. Lutyens' values seemed to chime perfectly with the national mood. Here was a clever young architect building something very modern, forward-thinking, but with absolute respect and knowledge of the past. His buildings played with the historical conventions of architecture, with an insistence on the vernacular that his Arts and Crafts forebears had established as quintessentially British. But with Lutyens there was nothing twee or chintzy. There was plainness and starkness but also comfort and – perhaps most importantly – wit. It was a thoroughly Edwardian mentality and attractive to a host of commissioners with new-found wealth who were looking to cement their social position. But, as one of the early 'lifestyle' magazines, *Country Life* was also simply a trendsetter. Commissioning a Lutyens house came to say something about you. To the readers of the magazine, a Lutyens house was not only a status symbol; it was a taste symbol. One of these readers was Herbert Johnson.

Lutyens' consultation style was in many ways contradictory. On the one hand, he would spend a lot of time with clients, getting to know them and sometimes befriending them. On the other hand, he would come up with designs quickly – often on the train home from a first meeting – and the built

design would rarely deviate far from these early sketches. Lutyens disliked the over-involvement of the client in the design, having a conviction that there was a right and a wrong way to do things. His way, of course, was the right way.

The archive of the Royal Institute of British Architects (RIBA) – the most prized architectural resource in the country – is housed at the Victoria & Albert Museum. Among its most important records is the correspondence between Edwin Lutyens and his wife Emily. It shows a marriage troubled and loving in equal measure. They were forced to spend a large amount of time apart because Lutyens – or Ned, as he signs himself in the letters – was away a lot visiting sites and clients. As an architectural record, the letters are at times frustrating, often concentrating on stories tangential to the architecture, but they fulfil a more interesting purpose – recording the daily details of Lutyens' career in a unique way, and painting a portrait of the man behind the architecture. From the visits they record to Marshcourt, they also paint a portrait of Herbert Johnson.

An early trip to see Johnnie at Marshcourt in August 1901 captures a typical weekend there while Johnnie was living in a farmhouse on the estate: 'There was a good rise last night and I killed one fish – lost two and another broke me entirely! Which was hard luck but nevertheless exciting. Tom Jefferson [Johnson's colleague at Wedd Jefferson] has just lost his eye – the end of a rope hit him – on his yacht and smashed the eye – it had to be

LEFT ABOVE *The drawing room, as published in Country Life in 1932 – the organ that promoted Lutyens and his country-house architecture.* LEFT BELOW *Country Life's owner and Lutyens' client Edward Hudson.* OPPOSITE *The Great Hall at Marshcourt – or Hall on the Lutyens plan – and not to be confused with the Great Hall or ballroom added to Marshcourt in the mid-1920s. This view, which first appeared in Country Life in 1906, shows the various historic styles that Lutyens fused in most original manner, and the spare nature of the room's furnishing.*

removed the same evening. We stayed on the river late and dined about 10 – and after up until 12 o'clock we looked over plans and Johnson is very nice about them and seems awfully pleased with them ... This morning we were up early and I had a gallop on the downs! I haven't ridden since my darling was my own! You would have been amused to see me perched up on top of a 17 hand hunter!'[6]

A letter the next day (Monday) is written from 29 Bloomsbury Square from an 'oh so stiff from riding'[7] Lutyens, struggling to get back on top of work, with a mountain of post to respond to. 'Yes, I loved Marshcourt,' he wrote to his wife, 'and how I envy the possession of it – in a nice way of course. I am stiff from riding – I can't imagine you on a horse – can you – me? I don't believe you can – own sweet love ... I do wish I could find a wife for Johnson. Would Emmy consent? He is very well off but not a kissy person at all.'[8]

Unfortunately, one thing these letters do little to explain is why Lutyens decided to build for Johnson the house he had promised to build for his new wife as their family home. Certainly, Lutyens and Johnson became firm friends, but at first Lutyens must have felt a few qualms. In a letter written to his wife on 20 April 1911 Lutyens remarked anxiously about his son Robert's 'vegetarianism and unboylike antipathies ... I should like a man like Herbert Johnson to take him up for summer holidays; endless exercise and a bit of discipline'.[9] We can speculate about Lutyens' and Johnson's characters – different in many respects but similar in some crucial areas: their shared sense of humour, their love of fishing, their matching routes to social betterment and fortune (outside of education and entirely of their own making), but none of this seems to quite fit. One is left with the conclusion that Lutyens simply loved the design he had made for Emily, accepted that he himself could not afford to build it and was willing to realize his 'ideal' design for Johnson – the man with sufficient finances to allow Lutyens' whimsy to run wild.

The few remaining sketches of Marshcourt are also held in the RIBA archive. True to Lutyens' usual design process, the earliest crayon drawing that survives is very like the house as built. The major difference is that it seems to show a thatched roof. It is a curious detail and one that was abandoned early on, almost certainly for reasons of practicality. However, you can see why Lutyens was drawn to the idea: there were many reed beds near the river Test, on estate land – fair game for an architect religiously devoted to vernacular materials.

The major building material of chalk clunch was also local to the site. Indeed, 'local' seems a bit of an understatement – you need only scrape the surface of the soil to hit chalk in this part of Hampshire. Lutyens' use of local materials made several points. First, it was a reflection of Arts and Crafts building philosophy that architecture should be firmly rooted to its site – orientated and responsive to the undulations of the land on which it stands, and built of materials that were, as far as possible, extracted from the site or from the immediate region – hence the chalk, the cut or knapped flint, the brick and tiles and the occasional stone blocks that form the façades of Marshcourt. In addition, for Johnson and Lutyens the use of chalk is a kind of jocular sporting reference to the bed of the river beyond the house. It is its chalk bed that makes fishing on the Test so remarkable. There is also another story about the choice, the origins of which have been lost, but it's said that Lutyens built using chalk because of a bet that he couldn't. He took up the challenge with relish. It seems a suitable origin for so macho a house.

The startling white of the chalk combined with red tile and brick and shiny black knapped flint is a brave and striking colour palette, and unusually saturated for a vernacular building. Interestingly, these colours – red, white and black – are the colours of early Modernism, of the Bauhaus, and worthy of its exponents Walter Gropius or De Stijl. These materials together – drawn from the landscape on which (and of which) the house is built – make a spectacle that is both theatrical and visually arresting. It is a thoroughly modern colour palette. Also modern, in a sense, is the fact that these materials are little more than skin deep. As with more conventional construction projects, the

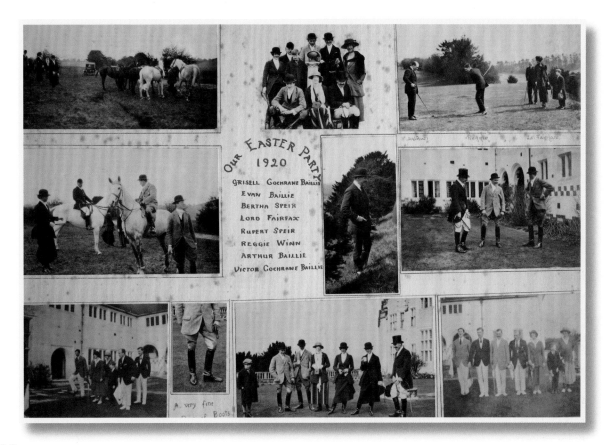

Our Easter Party 1920
Grisell Cochrane Baillie
Evan Baillie
Bertha Speir
Lord Fairfax
Rupert Speir
Reggie Winn
Arthur Baillie
Victor Cochrane Baillie

A very fine ... Boots.

> " The startling white of the chalk combined with red tile and brick and shiny black knapped flint is a brave and striking colour palette, and unusually saturated for a vernacular building…

ABOVE *Members of the Easter Day hunt in 1920 at Marshcourt.*
OVERLEAF *The south elevation, presiding over the terraced garden, with the striking landscape view to the west. The combination of white chalk walling, red tiles and staggered courses of black knapped flint makes a bold colour statement.*

traditional materials face and conceal more utilitarian materials, such as strong and cheap industrially made brick, which in obscurity do much of the structural work.

The approach to Marshcourt, along the tree-lined avenue and through the claustrophobic gorge, holds a revealing story about Lutyens' design process and his relationship with his clients. The winding gorge was an afterthought, dug when the house was all but completed after Johnson complained about the lack of an impressive drive. In response, Lutyens went down to the Kings Somborne labour exchange and took every man on the books into employment to create these earthworks. It took the men a year of digging – shovelling by hand[10] – and the effect is still breathtaking today as one emerges on to the final approach to Marshcourt, with Lutyens' barn-like garage and powerhouse flanking on either side, and signalling the imminent emergence of the house.

The north or entrance elevation of the house is

compressed below a heavy red-tile roof and, as is duly revealed, is designed and located to conceal, for those arriving for the first time, the drama of the site and the breathtaking vista beyond. This is baroque theatre at its best, and Lutyens wanted to expose the wonders of the site in a measured and controlled manner to achieve maximum surprise and delight – it simply would not do to reveal all at once!

The house forecourt is reached over a mock moat, the moat revealing the low-level footings of the bays on either side of the court. The footings are made of flint and stone, suggesting, playfully, a false building history – a whimsical fabrication intended to fool no-one – that the existing house was built on the footings of an older house. Once inside the forecourt, you are struck by the looming presence of the house, its deeply set Elizabethan-style mullioned windows, with serious-looking glazing bars. The squares of tile-creasing that punctuate the sleek elevations of white chalk are playing a similar game to that of the bay footings. They are pretending to be

filled putlog holes – a medieval technique of scaffolding, where holes were left in an elevation for the placing of horizontal timbers. Black flint squares also run in chequerboard patterns in near symmetry, stopping and starting inexplicably. It all gives an impression of something historic and lasting. Yet it is all very ironic, being ultimately and knowingly pastiche.

This front elevation is almost symmetrical, but not quite. Here again, the house responds to its site; as the western wing on the right-hand side is deeper due to the slope of the hillside, Lutyens elongates the windows to make a subtle asymmetry. The symmetry is also broken by the magnificent Elizabethan-style moulded-brick chimneys, which look from the northern side as if they have been supplanted directly from Hampton Court. From the western and southern garden sides of the house, where the hillside falls away, these chimneys rise triumphantly out of colossal chimney stacks, rich in flint, tile and brick chequerboard detailing, topped off with the ornate red chimneys themselves spiralling skywards.

On these western and southern garden elevations, the whole language of the house becomes more vertical than the horizontal lines of the entrance front. The small mullioned windows of the front become walls of leaded windows (Lutyens hated plate-glass windows and loved glazing bars). The double-storey bay window of the Great Hall and main bedroom breaks through the roofline, allowing the maximum amount of light

LEFT ABOVE *One of the finest details of the garden front is the loggia. It is a masterpiece of rich, refined and witty construction.*
LEFT BELOW *White chalk and putlog holes filled with knapped flint or tiles imply a complex*
and ancient building history for the house in a tongue-in-cheek manner.
OPPOSITE *A tall mullioned and transomed window, designed in Elizabethan manner, letting light flood into the Great Hall.*

There is a sense of ceremony as the visitor leaves the rendezvous lawn-front on the western side of the drive through a pair of ornate gateposts, led by stone-carved balustrades down the stairs to a low-level terrace. To the left, the white walls of the house are now at full stretch; to the right, there is lawn, then a yew hedge and beyond, the countryside. Underfoot, the surface changes frequently, from stone to herringbone brick to turf between stone slabs.

The gardens at Marshcourt were described in *Country Life* as 'one of the most fully worked-out garden schemes with which the names of Lutyens and Jekyll are associated'.[11] The impact of Jekyll at Marshcourt now leaves little trace, her planting schemes blurred or lost under years of replanting. Indeed, it appears that the original planting schemes for the gardens were not drawn up until much later (around 1915) anyway. However, Jekyll's influence on Lutyens more generally had been profound and lasting. When the two originally met, at Littleworth Cross in 1889, Jekyll was entering middle age. Already versed in the principles of the Arts and Crafts movement, and with a long list of connections, her gardening career remained in its early stages. She was a regular contributor to William Robinson's magazine *The Garden*, and her new garden at Munstead Wood had received a lot of attention, but she was far from the botanical doyenne she would become in later years. Jekyll and the young Lutyens became friends instantly, embarking on tours of Surrey to hunt down the local building techniques and cottage gardens they both loved. Lutyens was by this stage fearsomely devoted to his chosen career of architect, but was still inexperienced, having only recently left the prestigious office of Peto & George to set up on his own. Yet, in spite of Lutyens' inexperience, Jekyll eventually trusted her new friend to design a house for the plot of land she had bought in 1883, to match the already established garden. It was completed in 1896 and heralded by Jekyll as a

from the rooms' southern aspect to burst inside, as well as offering fine views of Johnson's beloved river Test in the valley below.

One of the finest details on the garden front is the loggia. It is a masterpiece of rich, refined and complex detail, as arch mouldings die into the column shaft, which is itself composed of a regular step pattern of chalk blocks and knapped flint panels. The column is sculptural in its three-dimensional perfection – all calculated and controlled, and a vernacular construction achieved (ironically) only through a vast number of precise working drawings.

THE GARDEN

Crucially, these powerfully composed south and west elevations rise above a landscape garden that is not only one of the glories of the house, but, by creating such a dramatic setting for its main elevations, actually defines it. The garden, designed by Gertrude Jekyll, is formed to weld the gradients of the site into a series of terraces that lead the

> **The garden ... is formed to weld the gradients of the site into a series of terraces that lead the visitor around the building in a kind of grand architectural promenade...**

great success. She would live there happily until her death in 1932. Her friendship with Lutyens would last just as long.

At the southwest corner of the building the visitor reaches a doorway leading to a sunken pool in a courtyard with stepped sides. It is a space of brilliant and controlled geometrical purity, the long rectangle of the lily pond radiating outwards and upwards in shallow stone steps, interrupted by square planters and beds backing on to the balustraded tops of the walls. Four lead-moulded hippocampi (seahorses) would have been arranged symmetrically on the outer margins of the pool, spouting water from their muzzles and adding to the drama of the space. At the centre of the sunken area is a leaden water tank to feed the cascade. It has an extraordinarily intricate geometrical pattern embossed on it, and is inscribed simply '1904 H J'. It is one of the few places on the site where the presence of Herbert Johnson is still tangible today.

At the other end of the sunken courtyard, circular

steps cascade down from a pair of imposing stone gateposts, offering a change of scene. From the top, the view suddenly opens up on to the Test valley, the hillside falling sharply away to the view of untamed nature beyond the garden. Along the lower length of this southern plot runs a terrace and an Italianate pergola. From this terrace, the view of the valley is framed by yew hedges, but from the higher 'sundial lawn', which meets the back door, the panorama is

visible. This kind of playing with space and light in the gardens, the contrasts achieved in the movement from intimate and enclosed to airy and exposed, were trademarks of Lutyens' work. The effect was even more intense indoors.

ENTERING MARSH COURT

The north entrance to Marshcourt is spectacular. Those entering the house pass into a wide vaulted porch that, in a superbly inventive manner, includes a stone arch suspended from three deeply projecting voussoirs. The vault of the porch is a chequerboard of different materials, and at its end is a stout front door with the motto above *Sis felix qui huc intres* (Happiness on all who enter). You duck through this seemingly low front door into an entrance hall that is also compressed in feeling – long, narrow, low-ceilinged – and on the floor is a chequerboard of black and rose marble parallelograms that seem to guide you towards a door on the left. This takes you from a dark and low world into the lofty and light-emblazoned heart of the house – the main axis formed by the interconnecting dining room, Great Hall and drawing room. Following the short north–south cross-axis from the entrance hall takes you between a screen of granite Doric columns supporting a sumptuously decorated domed archway to the door leading to the garden. Open this door and the spectacular view, across the terraces of the Jekyll-designed garden to the Arcadian valley in the distance, explodes before you.

The dining room is an incredible lesson in

LEFT ABOVE *The porch in the centre of the entrance elevation is a most witty affair in which Lutyens quietly reinvents the language of classical composition and construction. The central keystone and flanking voussoirs descend from the arch of the opening to help support a second and virtually free-standing arch.*

LEFT BELOW *Above the door within the arch is the motto Sis felix qui huc intres (Happiness on all who enter).* OPPOSITE *The entrance hall or vestibule is compressed – long, narrow and low-ceilinged – and the floor a chequerboard of black and rose marble parallelograms and squares.*

architectural geometry. It is a square room panelled on all sides with split walnut. The room has been likened to many things – the interior of a luxurious ship's cabin, or even a giant cigar box. The walnut panelling extends beyond the walls to the ceiling, where it forms a sixteen-sided piece of precision joinery that frames a white-plaster cove rising to meet a circle of plaster fruit and foliage. In the centre of the ceiling is the chandelier, and a further circle of lavish plasterwork runs in orbit around it, playing with the geometry of the room. It is warm, cosy and comforting, smacking of an old and expensive idea of England and Englishness, in spite of all the French polishing it might require.

On the other side of the domed and columned screen the building opens up. The ceiling height of the Great Hall is almost double that of the entrance hall, light flooding in from the southern bays. The decoration is extraordinarily lavish, but also playfully witty. Occupying the four corners of the room are pilasters of chalk and oak with Corinthian capitals. In this room Lutyens played what he later called the 'high game' of classicism. In a playful manner he shadows the wooden pilasters with chalk duplicates – half visible, recessed next to and behind their timber counterparts. It was a trick he obviously liked, replicating it almost exactly on the portico of the *Country Life* offices (also in 1904), this time solely in stone. The language of Lutyens' later 'Wrenaissance' style is beginning to find voice in Marshcourt, for much of the detailing in the Great Hall, plaster ceiling and fire surround are derived from the late seventeenth-century architecture of Christopher Wren.

The reintroduction of chalk into the interior further complicates this classical idea. The English vernacular classicism implied by the chalk, combined with the Tudor-style oak panelling and the erudite baroque plaster and timber details in the manner of Wren, set just the kind of apparent contradiction that Lutyens relished, implying the room is of different ages. The mix must have been calculated to give everything a richness and a pleasing complexity. Lutyens was playing a high game indeed, and a game played with skill and humour, especially when you take into account the chalk frieze running around the room. Here you see the same flowers and plants you have seen outside – oak and acorns, daisies, bellflowers and even ears of corn – a return to the bioregional vernacular of the Arts and Crafts cheek by jowl with Corinthian acanthus.

The hall flows into the drawing room – again with an extraordinary plasterwork ceiling, overly flamboyant in a way that even the Elizabethans never quite dared: the long loops of stems twisting and projecting from the relief of local flowers, predominately roses and dog roses. Owing much to the famous Wren-period carvings of Grinling Gibbons, this ceiling, in its excess, is almost a parody of late Stuart plasterwork. If overwrought and contrived, it is knowingly so, and so self-aware that you can forgive it. However, just when one thinks Lutyens has played his full hand, you discover he's been holding back his best card yet.

The billiard room was the male hub of any Edwardian country house. At Marshcourt the mammoth billiard table, mounted on a plinth of carved and polished chalk, is famous. There is also a humorous functionality: in looking for somewhere to chalk their cue, players would have to look no further than the table itself. Here too legend has proliferated in spite of the house's relatively young age. As the house lies on a slope, much of this room would have been below ground level – indeed, legend has it that this chalk plinth is an outcrop of the bedrock, the volume of the room having been chipped out around it. Looking at it closely, you can see that it has been given a façade of skilfully carved, well-polished chalk, but this anecdote somehow rings true. On the plan of the house that Lutyens sent in a letter to his friend and colleague Herbert Baker, drawn early on in the building process, the position of the billiard table is marked by a rectangle. There is no mere furniture marked on the plan; its elements are solely structural. Could the legend be true? In short, we will never know, but it is a telling feature of Lutyens' houses that these mythic stories seem to gravitate towards them.

The language of Lutyens' later 'Wrenaissance' style is beginning to find voice in Marshcourt, for much of the detailing in the Great Hall, plaster ceiling and fire surround are derived from the late seventeenth-century architecture of Christopher Wren...

ABOVE *The billiard room with its flamboyant, late seventeenth-century-style ceiling and its billiard table, seemingly made from a lump of chalk fashioned from the bedrock on which the house stands.*

NEVER NEVER LAND

These four rooms at Marshcourt – the dining room, Great Hall, drawing room and billiard room – are built for entertainment. With their intensely flamboyant decoration and shifting feelings of intimacy and exposure, they are designed to be theatrical. It is perhaps more than a coincidence that in 1904, as Lutyens finished the interiors of Marshcourt, he was also working on another project, designing stage sets for a new play a friend had recently completed. The friend was J.M. Barrie and the play was *Peter Pan*. Its opening set, the nursery of the Darlings' home, was almost a carbon copy of the nursery in Lutyens' home at 29 Bloomsbury Square. Allegedly, the ticking crocodile was Lutyens' idea. So was Nana the dog, if you believe his daughter Mary. Emily, his wife, maintained, 'it was through our night-nursery window at Bloomsbury Square that the Darling children flew to the Never Land'.[12]

Marshcourt, of course, was not a stage set –

although at times it distinctly feels like one – but rather a place to live. As such, Lutyens was keen to include all modern conveniences in the house. It is heated in four different ways. Of course it has a fireplace in every room, each one slightly different from its neighbour, utilizing stone and herringbone tiles in countless ways. The house also has radiators and early underfloor heating. Finally, and most remarkable, is the heating system in the corridors. Both upstairs and downstairs, running the length of the corridors and regularly spaced on either side, are small niches at ground level. Unexpectedly, they appear faintly North African in influence, and house

an early air exchange system: the niches in the exterior wall side draw in cold air, while those on the other side blow out warmed air. In 1904, this was revolutionary technology; indeed, it is still rarely seen today.

Of course, all these different heating systems required powering, and down in the basement of Marshcourt is the boiler room, which would have contained the house furnace. In the far corner of the room, high up the wall, is the shaft down which coal would have been directly delivered from the service courtyard above. It would have been like the engine room of the *Titanic* – even today, with modern boilers and after the technological advances of a century, the noise and heat is extraordinary.

In addition to the heating, there was, of course, electric lighting. This was still remarkably rare in 1904. As late as 1919, fewer than 6 per cent of homes in Britain were wired for electricity,[13] and Lutyens was part of the first generation of architects to build electrical lighting into his designs. Many of his trademark lights – light bulbs simply suspended from the ceiling on a long flex, with a halo ring of thin blue glass – survive along the upstairs corridor at Marshcourt. It was a design he stuck with, famously using it later to light the corridors of the Viceroy's House in New Delhi. The present owner of Marshcourt has had Lutyens' design for a light over the billiard table lovingly replicated from drawings at the RIBA.

The house also contained purpose-built bathrooms, with plumbed hot and cold water. They

LEFT ABOVE *A light fitting of Lutyens' design suspended simply from the ceiling on a long flex, with a halo ring of thin blue glass.*

LEFT BELOW *One of Marshcourt's original fourteen bathrooms – the epitome of modernity at the time in having*

plumbed hot and cold water.

OPPOSITE *The staircase rises from the 'fishing door' next to the billiard room and is made of solid carved oak in broadly Jacobean style. It is as much a masterpiece of highly crafted engineering as of design.*

boasted deep marble baths and fretted draining boards on the floor, while the walls are clad in bottle-green hand-glazed tiles. In the hall next to the dining room stands an extraordinary and unique addition to this array of modern conveniences – a warming cabinet, plumbed in to the central heating system, to keep food and plates warm.

Upstairs, Marshcourt is much simpler, with Lutyens' classical trickery being left – for the main part – downstairs. Here the feeling is much more medieval. The staircase that rises from the 'fishing door' next to the billiard room is of solid carved oak and is as much a masterpiece of engineering as it is of craftsmanship. Upstairs, there is peg-jointed oak everywhere, even when the pegging is fulfilling no structural purpose whatsoever. The bedrooms are of large proportions and arranged in suites to accommodate the needs of guests easily. The transverse corridor of the ground floor is mirrored above, and the vast bay window of the hall continues up into the master bedroom in a manner similar to

> **Upstairs, there is peg-jointed oak everywhere, even when the pegging is fulfilling no structural purpose whatsoever…**

ABOVE *Late in life Herbert Johnson fell in love with and married a widow, Violet Charlotte Meeking, who brought her two daughters with her when she moved to Marshcourt. A great affection grew within the family, and Johnson doted in most paternal manner upon his new daughters. Here the family is shown at Marshcourt during the First World War.*
OVERLEAF *The dining room is an incredible lesson in architectural geometry. Square in plan and panelled on all sides with walnut, it has been likened to many things, including a superior ship's cabin and a giant cigar box.*

the iconic bay windows of the early seventeeth-century Audley End House in Essex. Upstairs, the emphasis is on simplicity, comfort and craftsmanship. Even so, Lutyens couldn't help throwing in a barrel vault or two to keep visitors on their toes.

Few records survive of Herbert Johnson's life at Marshcourt immediately after it was built. One can only imagine the kind of sporting parties he would have hosted for his friends and partners from the City. Some stories have survived , such as that of the Prince of Wales (later Edward VIII) getting drunk and passing out on the billiard table and having to be carried by servants up to the nearest bedroom – known ever since as the Prince of Wales Room.

Of course, the dramas of the river Test remained constant. One particularly brilliant letter from Lutyens to his wife, written in September 1905, gives an evocative account of his dining alone in the house, remembering a day's fishing:

Here I am alone – in state.
The big red bed is ready for me.
Rich Oxtail Soup.
The next best thing to being with Emmieown is to write to her – a poor substitute I own.
Filleted sole.
I worked all the morning and then after lunch went out to fish. I caught 2 of 2½lb each v. good and lost 2 and touched one or two more – all good fun. Then a hurried tea and out again. I missed one or two and caught 2, which I put back. Going down the river we saw an Enormous trout – after tea we saw the trout again.

And Oh! Coming home in the dark we saw him again. So I fished for him – and for the fun of it. Suddenly, a dead steady pull at the line – and at a slow deliberate pace my reel unwound. It could not be the big one?!! The line slackened and I reeled in for all I was worth. And then almost at my feet was the Big – (Roast lamb) Trout.

The paper is not large enough to describe him!
He came close up alongside and Baker and myself we gasped. He saw us and went off – not at any great speed but just at a good deliberate pace and my reel clicked out its merry song. I feared he was going into some weeds so I

checked my reel – the speed did not vary. The weight of the fish was irresistible it seemed – and then slack the rod straightened – he was lost!!

He must have been 5lbs at least.

It was too dark to fish some more so I came home and played on the Aeolian 'the dead march in Saul.' So endeth my last fish for 1905.

Oh dear.

The day after tomorrow!! For I shall come Friday and it is so joyous. I think you as Nedisick as I am Emmiesick.

Pigeon and salad and then a savoury to come – Coffee – Port.

Too much – and it is such a bore – alone and a lot of different courses – why not a soup and another fat partridge and have done with it? Now I go round the house with Mrs Binns.

I am in bed and pray God Bless my darling and to keep and cherish her for I love her so very well and altogether.

Your own
Nedi[14]

In 1912 Herbert Johnson's life changed dramatically. First, he retired from the Stock Exchange, although he would continue to own shares for much of his life. Second, and possibly more momentous, in December 1912, at the age of fifty-six, he finally married. He had fallen in love with a widow, Violet Charlotte Meeking, who brought her two daughters with her when she moved to Marshcourt. The house now ceased to be the 'bachelor pad par excellence' it had always been, becoming for the first time in its short history a proper family home.

Violet's daughters were named Finola and Viola, and it is through them that we get to know the older Johnnie. Finola would eventually marry Lord Somers, and Viola Lord Apsley. As Lady Somers, Finola's home was Eastnor Castle in Malvern, and it is from their family archives that we get to see Marshcourt in these years. There we find photos in abundance of Johnnie, brilliantly cataloguing his later years; we find pictures of shooting parties, gatherings on the sundial lawn, a copy of *Herbert Johnson's Investment Tables* and a small fisherman's diary with 'a fisherman's prayer' on the cover:

Lord suffer me to catch a fish
So large that even I,
In talking of it afterwards
Shall have no need to lie.

They all help breathe life into the man. But among the archives of Eastnor, we also find records of the new role that Marshcourt would have in society – as a troop hospital during the First World War.

MARSHCOURT AT WAR

The optimism of the Edwardian age lasted just over a dozen years, the First World War cutting the party tragically and irrecoverably short in 1914. The new Mrs Johnson had brought fresh opinions on public life as well as a fresh philanthropy to Marshcourt. Her first husband had died of enteric fever at Bloemfontein, during the Boer War – one of about 18,000 of the 22,000 casualties in this war to succumb to disease rather than combat wounds.

It was, therefore, unsurprising that when the First World War began, Mrs Johnson turned Marshcourt into a troop hospital. It was something that many owners of large houses across Britain did for the war effort, but the Johnsons went further than most. They opened a second hospital – Marshcourt No. 2 – in Stockbridge itself, and financed the running of both hospitals entirely themselves.

The Eastnor photograph albums offer a remarkable insight into what wartime life was like at the house. There are brilliant posed photographs of the troops and hospital staff, the recovering troops shown in convalescent uniform – a blue flannel outfit with white lapels and a red necktie, which military authorities required convalescent troops of non-officer rank to wear at all times. Viola poses next to one of the Marshcourt ambulances in nurse's uniform. Finola lists the daily activities of the patients in blue ink: 'shooting, cricket, dancing, motoring, swimming, billiards, ratting, gramophone, concerts, badminton, fancy work, croquet, whist drives, stool ball, quoits'. Her own daily duties are listed in red – 'dressings, scrubbing, brushing, temperatures, medicines, calling, ambulance work, mendings, dusting, polishing, bedmaking, waiting, grates, bandaging, washing'.[15] It is a neat summary of a young woman's hard work in a wartime troop hospital.

Johnson, as well as financing the hospital out of his own pocket, gave the benefit of his financial knowledge to the Board of Trade as part of his national service. He seems to have played a vital role

LEFT ABOVE & BELOW *Herbert Johnson and his wife turned Marshcourt into a military hospital during the First World War. These photographs show patients and staff.*
OPPOSITE *Upstairs at Marshcourt there is peg-jointed oak everywhere, even when the pegging fulfils no obvious structural purpose.*

in aiding the successful sale of British Petroleum by the Anglo-Persian Company in 1917, in spite of BP being 'in a most difficult and precarious condition.'[16] Much less visible than his wife's work, this too was vitally important, ensuring the economic survival of Britain while war raged. But Johnnie, it seems, had other agendas. Keen to safeguard morale and fearing the decline of the rural Hampshire life he loved so much, he stepped into the breach as Master of the Hursley Hunt in 1916 when the incumbent master was forced to step down because of the demands of wartime service.

The convalescent uniforms seem to disappear from the pages of Finola's photograph albums quite suddenly. The Marshcourt hospitals closed on 31 December 1918, but the war had, of course, changed British society forever. The country had experienced carnage and horror unparalleled in its history, some of which must have been witnessed within the walls of the Marshcourt hospitals. Britain was in need of somewhere to direct its mourning for the dead, its thanks for their sacrifice and its relief in the face of victory. The government decided that, like France, they would commission a saluting monument for a memorial ceremony to be held on 19 July 1919. Only two weeks before, Lutyens was called to 10 Downing Street by the prime minister, David Lloyd George, and asked to come up with designs. As ever, it took him only a couple of hours to design the structure. Remembering a large, simple stone bench under a birch tree in Gertrude Jekyll's garden – the Cenotaph of Sigismunda – he designed a great warstone and named it the Cenotaph, meaning literally 'empty tomb'. The design received universal approval, and after the Peace Day celebrations, the decision was taken (despite Westminster Council's objections on traffic grounds) to rebuild the Cenotaph permanently in Whitehall in Portland stone.

Following the success of the Cenotaph, Lutyens became deeply involved in the expression of national remembrance and commemoration. He played a large role in executing designs for the War Graves Commission on the Continent, culminating in the gargantuan Thiepval Memorial on the Somme, which was not completed until the summer of 1932. Like many of Lutyens' country-house clients, Johnson commissioned him to build war memorials in the two villages that bordered the Marshcourt estate – Stockbridge and Kings Somborne. Tim Skelton and Gerald Gliddon in their book *Lutyens and the Great War* describe in detail the processes by which the memorials came about: 'A meeting to discuss the Kings Somborne memorial was held in the local schoolroom in February 1919 with Johnson in the chair, assisted by the local vicar.' Suggestions were heard and a representative committee formed, with promises of £100 (about £2000 today), including a contribution from Herbert Johnson. 'At the end of the meeting, a vote of thanks was given to Johnson for presiding over the meeting and in response he said that "it always gave him great pleasure to do anything he possibly could for the village and its inhabitants".'[17] The committees in both Stockbridge and Kings Somborne both decided on a simple Lutyens war cross of Portland stone, the only difference being that the Stockbridge monument stands on a circular coved base, while the one at Kings Somborne stands on a square coved base. Writing about the chosen design in the local paper, the *Hampshire Chronicle*, Johnson said: 'the Committee considered the cross they had chosen to be chaste and simple in character, dignified in appearance, while its proportions were beautiful and perfect, and of great artistic merit'.[18] The Stockbridge war memorial was unveiled by Mrs Johnson on 3 April 1921, the Kings Somborne monument having been unveiled by Rear Admiral Sir Godfrey Paine the week before.

The combination of marriage and the war had forced Johnson further into public life. In 1920 he became high sheriff and accepted a seat on the county council. To celebrate his new status, or perhaps to demonstrate his worthiness of such a role in county politics, that same year he applied for – and was granted – a coat of arms. The design, like so many created for new capitalists in the early twentieth century, is an old Johnson coat of arms, customized to suit its new bearer. The motto he chose is utterly bizarre – 'Come On'.

The First World War had been bitter and cruel for

all ranks of British society – none were spared its
pain and horror. For the Johnsons at Marshcourt,
tragedy did not end in 1918. On 26 October 1921,
after only nine years of marriage, Mrs Johnson
unexpectedly died. The cause of her death was
Encephalitis lethargica or 'sleepy sickness', a
devastating illness that swept the world in the
1920s. During the outbreak, almost a million people
died, and millions more suffered what was almost a
worse fate – being left speechless and motionless,
like living statues. Those who didn't die quickly
were institutionalized, frozen inside their useless
bodies. What made it worse was that at the time,
nobody knew the cause, let alone how to treat it.

Violet's funeral was held in Stockbridge on
31 October, while a memorial service was held at the
same time at St Paul's in Knightsbridge. Once again,
Johnson turned to Lutyens to commemorate the loss
in a gravestone and memorial cross. The memorial
is particularly fine – a four-point cross, hexagonal in

section, draped with a carved stone wreath, the focal point of the Winton Hill Cemetery in Stockbridge, at the eastern end of its single avenue of trees. Its inscription, in capital letters, reads touchingly:

Sacred to the memory of Violet Charlotte Johnson
MBE a gracious lady of England
Beloved of all who knew her for her rare qualities of
heart and mind endowed with every
capacity for the enjoyment of life, she gave herself to
the service of others and her solicitude
during the Great War for the wounded soldiers in
her hospitals at Marshcourt and
Stockbridge contributed to her untimely end

Erected by her husband Herbert Johnson Esq.
of Marshcourt

The souls of the righteous are in the hand of God
Dedicated 5th August 1923

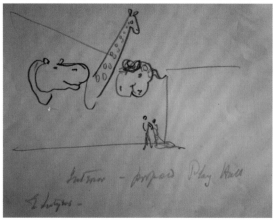

After Violet's death Herbert remained utterly devoted to his stepdaughters, even naming his yacht after Finola. That he, in turn, was held in great affection is shown by the Eastnor letters from Finola's children to 'grandpa Johnnie' and photographs of him well into his old age.

In the years after Violet's death, Johnnie pursued his sports activities even more. He served further spells as Master of the Hursley Hunt and also took to renting the Invercauld estate in Scotland for the hunting season, often dining with the king at Balmoral.

At Marshcourt, Johnson's leading role in the local hunt eventually manifested itself architecturally when he invited Lutyens back to build a ballroom fit to host the hunt balls. The ballroom was built between 1924 and 1926, and in order to finance it, Johnson was forced to make yet another fortune on the stock market. This appears to have begun in 1921, when he instructed his broker to make many more investments on his behalf.[19] The investments clearly paid off, and the site for the new ballroom was chosen to the east of the sundial lawn. The extension maintains the style of the rest of the house, as well as the limited palette of colours and materials. This was not always the case when Lutyens returned to his earlier designs for extensions, so it suggests that he remained happy with the scheme of Marshcourt more than twenty years after its initial design. In design terms, the only problem with the ballroom is its size and the bluntness of its shape. It breaks above the roofline

LEFT ABOVE *Johnson's leading role in the local hunt manifested itself architecturally when, in 1924, he commissioned Lutyens to add a large ballroom for hunt balls.*
LEFT BELOW *A sketch by Lutyens, showing trophies bagged in Africa by Johnson in* 1926. *Many of these found their way on to the walls of Marshcourt.*
OPPOSITE *The interior of the ballroom is finely detailed. In order to finance its construction, Johnson was obliged to make yet another fortune on the stock market.*

of the earlier house and fails to bed down into the hillside as the earlier house had done so skilfully.

Amid the archive at Eastnor are four little gems: early Lutyens sketches for the ballroom extension. On the plans Lutyens calls it the 'Play Hall' – a place for fun. The drawings themselves show views of the new 'Mulberry Courtyard from the northwest corner' and the 'new wing from the Tennis courts', all drawn with Lutyens' distinctive worm's-eye perspective in red, black and green crayon and pencil, with his trademark dark slitty windows. Inside, the ballroom feels just as vast as it appears outside. On the western wall there is a truly monumental fireplace of chalk, with acanthus-leaf scrolls on either side and a laurel wreath at its centre. Above this rises a huge, carved oak overmantel with a central recess and copies of the composite columns in the Great Hall flanking either side. To the left of the fireplace is a floor-to-ceiling window, deeply recessed with leaden glazing bars of course, perfectly positioned to catch the setting sun. To the right, ensuring symmetry, is an identical window, although with panes of mirrored glass

❝ Commissioning Lutyens to add to your house was an expensive game. Even the famous grocery fortune of Julius Drewe had been almost entirely consumed in the construction of Castle Drogo…

ABOVE *Lutyens' drawing of the 'new wing from [the] tennis court' shows the ballroom, or 'Play Hall' as he called it, rendered in his distinctive worm's-eye perspective.* OPPOSITE *Johnson posing next to yet another victim of his fine marksmanship – an African elephant.*

as the old office lies behind it. High windows run down the southern wall. The electric lights in this room are truly extraordinary, holding sixteen bulbs, with tassels above and blue glass dishes below, suspended from a gold and black chequerboard ring. It seems a neat colour scheme, reminiscent of the azure blue of Johnson's new coat of arms. It is a truly magnificent space.

Also at Eastnor is a photograph album given to Johnnie by his friend Dick, 'in memory of a wonderful trip and in admiration of a wonderful sportsman'.[20] It records a hunting trip the pair made to Africa between January and May 1926. It shows a 'Lion – shot by H. Johnson', 'Charging Rhino – shot by H. Johnson' and Johnnie posing next to another victim of his fine marksmanship, an African elephant. It makes the 1920s feel like a very distant time. With the other Lutyens ballroom drawings at Eastnor we discover one of the interior aptly titled 'Interior of proposed Play Hall'. What it shows, however is a cartoon of a man and a woman looking up at game trophies – a hippopotamus, a giraffe, a bison. What a delight it must have been when the hunter returned home with a host of trophies to furnish the new ballroom, testament to the brilliant shot he was! For a short time it must have seemed as if the old, careless lifestyle of pre-war Marshcourt had returned.

On Friday, 28 August 1931, Christopher Hussey, a writer for *Country Life*, picked up Lutyens from his offices at Eaton Gate in his Austin 6, setting out on a tour of some of Lutyens' early country houses for the magazine. By Saturday evening they had reached Andover, and Lutyens subsequently wrote to Emily:

The hotel most unappetising, so – let's telephone Johnnie; if in, might dine at Marshcourt. 'Mr Johnson out, but I am sure he will be delighted to see you.' So off we went Bumpty Bump down the valley of the Test – one of God's kindest and most gentle of his creations & there we got. 8:15 we dressed! Had our bags taken out, given rooms and a bath.

Johnnie very cordial with a glass eye – not an improvement – Apsley & his crippled wife who is in a lay down and can't move her legs... Lady Somers – her husband is in S. Africa. Stays there another month to save income tax

for the year! A man called Spears, ADC to Somers. Young and good fun as an ADC should possess.

We were so easy spinning after dinner. Persuaded to stay the night. So I had a good go round the house. Heard the organ in the new ballroom.

The garden – the mulberry is now nearly above the drawing room window. The clock I bought some 35 years ago – is a Bregnet! Talking of old times, Johnson is in bad economic luck. Spends no money. Reggie McKenner says now is the time to spend.

The proprietor – the Banker Johnnie was discovered telling the footman to lay dinner without light to save electricity. We dined in the Ballroom as it is easy for Lady Apsley in her long bed.

Slept sound. Call at 7. Off at 8:30. Bumpety Bumps. Reached 5 Eaton Gate at 10:15 instead of 10 sharp. So this was a very unexpected and exhilarating weekend.'[21]

Commissioning Lutyens to add to your house was an expensive game. Even the famous grocery fortune of Julius Drewe had been almost entirely consumed in the construction of Castle Drogo by Lutyens. Johnnie's financial troubles were more to do with philanthropy than self-indulgence. It was rumoured that he had never quite recovered from the expense of running the Marshcourt hospitals. Certainly the First World War had forever wrecked Britain's imperial buoyancy. Lutyens had, of course, ridden the wave of empire in its dying moments, designing the masterplan for the new imperial capital of New Delhi, as well as his *opus magnum*, the Viceroy's House, which had filled much of his time since 1913. Commissioned before the war, the project was a thorny one, the building being almost instantly redundant as the world changed around it. After the war, Lutyens' work abroad was at the mercy of Britain's paradoxical self-image – continuing the imperial plans of New Delhi, while creating monuments to commemorate its war dead.

The Depression that had started with the Wall Street Crash in late 1929, continued to sting well into the 1930s. This was one economic collapse where Johnson could not simply take out his ready reckoner and make back his money, as he had done

so many times before. In 1931 he sold his beloved Daimler, and in 1932 the house was put on the market. Lutyens made one final visit to Marshcourt in May of that year. He wrote about it very briefly to his wife – on Marshcourt headed notepaper – with more than a note of sadness: 'The house here is shut up, no one but Johnnie. Apsley came here yesterday – this place will have to be sold. Johnnie said last night at dinner: "It doesn't matter what happens to a man but what does matter is how he takes it."'[22]

By the beginning of the Second World War, Johnson was forced to sell the freehold of the house, only for it to be swiftly requisitioned by the War Office. A four-day auction was held at the house between 15 and 18 October 1941, selling off almost all of its precious contents, right down to the curtains.

By now, Johnson's health was failing. Just over eighty in 1938, he was now totally blind and partially deaf. Nonetheless, he managed to maintain a good quality of life, sustaining his relationship with the river – crossing over his beloved river Test on a plank unaided. He died on 2 April 1949. His lengthy obituary in *The Times* spoke warmly of a man at the heart of a community into which he had come as a London city dweller over fifty years earlier: 'Hampshire society of the last 50 years will feel a void by the death of Herbert Johnson – "Johnnie" to his intimates ... In 1904, though still a bachelor, he began the erection of the great flint and chalk mansion designed by Lutyens, which was for the rest of his life the very symbol of himself and every stone of which he loved ... In short, as one of his

LEFT ABOVE AND BELOW
After the war Marshcourt passed into the hands of a Mr Wright, who converted it into a boys' prep school. Under his stewardship, and later that of Mr Broadbent, the school ran for over forty years.
OPPOSITE *The garden is finely tuned to evoke different moods, to respond to the potential of the site and to complement the architecture of the house and offer dramatic vignettes. Particularly successful is the way in which the garden is terraced, with sections walled and secluded – such as this court, seemingly inspired by Indian step-tanks – to offer an eventful journey around the perimeter of the house.*

servants said, "We shall never see a Mr. Johnson again." But we are glad we have seen him.'[23]

It seems almost too romantic to suggest that, without the house, Johnnie had little to live for. It had been a labour of love, a life's work that had cost a life's fortune. But the house, naturally, lived on without Johnnie. After the war, Marshcourt passed into the hands of a Mr Wright, who converted it into a boys' prep school. Under his stewardship, and later that of a Mr Broadbent, the school ran for over forty years.

In many ways, and unlike the fate of so many other country houses, Marshcourt was kept alive by the school: it kept a roof on, kept it heated, but more than that, it kept it occupied and lived in. The playfulness of Lutyens' architecture lent itself to the boys' imagination, as did the pursuits of Herbert Johnson, whose shooting trophies remained in the house, becoming the mascots and names for the dormitories. The eldest boys slept in 'Rhino', and the younger ones in 'Gazelle', 'Buffalo', 'Eland', 'Swordfish' and 'Wildebeest', each with its accompanying trophy. On the first-floor corridor a large storage cupboard was converted into a tuck shop and opened every break time. The door, with custom-made medieval hinges and an unexpected squirrel carved into the banister above, is one of those exquisitely carved details where Lutyens allowed craftsmanship to shine through.

The boys used to tell a story that Mr Wright had killed a German during the war by throwing him off the top of the stairs. The German stormtrooper was no match for an English headmaster at full tilt, and it was said that he fell on one of the coat hooks and had his throat ripped out. The ghost of this particular Hun was rumoured to walk the school at night, and the discovery of a silver Reichsmark coin under the floorboards of Rhino dormitory added spice to the story.[24]

When the school closed in the 1980s, the house found itself a saviour in the shape of Geoffrey Robinson, then a front-bench MP for the Labour Party in the opposition to Thatcher's government. Robinson's passion for Lutyens is as strong today as it ever was. The restoration task was mammoth, the biggest problem being the damp, which over the years had seeped into the porous chalk walls, doing much damage. Much had to be replaced using chalk quarried from a local pit in the Test valley, only a few miles from the house. Partition walls had to be taken down and the plasterwork on the ceiling reinstated where it had been cut away to accommodate them; the walnut panelling in the dining room desperately needed restoring after forty years of steam from school dinners; all this in addition to removing asbestos from the house, a considerable task that continues to this day.

Since Mr Robinson's tenure, owners of Marshcourt have continued the restoration work where he left off, not least the current owners, who have reinstated many lost features with bespoke replicas. Today the theatricality of the Lutyens architecture is twinned with an eclectic array of contemporary furnishings; the house feels thoroughly modern again, and as luxurious as it should.

Lutyens' last ever country house was Middleton Park in 1938 for Lady Jersey – best known later for her brief marriage to Cary Grant. The house, with fourteen bathrooms and based on a late seventeenth-century plan-type, was only briefly and rarely used. Later, symbolically, it was converted into flats. Lutyens' most interesting residential project of this late period was the Page Street Flats, built for Westminster City Council to replace a set of Pimlico tenements destroyed by flooding in 1928. Between 1929 and 1935 Lutyens built 616 flats on the site, in seven U-plan blocks each five or six storeys high. They are still desirable today. What makes them particularly striking is their chequerboard walls, a more modern, if not modernist, abstraction of the flint and chalk chequerboards at Marshcourt. In terms of setting and client, they couldn't be more different, but for some reason the Page Street Flats seem to have inherited this design; what they share is Lutyens' distinctive architectural quality and flair.

Lutyens' career neatly embodied the last golden age of country house building in Britain. For him, the country house had been an arena of architectural fancy, of witty contrasts and luxurious fittings, but it had also been an apprenticeship where he had

> It seems almost too romantic to suggest that, without the house, Johnnie had little to live for. It had been a labour of love, a life's work that had cost a life's fortune...

ABOVE *Middleton Park, Oxfordshire, was designed in 1938 for Lady Jersey, the American former actress Virginia Cherrill and ex-wife of Cary Grant. This was the last country house designed by Lutyens – he died six years later – and architecturally represents a long and not entirely successful journey from the youthful magic of Marshcourt.*

honed his distinctive architectural style. The Edwardian economy had supplied an abundance of wealthy clients eager to affirm their place in society through property, and by one route or another many such clients had found their way to Lutyens. Johnson, of course, had been one of the many, but he was also remarkable. Because of Lutyens' techniques, and because of where it was, Marshcourt became the house it was. The site was Johnson's real passion – the best piece of land that any Edwardian sportsman adventurer could hope for. Despite Marshcourt being a new house, Johnson took pains to link it to the village communities that bordered its land. He must have believed that certain duties accompanied his elevated social rank, but he fulfilled them (especially in time of war) far beyond what was merely necessary. His were old-fashioned actions, based on old-fashioned values, but perhaps they have much to teach us today ❖

ENDNOTES

All money conversions in the book have been calculated using www.nationalarchives.gov.uk/currency.

INTRODUCTION

1 Giles Worsley, 'Country Houses: the Lost Legacy', *Daily Telegraph*, 15 June 2002; Giles Worsley, *England's Lost Houses: From the Archives of Country Life*, Aurum Press, London, 2002, p. 7; and 'SAVE Britain's Heritage: Thirty Years of Campaigning', V&A exhibition, November 2005. Ian Gow in *Scotland's Lost Houses*, Aurum Press/National Trust for Scotland, London, 2006, states that since 1945 it has been estimated that over 200 'major houses' have been demolished in Scotland.

CHAPTER 1
SOUTH WRAXALL

1 Walter Chitty, *The Old Manor, South Wraxall*, Bath, 1893, p. 5; also R.B. Pugh (ed.), *History of Wiltshire*, Victoria County History, Vol. 7: *Bradford Hundred*, OUP/Boydell & Brewer, Woodbridge, 1953, p. 21.

2 Thomas Larkins Walker, *The History and Antiquities of the Manor House, at South Wraxall and Church of Saint Peter, at Biddestone, Wiltshire; the former property of Walter Long, Forming Part III of Examples of Gothic Architecture*, London, 1838, p. 2.

3 Chitty, op. cit., p. 6.

4 Walker, op. cit., p. 2.

5 J.S. Roskell, Linda Clark and Carole Rawcliffe (eds), *History of Parliament: The Commons, 1386–1421*, Alan Sutton for the History of Parliament Trust, Stroud, 1992/3, p. 616; also Pugh, *Bradford Hundred*, p. 22.

6 John Leland, *The itinerary of John Leland in or about the years 1535–1543*, ed. Lucy Toulmin Smith, Centaur Press, London, 1964, p. 616.

7 Roskell et al, op. cit., p. 617.

8 Information thanks to David Gelber, formerly of the College of Arms, City of London.

9 Tim Couzens, *The Hand of Fate*, ELSP, Bradford on Avon, 2001, p. 29.

10 Roskell et al, *History of Parliament*, p. 543.

11 Couzens, op. cit., p. 29, and interview.

12 Foreword by Mark Girouard in *The Tudor and Jacobean Country House* by Malcolm Airs, Alan Sutton, Stroud, 1995, p. ix.

13 William Harrison, *Description of Englande, within Raphaell Holinshed's Chronicles of England, Scotlande and Irelande*, London, 1577. See also George Edelen (ed.), *The Description of England*, Courier/Dover, New York, 1994, p. 431.

14 Andrew Boorde, *Dyetary of Helth*, 1542, ed. F.J. Furnivall, 1870, reprinted by Elibron Classics, London, 2005, pp. 236–7.

15 Walker, *History and Antiquities*, p. 9.

16 Exodus 20:4.

17 Ibid., 20:5.

18 Walker, op. cit., p. 18.

19 Ibid., pp. 12–13.

20 National Archives, State Papers (Domestic), SP 12/251/f211 and SP 12/219/f198; also Francis Macnamara, *Memorials of the Danvers Family, of Dauntsey and Culworth*, Hardy & Co., London, 1895, p. 303; also Lansdowne MSS, No. 827, British Library.

21 Reverend J.E. Jackson, 'Murder of Henry Long Esq. AD 1594: An Inquisition held at Corsham, 5th October 36 Elizabeth (1594)', *Wiltshire Archaeological and Natural History Magazine*, March 1854, p. 320.

22 Couzens, *Hand of Fate*, p. 34; Reverend J.E. Jackson, *Wiltshire Archaeological and Natural History Magazine*, Vol. 1, 1864, pp. 239–40.

23 Insights about Florio and Shakespeare courtesy of Jonathan Bate, professor of Shakespeare and Renaissance literature at the University of Warwick.

24 Wiltshire Record Office: 947/1373/1–2.

25 John Aubrey, *Wiltshire Topographical Collections (1659–70)*, corrected and enlarged by John Edward Jackson, Devizes, 1862; Aubrey MS 3, copy in the Bodleian Library, Oxford.

CHAPTER 2
KINROSS HOUSE

1 N.H. Walker, *Kinross House*, published privately, Kinross-Shire Antiquarian Society, 1990, p. 50.

2 Mark Girouard, *Country Life*, 25 March 1965 and 1 April 1965.

3 Charles Wemyss, *A Study of Aspiration and Ambition*, PhD thesis, 2 vols, University of Dundee, December 2008, Vol. 1, p. 3.

4 Ibid, Vol. 1, pp. 1–2.

5 Bruce Papers, GD29/263/10 (B.181), National Archives, Edinburgh.

6 Walker, *Kinross House*, p. 33.

7 Annotated plans of the house, University of Edinburgh, KRD/5/10-11, also reproduced in Walker, *Kinross House*, pp. 14–16.

8 Plan of the house in its setting, ibid., KRD/5/9a, and in Walker, *Kinross House*, p. 12.

9 Girouard, *Country Life*, 25 March 1965.

10 J. Gifford, *The Buildings of Scotland: Perth and Kinross* (Pevsner's Architectural Guides), Yale University Press, New Haven and London, 2007, pp. 484–94.

11 Walker, *Kinross House*, p. 29.

12 Ibid., p. 17.

13 Ibid.

14 Wemyss, *A Study of Aspiration and Ambition*, Vol. 1, p. 86.

15 Bruce Papers, 29/432/4 (51), National Archives, Edinburgh.

16 Walker, *Kinross House*, p. 57.

17 Bruce Papers, GD 26/7/103, item viii, National Archives, Edinburgh.

18 Quoted in *BBC History Magazine*, July 2001.

19 David Hayton, Eveline Cruickshanks and Stuart Hawley (eds), *The House of Commons, 1690–1715*, Cambridge University Press, Cambridge, 2002, Vol. 2, p. 370.

20 *BBC History Magazine*, July 2001.

21 Walker, *Kinross House*, p. 62.

22 Ibid., p. 58.

23 Bruce Papers, GD 26/7/128/5, National Archives, Edinburgh.

24 Daniel Defoe, *Tour thro' the Whole Island of Britain*, 3 vols, G. Strahan, London, 1724–7.

25 Dr Thomas Ross, *Notes on Kinross House and Sir William Bruce*, 1903, manuscript copy in Charter Room, Kinross House.

CHAPTER 3

EASTON NESTON

1 From Hawksmoor's obituary, probably by his son-in-law Nathaniel Blackerby, quoted in Kerry Downes, *Hawksmoor*, Zwemmer, London, 1959, p. 7.

2 Nicholas Hawksmoor to the Earl of Carlisle, 4 October 1731, in *The Nineteenth Volume of the Walpole Society 1930–1931*, OUP, Oxford, 1931, p. 126.

3 Ibid., p. 136.

4 Letter from the Duchess of Marlborough to Lord Chief Justice Parker, 23 December 1715, quoted in Downes, *Hawksmoor*, p. 272 in 1979 edition.

5 Nicholas Hawksmoor to the Earl of Carlisle, 4 October 1731, in *Walpole Society*, p. 126. Earlier English houses or architectural compositions to incorporate a Giant order include houses of the 1640s in Great Queen Street, Covent Garden (demolished), and in Lincoln's Inn Fields, where Lindsey House survives, and the remarkable Lees Court, Kent, of c.1640. Dendrochronological dating carried out in 2010 and January 2011 date the felling of roof timbers used in the wing to 1683–6, and for the main house to the spring of 1700–01.

6 Kerry Downes, 'Hawksmoor's House at Easton Neston', *Architectural History*, Vol. 30, 1987, p. 55.

7 D.E.L Haynes, *The Arundel Marbles*, Ashmolean Museum, Oxford, 1975.

8 John Summerson, *Architecture in Britain 1530 to 1830*, Penguin Books, London, 1953, p. 186.

9 Downes, 'Hawksmoor's House', p. 63.

10 Ibid.

11 Nancy H. Ramage, 'Restorer and Collector: Notes on Eighteenth-century Re-creations of Roman Statues' in *Memoirs of the American Academy in Rome: Supplementary Volumes, Vol. 1: The Ancient Art of Emulation: Studies in Artistic Originality and Tradition from the Present to Classical Antiquity*, ed. Elaine K. Gazda, University of Michigan Press, Ann Arbor, 2002, p. 71.

12 Howard Colvin, *Country Life*, 15 October 1970, p. 968.

13 Hawksmoor to the Dean of Westminster, 8 March 1735, quoted in Downes, *Hawksmoor*, p. 260.

14 Nicholas Hawksmoor to the Earl of Carlisle, 4 October 1731, in *Walpole Society*, p. 137.

15 Colen Campbell, *Vitruvius Britannicus*, Dover Publications, New York, 2007, p. 1.

16 Ibid.

17 Ibid., p. 7.

18 Nicholas Hawksmoor to the Earl of Carlisle, 4 October 1731, in *Walpole Society*, p. 126.

19 Downes, 'Hawksmoor's House', p. 55.

20 Quoted in Downes, *Hawksmoor*, p. 7.

21 Helen Davies, *Times Online*, 17 July 2005.

CHAPTER 4

WENTWORTH WOODHOUSE

1 Geoffrey Howe, *The Wentworths of Wentworth: The Fitzwilliam (Wentworth) Estates and the Wentworth Monuments*, Trustees of the Fitzwilliam Wentworth Amenity Trust, Rotherham, 2002, p. 126.

2 Ibid., p. 129.

3 Letter dated 9 February 1711/12 in Jonathan Swift, *Journal to Stella*, 1766, ed. Harold Williams, Blackwell, Oxford, 1974, Vol. II, p. 489.

4 Information from Patrick Eyres, editor of *New Arcadian Journal*, in conversation with author.

5 Contract in British Library, Add Mss. 22329.

6 Lord Shaftesbury, *Letter concerning Art, or Science of Design*, 1712, published in *Essays in Characteristics of Men, Manners etc.*, John Darby, London, 1714.

7 When speaking of the origin of classical architecture, Robert Morris wrote in his *Essay in Defence of Ancient Architecture* (London, 1728, pp. 19–20): 'The Grecians were the first happy Inventers, they extracted the beauteous Ideas of it from rude and unshapen Trees, the Product of Nature, and embellish'd it, by degrees of Perfectness, with those necessary Ornaments (since) collected by the indefatigable Care and Industry of Palladio.'

8 Colen Campbell, *Vitruvius Britannicus*, Dover Publications, New York, 2007, p. 1–2.

9 Giacomo Leoni (trans), *The Architecture of Leon Battista Alberti in Ten Books*, 3 vols, Thomas Edlin, London, 1726. See volume 3, which includes '… Designs for buildings … by James Leoni' along with a text 'To the Reader' (no page numbers) and which discusses 'Moderns' who forget or neglect the 'great Masters' and praises Inigo Jones.

10 Tim Couzens, *The Hand of Fate*, ELSP, Bradford on Avon, 2001, pp. 60–1.

11 Isaac Ware (trans), *The Four Books of Architecture by Andrea Palladio*, London, 1738, pp. 29–30.

12 Account Book, WWM/A-1273, City of Sheffield archives.

13 John Trussler, *The Honours of the Table … with the whole art of carving*, London, 1788, p. 6.

14 Richard Hewlings, *Country Life*, 24 February 2010.

15 George Sheeran, 'The Hoober Stand: A Masonic Perspective', *New Arcadian Journal*, no. 59/60, 2006, Part I, pp. 28–50.

16 'The Patriotism and Improvement of a Classic Whig Landscape', *New Arcadian Journal*, no. 59/60, 2006, Part II, pp. 54–105.

17 Letter from Joe Hall to Clement Attlee, 8 April 1946, National Archives, 8/728.

18 Sale catalogue from Henry Spencer & Sons, Worksop, July 1949.

CHAPTER 5
CLANDEBOYE HOUSE

1 Mike Chappell, *Wellington's Peninsula Regiments*, Vol. 1: The Irish, Osprey, Oxford, 2003, p. 5.

2 Public Record Office Northern Ireland (PRONI), Dufferin Papers, D1071, D1231, MIC22, ed. Dr A.T. Harrison, November 2007, p. 4.

3 Mark Bence-Jones, *Burke's Guide to Country Houses: Ireland*, Burke's Peerage Ltd, London, 1978, p. xxiii.

4 William Maguire, *The Blackwoods of Ballyleidy*, Clandeboye booklet, p. 35.

5 Letter in Clandeboye House library.

6 Quoted in Sir Alfred Lyall, *The Life of the Marquis of Dufferin and Ava*, John Murray, London, 1905, Vol. 1, p. 44.

7 As expressed by Charles Trevelyan, assistant secretary to the Treasury, who was in charge of administering famine relief in Ireland.

8 Lyall, op. cit., p. 47.

9 PRONI, Dufferin Papers, p. 6.

10 Quoted in Harold Nicolson, *Helen's Tower*, Constable, London, 1937, p. 91.

11 Dufferin's journal, 1855–8, in Clandeboye House library, p. 20.

12 Ibid., p. 97.

13 I.E.S. Edwards, 'Lord Dufferin's Excavations at Deir el-Bahri', *Journal of Egyptian Archaeology*, Vol. 51, December 1965, pp. 16–28, published by the Egypt Excavation Society.

14 Helen's death journal in Clandeboye library, pp. 26–7.

15 Lord Dufferin, *Irish Emigration and the Tenure of Land in Ireland*, Willis, Sotheran & Co. London, 1867, pp. 1–45.

16 Lord Dufferin, *Mr. Mill's Plan for the Pacification of Ireland Examined by Lord Dufferin*, John Murray, London, 1868.

17 Ibid., p. 3.

18 Catalogue of sale of 'Egyptian classical statues' by Messrs Christie, Manson & Wood, King Street, St James's, 31 May 1937: Mummy case and lid, 8 ft high, sold for £22.1s.0d. and then sold subsequently to King of Egypt for £20, and a 'Figure of a king in hard white limestone, probably King Amenhetep II as God Amen-Ra, throne symbol of Isis, girder belt of Isis, left hand clenching Ankh. 34 inches high, XVIII dynasty.' Sold for £1081.10s.0d to 'Archer', as written by hand in copy of the catalogue in Clandeboye House. A total of 42 items were sold, making a sum of £1440.3s.0d (about £53,000 today).

19 Transcript in Muniments Room archive, Clandeboye House.

20 Mark Bence-Jones, *Country Life*, 8 October 1970, p. 902.

21 Transcript of letter from Dufferin in India to Lynn in 1887, copy in Muniments Room archive, Clandeboye House.

22 PRONI, Dufferin Papers, p. 7.

23 Ibid., pp. 7–9.

24 John Gray, The Dufferins in Canada, 1872–1878,

Linen Hall Library, Belfast, 1997, p. 8.

25 See ledger in Muniments Room archive, Clandeboye House.

26 Lord Dufferin's papers, 1884–1888, 'Correspondence with Her Majesty the Queen Empress', transcription volume, p. 2, in Clandeboye House library.

27 Transcript of letters in Muniments Room archive, Clandeboye House.

28 Ibid.

29 Bence-Jones, *Country Life*, 8 October 1970, p. 902.

30 PRONI, Dufferin Papers, p. 32.

CHAPTER 6
MARSHCOURT

1 *Wedd Durlacher Mordaunt and Co., Members of the Stock Exchange, London*, The Company, London, 1984 – a short, self-published company pamphlet held at the Guildhall Library, City of London.

2 *Western Mail* newspaper, 2 December 1893.

3 Wedd Durlacher, op. cit.

4 Mary Comyns Carr, 'Marshcourt – Lutyens' masterpiece in chalk', *Hampshire Magazine*, October 1985, pp. 41–2.

5 Marshcourt sale catalogue, Eastnor Castle archives.

6 Letter from Edwin Lutyens to his wife, Lady Emily, 18 August 1901, RIBA Archive, LuE/15/3/6.

7 Letter from Edwin Lutyens to his wife, Lady Emily, 19 August 1901, RIBA Archive, LuE/15/3/7.

8 Letter from Edwin Lutyens to his wife, Lady Emily, 20 August 1901, RIBA Archive, LuE/15/3/10.

9 Clayre Percy and Jane Ridley (eds), *Letters of Edwin Lutyens to His Wife Lady Emily*, Collins, London, 1985, p. 217.

10 Conversation with Dave Webb, a land surveyor, from Stockbridge, Hampshire.

11 Christopher Hussey, *Country Life*, 19 March 1932, pp. 316–22.

12 Cited in Jane Ridley, *Edwin Lutyens – His Life, His Wife, His Work*, Pimlico, London, 2003, p. 153.

13 Rex Pope, *Atlas of British Social and Economic History Since c.1700*, Routledge, London, 1989, p. 89.

14 Letter from Edwin Lutyens to his wife, Lady Emily, 13 September 1905, RIBA Archive, LuE/7/9/13.

15 Finola Somers' photograph album, Eastnor Castle archive.

16 Letter from the Board of Trade to Herbert Johnson, 8 June 1917, Eastnor Castle archive.

17 Gerald Gliddon and Timothy Skelton, Lutyens and the Great War, Frances Lincoln, London, 2008, p. 80.

18 *Hampshire Chronicle*, 2 April 1919, cited in Gliddon and Skelton, op. cit., p. 80.

19 Letter from Sir Henry Paget-Cooke to Herbert Johnson, 15 December 1921.

20 Johnson hunting photograph album, Eastnor Castle archive.

21 Letter from Edwin Lutyens to his wife, Lady Emily, 31 August 1931, RIBA Archive, LuE/19/17/8.

22 Letter from Edwin Lutyens to his wife, Lady Emily, 16 May 1932, RIBA Archive, LuE/20/1/11.

23 *The Times*, London, 13 April 1949.

24 Conversation with Simon Miller, pupil at Marshcourt School in the 1970s.

GLOSSARY

Barrel vault Ceiling or roof of semi-cylindrical form.

Caryatid A supporting column sculpted in the form of a draped female figure, Grecian in origin.

Chamfer A flat surface made by cutting off the edge or corner of a block of wood or other material.

Clerestory The upper part of the nave, transepts and choir of a church, containing windows.

Closet A small private room used for study, intimate meetings or prayer. Occasionally, the location for a close-stool (commode).

Clunch A block of chalk, used in building.

Coffering A decorative sunken panel in a ceiling, dome, soffit or vault.

Composite The most elongated of the five orders of architecture, Roman in origin and combining elements of the Grecian Ionic and Corinthian orders. See *Orders*.

Corbel A bracket of stone, wood, brick or other building material projecting from the face of a wall and generally used to support a lintel post or arch.

Corinthian The most ornate of the three main orders of classical Greek architecture, characterized by a slender fluted column having an ornate, bell-shaped capital decorated with acanthus leaves. See *Orders*.

Cusp The point of intersection of two ornamental arcs or curves, such as the inner points of a trefoil.

Doric The simplest of the three main orders of classical Greek architecture. Grecian Doric is characterized by heavy fluted columns with plain, saucer-shaped capitals and no base. Roman Doric is slightly more ornate, including columns of more slender girth and with bases. See *Orders*.

Enfilade A linear arrangement of a series of interior doors, usually serving as a suite of rooms, to provide a vista when the doors are open.

Entablature The upper horizontal element of a classical building, often actually or visually supported by pilasters or columns and consisting of architrave, frieze and cornice. See *Orders*

Gargoyle A sculpture, usually serving as a waterspout, carved in the form of a grotesque face or creature and projecting from the building, especially in a Gothic building.

Giant or Colossal order Columns or pilasters rise through more than one storey of a building, usually from ground level to the eaves of the roof or parapet.

Grisaille A style of monochromatic painting in shades of grey, used especially for representation of relief sculpture.

Groin vault A vault caused by the intersection at right angles of two barrel vaults, the edges meeting in a cross.

Intercolumniation The space between columns, dictated by canons of classical architecture

Ionic An order in which the type of Greek column is characterized by scroll-like decorations. See *Orders*.

Keystone A wedged shape block at the crown of an arch, curved or slightly cambered, to consolidate its structure.

Loggia A covered area on the side of a building, especially one that includes a colonnade and serves as a porch.

Nonce order Usually based upon the Composite order and varying only in the design of the capitals, nonce orders have been invented under the inspiration of specific occasions, but have not been used again.

Orders By the Roman period there were five 'orders' of classical architecture, ranging from the simple Tuscan through the progressively elongated and ornate Doric, Ionic and Corinthian to the Composite. The Doric, Ionic and Corinthian are of Grecian origin, the Tuscan and Composite Roman. Each order possesses its own sets of proportions, ornaments and attributes, but all include plinths, columns, capitals and entablatures of varied proportion, profiles and ornamentation. All entablatures comprise three elements that, from the bottom, are the architrave, the frieze and the cornice. Although largely symbolic and ornamental, by the Roman period the entablature – like many elements of the orders – was functional in its origin. The cyma, or serpentine, mouldings of the cornice were originally placed at the eaves of the pitched roof and contrived to throw rainwater off the walls below.

Oriel window A bay window, especially one that projects from a wall and is supported on brackets or corbels. Usual in Gothic architecture.

Piano nobile The main floor of a large house, containing the reception rooms; usually of lofty proportions.

Pilaster A shallow rectangular projection attached to the face of a wall, corresponding in its details to columns of one of the five orders of classical architecture.

Putlog holes Small holes deliberately left in a wall in the medieval period to use, during construction or maintenance work, for the insertion of horizontal scaffolding timbers.

Quadrant link building A structure of quadrant plan

form, linking the main body of a building to its flanking wings.

Scagliola Imitation marble made of glued gypsum plaster with a polished surface of coloured stone, dyed plaster or marble dust.

Soffit The visible underside of an arch, beam, architrave or any horizontally laid element, such as a stair tread.

Spandrel An approximately triangular surface defined by the outer curve of an arch, a horizontal line projecting from its top and a vertical line rising from its springing. Also known as a haunch.

Springing The base of an arch, the place where an arch or vault starts to rise, curve or 'spring' from the horizontal and vertical levels on which it sits.

Term A figure composed of a human head and torso emerging from a tapering, pier-like form. If the bust is of Hermes, the feature is called a herm, and the tapering pier usually furnished with male genitalia at the appropriate height. Hermes was the Greek god who protected boundaries; Terminus was the name of the Roman god who fulfilled the same function. Terms or herms are usually disposed as free-standing garden ornaments, but also used as columns or pilasters in the composition of porches or fire surrounds.

Tile-creasing Tiles laid in mortar in the manner of bricks to form walling or, more usually, to repair or fill a hole in stonework.

Tracery A pattern of interlacing ribs, especially as used in Gothic windows.

Truss A rigid structural framework, usually of timber or metal and rectangular or arched in form, bridging a space, with each end resting on supports at regular intervals.

Volume The amount of space occupied by a three-dimensional object, or a region of space.

Volute Also called a helix, this is a carved ornament, especially as used in an Ionic or Composite capital. See *Orders*.

Voussoir A wedge-shaped element, typically a stone used in building an arch or vault.

Wind-braces Diagonal braces that tie the rafters of a roof together and prevent racking. In the better sort of medieval roofs they are arched, and run from the principal rafters to the purlins.

SELECT BIBLIOGRAPHY

INTRODUCTION

Gow, Ian, *Scotland's Lost Houses*, Aurum Press/National Trust for Scotland, London, 2006.

Worsley, Giles, *England's Lost Houses: From the Archives of Country Life*, Aurum Press, London, 2002.

CHAPTER 1
SOUTH WRAXALL

Airs, Malcolm, *The Tudor and Jacobean Country House: A Building History*, Alan Sutton, Stroud, 1995.

Architecture & Surveying Institute, *South Wraxall Manor, Wiltshire: Archaeological Assessment, April–May 2002*, ASI, 2002.

Aubrey, John, *Wiltshire Topographical Collections (1659–70)*, corrected and enlarged by John Edward Jackson, Devizes, 1862.

Boorde, Andrew, *A Dyetary of Helth*, 1542, ed. F.J. Furnivall, 1870, reprinted by Elibron Classics, London, 2005.

Chitty, Walter, *The Old Manor, South Wraxall*, Bath, 1893.

Cooper, Nicholas, *Houses of the Gentry, 1480–1680*, Paul Mellon Center for Studies in British Art in association with English Heritage, Yale University Press, New Haven and London, 1999.

Couzens, Tim, *The Hand of Fate: The History of the Longs, Wellesleys and the Draycot Estate in Wiltshire*, ELSP, Bradford on Avon, 2001.

Edelen, George (ed.), *The Description of England*, Courier/Dover, New York, 1994.

Emery, Anthony, *Greater Medieval Houses of England and Wales, 1300–1500*, Cambridge University Press, Cambridge, 1996.

Garner, E. and A. Stratton, *Domestic Architecture during the Tudor Period*, Vol. 1, Batsford, London, 1911.

Girouard, Mark, *Elizabethan Architecture: Its Rise and Fall, 1540–1640*, Yale University Press, New Haven and London, 2009.

Girouard, Mark, *Life in the English Country House*, Yale University Press, New Haven and London. 1978.

Girouard, Mark, *Robert Smythson and the Architecture of the Elizabethan Era*, Country Life, London, 1966.

Harrison, William, *Description of Englande: An historicall description of the Islande of Britayne*, 1577, companion to Raphaell Holinshed's Chronicles of England, Scotlande and Irelande, London, 1577.

Heal, Felicity and Clive Holmes, *The Gentry in England and Wales, 1500–1700*, Macmillan, Basingstoke, 1994.

Howard, Maurice, *The Early Tudor Country House: Architecture and Politics, 1490–1550*, George Philip, London, 1987.

Leland, John, *The itinerary of John Leland in or about the years 1535–1543*, ed. Lucy Toulmin Smith, Centaur Press, London, 1964.

Mack, Phyllis, *Politics and Culture in Early Modern Europe*, Cambridge University Press, Cambridge, 1987.

Macnamara, Francis Nottidge, *Memorials of the Danvers Family, of Dauntsey and Culworth: their ancestors and descendants from the Conquest till the termination of the eighteenth century*, Hardy & Co., London, 1895.

Parker, Vanessa Brett, *South Wraxall: A Book for the Year 2000*, privately published by South Wraxall Parish Council, Midsomer Norton, 2001.

Pevsner, Nikolaus, *Buildings of England: Wiltshire*, Penguin, London, 1975.

Ponting, C.E., 'Notes on South Wraxall Manor House', *The Reliquary and Illustrated Archaeologist: A quarterly journal and review devoted to the study of early pagan and Christian antiquities of Great Britain*, Vol. II (new series), 1888, p. 91.

Pugh, R.B. (ed.), *History of Wiltshire*, Victoria County History, Vol. 7: Bradford Hundred, OUP/Boydell & Brewer, Woodbridge, 1953.

Roskell, J.S., Linda Clark and Carole Rawcliffe (eds), *History of Parliament: The Commons, 1386–1421*, Alan Sutton for the History of Parliament Trust, Stroud, 1992/3.

Rowse, A.L., *Shakespeare's Southampton; Patron of Virginia*, Macmillan, London, 1965.

Stopes, Charlotte Carmichael, *The Life of Henry, Third Earl Southampton, Shakespeare's Patron*, Cambridge University Press, Cambridge, 1922.

Walker, Thomas Larkins, *The History and Antiquities of the Manor House, at South Wraxall and Church of Saint Peter, at Biddestone, Wiltshire; the former property of Walter Long, Forming Part III of Examples of Gothic Architecture*, London, 1838.

Wedgwood, Josiah C., *History of Parliament: Biographies of the Members of the Commons House, 1439–1509*, HMSO, London, 1936–38.

Yates, Francis A., *John Florio*, Cambridge University Press, Cambridge, 1934.

CHAPTER 2
KINROSS HOUSE

Defoe, Daniel, *Tour thro' the Whole Island of Britain*, 3 vols, G. Strahan, London, 1724–7.

Hayton, David, Eveline Cruickshanks and Stuart Hawley (eds), *The House of Commons, 1690–1715*, Vol. 2, Cambridge University Press, Cambridge, 2002.

Gifford, J., *The Buildings of Scotland: Perth and Kinross* (Pevsner's Architectural Guides), Yale University Press, New Haven and London, 2007.

Girouard, Mark, *Country Life*, 25 March 1965 & 1 April 1965.

Walker, N.H., *Kinross House*, published privately, Kinross-Shire Antiquarian Society, 1990.

Wemyss, Charles, *A Study of Aspiration and Ambition*, PhD thesis, 2 vols, University of Dundee, December 2008.

CHAPTER 3
EASTON NESTON

Baker, Christopher, 'Talman, Aldrich and the Oxford Virtuosi' in *John Talman: An Early English Connoisseur*, ed. Cinzia Maria Sicca, Yale University Press, London and New Haven, 2008.

Campbell, Colen, *Vitruvius Britannicus, or the British Architect, containing the plans, elevations, and sections of the regular buildings, both publick and private, in Great Britain, with variety of new designs; in … large folio plates [with explanations] … Vitruvius Britannicus, ou l'Architecte britannique*, 3 vols, London, 1715, 1717, 1725, and Dover Publications, New York, 2007.

Colvin, Howard, *A Biographical Dictionary of British Architects 1600–1840*, John Murray, London, 1978.

Colvin, Howard, 'Easton Neston Reconsidered', *Country Life*, Vol. CXCIX, 15 October 1970.

Cornforth, John, 'Drayton House', *Country Life*, Vol. CXXXVII, 27 May 1965.

Downes, Kerry, *English Baroque Architecture*, Zwemmer, London, 1966.

Downes, Kerry, *Hawksmoor*, Zwemmer, London, 1959.

Downes, Kerry, 'Hawksmoor's House at Easton Neston', *Architectural History*, Vol. 30, 1987.

Du Prey, Pierre de la Ruffinière, *Hawksmoor's London Churches: Architecture and Theory*, University of Chicago Press, Chicago and London, 2000.

Gazda, Elaine K. (ed.), *Memoirs of the American Academy in Rome: Supplementary Volumes, Vol. 1: The Ancient Art of Emulation: Studies in Artistic Originality and Tradition from the Present to Classical Antiquity*, University of Michigan Press, Ann Arbor, 2002.

Harris, John, 'William and John Talman: Architecture and a Partnership' in *Sicca, John Talman*.

Harris, John, *William Talman: Maverick Architect*, George Allen & Unwin, London, 1982.

Hart, Vaughan, *Nicholas Hawksmoor: Rebuilding Ancient Wonders*, Yale University Press, New Haven and London, 2002.

Hart, Vaughan, *Sir John Vanbrugh: Stories in Stone*, Yale University Press, New Haven and London, 2008.

Haynes, D.E.L., *The Arundel Marbles*, Ashmolean Museum, Oxford, 1975.

Kieven, Elisabeth, 'Models of Perfection: John Talman and Roman Baroque Architecture' in *Sicca, John Talman*. *Oxford Dictionary of National Biography*, online edition, Oxford University Press, Oxford and London, 2004.

Summerson, John, *Architecture in Britain 1530 to 1830*, Penguin Books, London, 1953.

Tyack, Geoffrey, Simon Bradley and Nikolaus Pevsner, *The Buildings of England: Berkshire*, Yale University Press, New Haven and London, 2010.

Walpole Society, *The Nineteenth Volume of the Walpole Society 1930–1931*, Oxford University Press, Oxford, 1931.

Watkin, David (ed.), *Sir John Soane: The Royal Academy Lectures*, Cambridge University Press, Cambridge, 2000.

Watkin, David (ed.), *The Sale Catalogue of Libraries of Eminent Persons, Vol. IV: Architects*, London, 1972.

Whistler, L., 'Talman and Vanbrugh: episodes in an architectural rivalry', *Country Life*, Vol. 112, 21 November 1952.

Woodman, Ellis, *Modernity and Reinvention: The Architecture of James Gowan*, Black Dog Publishing, London, 2008.

Worsley, Giles, *Classical Architecture in Britain: The Heroic Age*, Yale University Press, New Haven and London, 1995.

Worsley, Giles, 'Taking Hooke Seriously', *Georgian Group Journal*, Vol. XIV, 2004.

Worsley, Giles, 'The Puzzle of Easton Neston', *Country Life*, Vol. 199, 25 August 2005.

CHAPTER 4
WENTWORTH WOODHOUSE

Bailey, Catherine, *Black Diamonds: The Rise and Fall of an English Dynasty*, Viking, London, 2007.

Campbell, Colen, op. cit., chapter 3.

Couzens, Tim, op. cit., chapter 1.

Gotch, J.A., *Inigo Jones*, Methuen, London, 1928.

Hewlings, Richard, *Country Life*, 24 February 2010.

Howe, Geoffrey, *The Wentworths of Wentworth: The Fitzwilliam (Wentworth) Estates and the Wentworth Monuments*, Trustees of the Fitzwilliam Wentworth Amenity Trust, Rotherham, 2002.

Leoni, Giacomo (trans), *The Architecture of Leon Battista Alberti in Ten Books*, 3 vols, Thomas Edlin, London, 1726.

Morris, Robert, *Essay in Defence of Ancient Architecture*, London, 1728.

Shaftesbury, Lord (Anthony Ashley Cooper, 3rd Earl of

Shaftesbury), *Letter concerning Art, or Science of Design*, 1712, in *Essays in Characteristics of Men, Manners etc.*, John Darby, London, 1714.

Swift, Jonathan, *Journal to Stella*, 1766; 1974 edition, 2 vols, ed. Harold Williams, Blackwell, Oxford, 1974.

Trussler, John, *The Honours of the Table, or, Rules of behaviour during meals; with the whole art of carving*, London, 1788.

Ware, Isaac (trans), *The Four Books of Architecture by Andrea Palladio*, London, 1738.

CHAPTER 5
CLANDEBOYE HOUSE

Bence-Jones, Mark, *Burke's Guide to Country Houses: Ireland*, Burke's Peerage Ltd, London, 1978.

Chappell, Mike, *Wellington's Peninsula Regiments, Vol. 1: The Irish*, Osprey, Oxford, 2003.

Dean, Ptolemy, *Country Life*, 2 December 2008, pp48–51.

Dufferin, Lord (Frederick Hamilton-Temple-Blackwood, 1st Marquess of Dufferin and Ava), *Irish Emigration and the Tenure of Land in Ireland*, Willis, Sotheran & Co. London, 1867.

Dufferin, Lord (Frederick Hamilton-Temple-Blackwood, 1st Marquess of Dufferin and Ava), *Mr. Mill's Plan for the Pacification of Ireland Examined*, John Murray, London, 1868.

Dufferin, Lord (Frederick Hamilton-Temple-Blackwood, 1st Marquess of Dufferin and Ava), *Letters from high latitudes: being some account of a voyage in the schooner yacht 'Foam'*, John Murray, London, 1857.

Goodall, John, *Country Life*, 9 December 2008, pp. 46–51.

John Gray, *The Dufferins in Canada, 1872–1878*, Linen Hall Library, Belfast, 1997.

Lyall, Sir Alfred, *The Life of the Marquis of Dufferin and Ava*, 2 vols, John Murray, London, 1905.

Nicolson, Harold, *Helen's Tower*, Constable, London, 1937.

Public Record Office of Northern Ireland, *Dufferin Papers*, ed. A.T. Harrison, Crown, Belfast, 2007.

Purdue, Olwen Ruth, *Challenge and Change: The Big House in North-eastern Ireland: Land, power and social elites, 1878–1960*, electronic resource, Queen's University Belfast, 2008.

CHAPTER 6
MARSHCOURT

Brown, Jane, *Gardens of a Golden Afternoon*, London, Penguin, 1985.

Brown, Jane, *Lutyens and the Edwardians*, London, Viking, 1997.

Butler, A.S.G., *The Domestic Architecture of Sir Edwin Lutyens*, Country Life, 1950, facsimile by Antique Collectors' Club, London, 1989.

Gliddon, Gerald and Timothy Skelton, *Lutyens and the Great War*, Frances Lincoln, London, 2008.

Greenberg, Allan, *Lutyens and the Modern Movement*, Papadakis, London, 2007.

Hill, Oliver, 'An Architect's Debt to Country Life', *Country Life*, Vol. CXLI, 12 January 1967.

Hill, Oliver, 'The Genius of Edwin Lutyens', *Country Life*, Vol. CXLV, 27 March 1969.

Hussey, Christopher, *The Life of Sir Edwin Lutyens*, Country Life & Scribners, London, 1950.

Hussey, Christopher, 'Marshcourt I', *Country Life*, Vol. XXLI, 19 March 1932.

Hussey, Christopher, 'Marshcourt II', *Country Life*, Vol. LXXI, 26 March 1932.

Hussey, Christopher, 'Marshcourt III', *Country Life*, Vol. LXXI, 2 April 1932.

Hynes, Samuel, *The Edwardian Turn of Mind*, London, Pimlico, 1991.

Inskip, Peter, *Edwin Lutyens*, Architectural Monographs, Academy Editions, London, 1979.

Jeykll, Gertrude and Laurence Weaver, *Arts and Crafts Gardens*, Garden Art Press, Suffolk, 1999.

Johnson, Herbert, *Investment tables shewing the return per cent. per annum on the market price of stocks or perpetual debentures paying rates of interest varying (in ¼%) from 1 to 10 per cent. per annum*, F.C. Mathieson & Sons, London, 1893.

Percy, Clayre and Jane Ridley (eds), *Letters of Edwin Lutyens to His Wife Lady Emily*, Collins, London, 1985.

Phillipps, L. March, 'Marshcourt', *Country Life*, Vol. XX, 1 September 1906.

Pope, Rex, *Atlas of British Social and Economic History Since c.1700*, Routledge, London, 1989.

Ridley, Jane, *Edwin Lutyens – His Life, His Wife, His Work*, Pimlico, London, 2003.

Stamp, Gavin, *Edwin Lutyens: Country Houses*, Aurum Press, London, 2001.

Weaver, Lawrence, *Houses and Gardens by E.L. Lutyens*, Antique Collectors' Club, London, 1981.

Wilhide, Elizabeth, *Sir Edwin Lutyens – Designing in the English Tradition*, Pavilion, London, 2000.

INDEX

ACKNOWLEDGEMENTS

I would like to thank Janice Hadlow, controller of BBC2, and Mark Bell, commissioner for arts at the BBC, for commissioning the BBC television series that this book accompanies, and for their enthusiasm and encouragement. I would also like to thank Lorna Russell, editorial director at BBC Books, for her energy, skill and guidance in the production of the book, Trish Burgess for her sterling work on the text, Caroline McArthur for her work on illustrations, and Sarah Cuttle for her beautiful photographs. At the production company that made the series for BBC2 – Oxford Film and Television – I would in particular like to thank Stephanie Collins and Patrick Forbes who acted as executive producers and most skillfully and adroitly steered the project through from conception to completion, Annabel Lee as director of production, and the production team Marisa Erftemeijer, Marisa Verazzo and Scarlet Mehta for their logistical support. The content and arrangement of the chapters of the book owe a huge debt to the director/producers Jenny Dames, David Jeffcock, Ian Macmillan and Philip Smith, and to the assistant producers Jessica Cobb, Tilly Cowan, James Evans and Charlotte Sacher.

My very special thanks are due to Jonathan Parker, who researched each of the country houses featured in the book and television series and drafted the chapter on Marshcourt. My very special thanks are also due to Otto Saumarez Smith, who undertook much research on Hawksmoor and drafted the chapter on Easton Neston. Thanks also to Marenka Gabler for her research assistance on South Wraxall and the bibliography, and to Geraldine Roberts for her research notes on Wentworth Woodhouse. Also to Ptolemy Dean for revelations about Easton Neston and to Robert Howard of Nottingham tree-ring dating laboratory for information about the roof at Easton Neston, to Patrick Eyres for insights about Wentworth Woodhouse and the second Marquess of Rockingham, to Jonathan Bate for thoughts on Shakespeare and the Longs of South Wraxall, to Tim Couzens for information about the Long family of South Wraxall, to James Hervey-Bathhust and Jane Ridley for assistance with the chapter on Marshcourt, to Charles Wemyss for information on Kinross House, and to Marcus Binney.

At the individual houses I would like to thank the owners for allowing me to explore and write about their very special homes – Gela Nash-Taylor and John Taylor at South Wraxall; Jamie and Lizzie Montgomery at Kinross House; Leon Max at Easton Neston; Clifford and Giles Newbold at Wentworth Woodhouse; and Lady Dufferin at Clandeboye. For their assistance at each house I am delighted to thank Sue Edwards and Bob Loudan (South Wraxall); Roy Goodgers (Easton Neston); Tom McWilliams (Wentworth Woodhouse); John Witchell and Lola Armstrong (Clandeboye House); and Neil Simpson (Marshcourt).

Finally, I would like to thank the film crews, who made tough shoots as congenial as humanly possible: Tim Cragg, Simon Farmer, Neil Harvey, Simon Parmenter, Jonathan Partridge and Adam Prescod. And, as always, my agents Charles Walker and Katy Jones for doing so much to make both television series and book possible.

PICTURE CREDITS

All photography by Sarah Cuttle © Woodlands Book Ltd except for the following:

Dan Cruickshank: 8, 10–11, 12, 14l, 17, 20–21, 22, 23, 27, 28, 34t, 36, 37, 43l, 48–49, 50–51, 56, 57, 68, 86, 100–101, 102, 105, 120b, 124t, 128l, 129, 144b, 145, 146, 149, 170b, 175, 178–179, 181, 192b, 198b, 200, 210, 214–215, 228, 231, 235, 247, 248b, 251. **AKG Images**: akg-images/A.F.Kersting 113t; akg-images/Erich Lessing 116t & b. **Alamy**: Classic Image/Alamy 18br, 38; Angelo Hornak/Alamy 130, 152t; Antiques & Collectables/Alamy 34bl & br; Art Directors & TRIP/Alamy 113l; Ben Ramos/Alamy 72t; Classic Image/Alamy 144t; David Lyons/Alamy 187; INTERFOTO/Alamy 26t, 40t; Jim Henderson/Alamy 198t; Les. Ladbury/Alamy 60b; Mary Evans Picture Library/Alamy 18t, 26b, 40b, 106t, 140b, 188b; Michael Jenner/Alamy 152b; Stuart Robertson/Alamy 60t; The Art Gallery Collection/Alamy 41, 148; The Bridgeman Art Library/Getty Images 52b, 59; The Print Collector/Alamy 18bl, 75, 192t; Walker Historical Picture Archive/Alamy 188t; World History Archive/Alamy 140t. **City of Sheffield Archives**: 162. **Country Life**: 72b, 135, 146, 154, 163, 164, 170t, 171, 172, 177, 183, 185, 203, 225, 234, 237tr & br, 242, 243, 250, 256t, 257, 266t, 273. **Tim Cragg**: 3–4, 6. **Dufferin and Ava Archive** 4t, 180, 184, 186, 194, 202, 204, 206, 209, 212, 219, 220, 222, 224, 227. **Domestic Architecture of Sir Edwin Lutyens, by A.S.G. Butler, 1950**: 240. **Eastnor Castle Archive**: 245, 258, 262, 269. **English Heritage**: 118. **Getty Images**: 108; Popperfoto/Getty Images 136. **Hulton-Deutsch Collection/CORBIS** 237l. **Lutyens Estate** 266b, 268. **National Portrait Gallery**: 111b. **Private collections**: 16, 52t, 70, 82, 108, 110, 111t, 156, 238, 246, 270. **RIBA Library Drawings Collection** 113b. **Royal Commission on the Ancient and Historical Monuments of Scotland**: 67. **Courtesy of Sothebys Picture Library** 106b. **The British Library Board**: 151. 109 taken from Kerry Downes, *English Baroque Architecture*, Zwemmer, London, 1966.

This book is published to accompany the television series entitled *The Country House Revealed*, produced by Oxford Film & Television and first broadcast on BBC2 in 2011.
EXECUTIVE PRODUCERS Stephanie Collins and Patrick Forbes

1 3 5 7 9 10 8 6 4 2

Published in 2011 by BBC Books, an imprint of Ebury Publishing. A Random House Group Company

The Random House Group Limited Reg. No. 954009

Addresses for companies within the Random House Group can be found at www.randomhouse.co.uk

A CIP catalogue record for this book is available from the British Library.

ISBN 978 1 84 990206 9

The Random House Group Limited supports the Forest Stewardship Council (FSC), the leading international forest certification organisation. All our titles that are printed on Greenpeace approved FSC certified paper carry the FSC logo. Our paper procurement policy can be found at www.rbooks.co.uk/environment

FSC
www.fsc.org
MIX
Paper from responsible sources
FSC® C023561

COMMISSIONING EDITOR Lorna Russell
EDITOR Caroline McArthur
COPY-EDITOR Trish Burgess
DESIGNER Andrew Barron
PHOTOGRAPHER Sarah Cuttle
PRODUCTION Antony Heller

Printed and bound in the UK by Butler, Tanner and Dennis

To buy books by your favourite authors and register for offers, visit www.rbooks.co.uk